Beginning Spring Boot 2

Applications and Microservices
with the Spring Framework

K. Siva Prasad Reddy

Apress®

Beginning Spring Boot 2: Applications and Microservices with the Spring Framework

K. Siva Prasad Reddy
Hyderabad, India

ISBN-13 (pbk): 978-1-4842-2930-9
DOI 10.1007/978-1-4842-2931-6

ISBN-13 (electronic): 978-1-4842-2931-6

Library of Congress Control Number: 2017955551

Cover image by Freepik (`www.freepik.com`)

Managing Director: Welmoed Spahr
Editorial Director: Todd Green
Acquisitions Editor: Steve Anglin
Development Editor: Matthew Moodie
Technical Reviewer: Massimo Nardone
Coordinating Editor: Mark Powers
Copy Editor: Kezia Endsley

Distributed to the book trade worldwide by Springer Science+Business Media New York, 233 Spring Street, 6th Floor, New York, NY 10013. Phone 1-800-SPRINGER, fax (201) 348-4505, e-mail orders-ny@springer-sbm.com, or visit `www.springeronline.com`. Apress Media, LLC is a California LLC and the sole member (owner) is Springer Science + Business Media Finance Inc (SSBM Finance Inc). SSBM Finance Inc is a **Delaware** corporation.

For information on translations, please e-mail rights@apress.com, or visit `http://www.apress.com/rights-permissions`.

Apress titles may be purchased in bulk for academic, corporate, or promotional use. eBook versions and licenses are also available for most titles. For more information, reference our Print and eBook Bulk Sales web page at `http://www.apress.com/bulk-sales`.

Any source code or other supplementary material referenced by the author in this book is available to readers on GitHub via the book's product page, located at `www.apress.com/9781484229309`. For more detailed information, please visit `http://www.apress.com/source-code`.

Contents at a Glance

Contents

About the Author

K. Siva Prasad Reddy has more than 11 years of experience in building enterprise software systems on the Java platform. He worked on building scalable distributed enterprise applications in banking and e-commerce domains using Java, Spring, RESTful web services, JPA, and NoSQL technologies. He is also the author of *Java Persistence with Mybatis 3* and *PrimeFaces Beginners Guide* with other publishers.

His current technical focus is on modern architectures, including microservices, continuous integration and continuous delivery (CI/CD), and DevOps. He enjoys coding in Java 8, Kotlin, and Spring Boot, and has a passion for automating repetitive work.

He blogs regularly at `http://sivalabs.in`, or you can follow him on Twitter `@sivalabs` and GitHub `https://github.com/sivaprasadreddy`.

About the Technical Reviewer

Massimo Nardone has more than 23 years of experience in security, web/mobile development, and cloud and IT architecture. His true IT passions are security and Android.

He has been programming and teaching people how to program with Android, Perl, PHP, Java, VB, Python, C/C++, and MySQL for more than 20 years.

He holds a Master of Science degree in Computing Science from the University of Salerno, Italy.

He has worked as a project manager, software engineer, research engineer, chief security architect, information security manager, PCI/SCADA auditor, and senior lead IT security/cloud/SCADA architect for many years.

His technical skills include security, Android, cloud, Java, MySQL, Drupal, Cobol, Perl, web and mobile development, MongoDB, D3, Joomla, Couchbase, C/C++, WebGL, Python, Pro Rails, Django CMS, Jekyll, Scratch, etc.

He worked as visiting lecturer and supervisor for exercises at the Networking Laboratory of the Helsinki University of Technology (Aalto University). He also holds four international patents (in the PKI, SIP, SAML, and Proxy areas).

He currently works as a Chief Information Security Officer (CISO) for CargotecOyj and is member of ISACA Finland chapter board.

Massimo has reviewed more than 40 IT books for different publishers and is the coauthor of *Pro Android Games* (Apress, 2015).

Acknowledgments

I would like to thank my wife Neha Jain and my family members for their continuous support all the days I spent writing this book.

I would like to express my gratitude to the Apress team, specifically to Steve Anglin and Mark Powers, for their continuous support throughout the journey. I would also like to thank the reviewers for providing valuable feedback that helped improve the quality of the content.

Introduction

Spring is the most popular Java-based framework for building enterprise applications. The Spring framework provides a rich ecosystem of projects to address modern application needs, like security, simplified access to relational and NoSQL datastores, batch processing, integration with social networking sites, large volume of data streams processing, etc. As Spring is a very flexible and customizable framework, there are usually multiple ways to configure the application. Although it is a good thing to have multiple options, it can be overwhelming to the beginners. Spring Boot addresses this "Spring applications need complex configuration" problem by using its powerful autoconfiguration mechanism.

Spring Boot is an opinionated framework following the "Convention Over Configuration" approach, which helps build Spring-based applications quickly and easily. The main goal of Spring Boot is to quickly create Spring-based applications without requiring the developers to write the same boilerplate configuration again and again.

In recent years, the microservices architecture has become the preferred architecture style for building complex enterprise applications. Spring Boot is a great choice for building microservices-based applications using various Spring Cloud modules.

This book will help you understand what Spring Boot is, how Spring Boot helps you build Spring-based applications quickly and easily, and the inner workings of Spring Boot using easy-to-follow examples.

What This Book Covers

This book covers the following topics:

- What is Spring Boot and how does it improve developer productivity?
- How does Spring Boot autoconfiguration work behind the scenes?
- How do you create custom Spring Boot starters?
- Working with databases using JdbcTemplate, MyBatis, JOOQ, and Spring Data JPA
- Working with the MongoDB NoSQL database
- Developing web applications using Spring Boot and Thymeleaf
- Developing Reactive Web Applications using Spring WebFlux
- Developing REST API using Spring Boot
- Securing web applications using SpringSecurity
- Monitoring Spring Boot applications with Spring Boot Actuator
- Testing Spring Boot applications
- Developing Spring Boot applications in Groovy, Scala, and Kotlin
- Running Spring Boot applications in the Docker container

What You Need for This Book

To follow the examples in this book, you must have the following software installed:

- JDK 1.8
- Your favorite IDE
  - Spring Tool Suite
  - IntelliJ IDEA
  - NetBeans IDE
- Build tools
  - Maven
  - Gradle
- Database server
  - MySQL
  - PostgreSQL

CHAPTER 1

Introduction to Spring Boot

The Spring framework is a very popular and widely used Java framework for building web and enterprise applications. Spring at its core is a dependency injection container that provides flexibility to configure beans in multiple ways, such as XML, Annotations, and JavaConfig. Over the years, the Spring framework grew exponentially by addressing the needs of modern business applications like security, support for NoSQL datastores, handling big data, batch processing, integration with other systems, etc. Spring, along with its sub-projects, became a viable platform for building enterprise applications.

The Spring framework is very flexible and provides multiple ways of configuring the application components. With a rich set of features combined with multiple configuration options, configuring Spring applications become complex and error-prone. The Spring team created Spring Boot to address the complexity of configuration through its powerful AutoConfiguration mechanism.

This chapter takes a quick look at the Spring framework. You'll develop a web application using SpringMVC and JPA the traditional way (without using Spring Boot). Then you will look at the pain points of the traditional way and see how to develop the same application using Spring Boot.

Overview of the Spring Framework

If you are a Java developer, then there is a good chance that you have heard about the Spring framework and have used it in your projects. The Spring framework was created primarily as a dependency injection container, but it is much more than that. Spring is very popular for several reasons:

- Spring's dependency injection approach encourages writing testable code

- Easy-to-use and powerful database transaction management capabilities

- Spring simplifies integration with other Java frameworks, like the JPA/Hibernate ORM and Struts/JSF web frameworks

- State-of-the-art Web MVC framework for building web applications

Along with the Spring framework, there are many other Spring sub-projects that help build applications that address modern business needs:

- **Spring Data:** Simplifies data access from relational and NoSQL datastores.

- **Spring Batch:** Provides a powerful batch-processing framework.

- **Spring Security:** Robust security framework to secure applications.

© K. Siva Prasad Reddy 2017
K. S. Prasad Reddy, *Beginning Spring Boot 2*, DOI 10.1007/978-1-4842-2931-6_1

- **Spring Social:** Supports integration with social networking sites like Facebook, Twitter, LinkedIn, GitHub, etc.

- **Spring Integration:** An implementation of enterprise integration patterns to facilitate integration with other enterprise applications using lightweight messaging and declarative adapters.

There are many other interesting projects addressing various other modern application development needs. For more information, take a look at http://spring.io/projects.

Spring Configuration Styles

Spring initially provided an XML-based approach for configuring beans. Later Spring introduced XML-based DSLs, Annotations, and JavaConfig-based approaches for configuring beans. Listings 1-1 through 1-3 show how each of those configuration styles looks.

Listing 1-1. Example of XML-Based Configuration

```
<bean id="userService" class="com.apress.myapp.service.UserService">
    <property name="userDao" ref="userDao"/>
</bean>

<bean id="userDao" class="com.apress.myapp.dao.JdbcUserDao">
    <property name="dataSource" ref="dataSource"/>
</bean>

<bean id="dataSource" class="org.apache.commons.dbcp.BasicDataSource" destroy-
method="close">
    <property name="driverClassName" value="com.mysql.jdbc.Driver"/>
    <property name="url" value="jdbc:mysql://localhost:3306/test"/>
    <property name="username" value="root"/>
    <property name="password" value="secret"/>
</bean>

<!-- DSL based configuration  -->
<beans>
    <jee:jndi-lookup id="entityManagerFactory" jndi-name="persistence/defaultPU"/>
</beans>
```

Listing 1-2. Example of Annotation-Based Configuration

```
@Service
public class UserService
{
    private UserDao userDao;
    @Autowired
    public UserService(UserDao dao){
        this.userDao = dao;
    }
    ...
    ...
}
```

```
@Repository
public class JdbcUserDao
{
    private DataSource dataSource;
    @Autowired
    public JdbcUserDao(DataSource dataSource){
        this.dataSource = dataSource;
    }
    ...
    ...
}
```

Listing 1-3. Example of a JavaConfig-Based Configuration

```
@Configuration
public class AppConfig
{
    @Bean
    public UserService userService(UserDao dao){
        return new UserService(dao);
    }
    @Bean
    public UserDao userDao(DataSource dataSource){
        return new JdbcUserDao(dataSource);
    }
    @Bean
    public DataSource dataSource(){
        BasicDataSource dataSource = new BasicDataSource();
        dataSource.setDriverClassName("com.mysql.jdbc.Driver");
        dataSource.setUrl("jdbc:mysql://localhost:3306/test");
        dataSource.setUsername("root");
        dataSource.setPassword("secret");
        return dataSource;
    }
}
```

As you can see, Spring provides multiple approaches for configuring application components and you can even mix the approaches as well. For example, you can use JavaConfig- and Annotation-based configuration styles in the same application. That is a lot of flexibility, which is good and bad. People who are new to the Spring framework may get confused about which approach to follow.

As of now, the Spring community is suggesting you follow the JavaConfig-based approach, as it gives you more flexibility. But there is no one-size-fits-all kind of solution. You have to choose the approach based on your own application needs.

Now that you've had a glimpse of how various styles of Spring Bean configurations look, you'll take a quick look at the configuration of a typical SpringMVC and JPA/Hibernate-based web application configuration.

Developing Web Application Using SpringMVC and JPA

Before getting to know Spring Boot and learning what kind of features it provides, we'll take a look at how a typical Spring web application configuration looks and learn about the pain points. Then, we will see how Spring Boot addresses those problems.

The first thing to do is create a Maven project and configure all the dependencies required in the pom.xml file, as shown in Listing 1-4.

Listing 1-4. The pom.xml File

```xml
<?xml version="1.0" encoding="UTF-8"?>
<project xmlns="http://maven.apache.org/POM/4.0.0"
         xmlns:xsi="http://www.w3.org/2001/XMLSchema-instance"
         xsi:schemaLocation="http://maven.apache.org/POM/4.0.0
                       http://maven.apache.org/maven-v4_0_0.xsd">
    <modelVersion>4.0.0</modelVersion>
    <groupId>com.apress</groupId>
    <artifactId>springmvc-jpa-demo</artifactId>
    <packaging>war</packaging>
    <version>1.0-SNAPSHOT</version>
    <name>springmvc-jpa-demo</name>
    <properties>
        <project.build.sourceEncoding>UTF-8</project.build.sourceEncoding>
        <maven.compiler.source>1.8</maven.compiler.source>
        <maven.compiler.target>1.8</maven.compiler.target>
        <failOnMissingWebXml>false</failOnMissingWebXml>
    </properties>
    <build>
        <plugins>
            <plugin>
                <groupId>org.apache.tomcat.maven</groupId>
                <artifactId>tomcat7-maven-plugin</artifactId>
                <version>2.2</version>
            </plugin>
        </plugins>
    </build>
    <dependencies>
        <dependency>
            <groupId>org.springframework</groupId>
            <artifactId>spring-webmvc</artifactId>
            <version>4.3.7.RELEASE</version>
        </dependency>
        <dependency>
            <groupId>org.springframework.data</groupId>
            <artifactId>spring-data-jpa</artifactId>
            <version>1.11.1.RELEASE</version>
        </dependency>
        <dependency>
            <groupId>org.slf4j</groupId>
            <artifactId>jcl-over-slf4j</artifactId>
            <version>1.7.22</version>
        </dependency>
        <dependency>
            <groupId>org.slf4j</groupId>
            <artifactId>slf4j-api</artifactId>
            <version>1.7.22</version>
```

```xml
        </dependency>
        <dependency>
            <groupId>org.slf4j</groupId>
            <artifactId>slf4j-log4j12</artifactId>
            <version>1.7.22</version>
        </dependency>
        <dependency>
            <groupId>log4j</groupId>
            <artifactId>log4j</artifactId>
            <version>1.2.17</version>
        </dependency>
        <dependency>
            <groupId>com.h2database</groupId>
            <artifactId>h2</artifactId>
            <version>1.4.193</version>
        </dependency>
        <dependency>
            <groupId>commons-dbcp</groupId>
            <artifactId>commons-dbcp</artifactId>
            <version>1.4</version>
        </dependency>
        <dependency>
            <groupId>mysql</groupId>
            <artifactId>mysql-connector-java</artifactId>
            <version>5.1.38</version>
        </dependency>
        <dependency>
            <groupId>org.hibernate</groupId>
            <artifactId>hibernate-entitymanager</artifactId>
            <version>5.2.5.Final</version>
        </dependency>
        <dependency>
            <groupId>javax.servlet</groupId>
            <artifactId>javax.servlet-api</artifactId>
            <version>3.1.0</version>
            <scope>provided</scope>
        </dependency>
        <dependency>
            <groupId>org.thymeleaf</groupId>
            <artifactId>thymeleaf-spring4</artifactId>
            <version>2.1.4.RELEASE</version>
        </dependency>
    </dependencies>
</project>
```

We have configured all the Spring MVC, Spring Data JPA, JPA/Hibernate, Thymeleaf, and Log4j dependencies in the Maven `pom.xml` file.

Configure the service/DAO layer beans using JavaConfig, as shown in Listing 1-5.

Listing 1-5. The com.apress.demo.config.AppConfig.java File

```java
package com.apress.demo.config;

import java.util.Properties;

import javax.persistence.EntityManagerFactory;
import javax.sql.DataSource;

import org.apache.commons.dbcp.BasicDataSource;
import org.springframework.beans.factory.annotation.Autowired;
import org.springframework.context.annotation.Bean;
import org.springframework.context.annotation.Configuration;
import org.springframework.context.annotation.PropertySource;
import org.springframework.context.support.PropertySourcesPlaceholderConfigurer;
import org.springframework.core.env.Environment;
import org.springframework.core.io.ClassPathResource;
import org.springframework.data.jpa.repository.config.EnableJpaRepositories;
import org.springframework.instrument.classloading.InstrumentationLoadTimeWeaver;
import org.springframework.jdbc.datasource.init.DataSourceInitializer;
import org.springframework.jdbc.datasource.init.ResourceDatabasePopulator;
import org.springframework.orm.hibernate4.HibernateExceptionTranslator;
import org.springframework.orm.jpa.JpaTransactionManager;
import org.springframework.orm.jpa.LocalContainerEntityManagerFactoryBean;
import org.springframework.orm.jpa.vendor.HibernateJpaVendorAdapter;
import org.springframework.transaction.PlatformTransactionManager;
import org.springframework.transaction.annotation.EnableTransactionManagement;

@Configuration
@EnableTransactionManagement
@EnableJpaRepositories(basePackages="com.apress.demo.repositories")
@PropertySource(value = { "classpath:application.properties" })
public class AppConfig
{

    @Autowired
    private Environment env;

    @Bean
    public static PropertySourcesPlaceholderConfigurer placeHolderConfigurer()
    {
        return new PropertySourcesPlaceholderConfigurer();
    }

    @Bean
    public PlatformTransactionManager transactionManager()
    {
        EntityManagerFactory factory = entityManagerFactory().getObject();
        return new JpaTransactionManager(factory);
    }
```

```
@Bean
public LocalContainerEntityManagerFactoryBean entityManagerFactory()
{
    LocalContainerEntityManagerFactoryBean factory = new
    LocalContainerEntityManagerFactoryBean();

    HibernateJpaVendorAdapter vendorAdapter = new HibernateJpaVendorAdapter();
    vendorAdapter.setShowSql(Boolean.TRUE);

    factory.setDataSource(dataSource());
    factory.setJpaVendorAdapter(vendorAdapter);
    factory.setPackagesToScan(env.getProperty("packages-to-scan"));

    Properties jpaProperties = new Properties();
    jpaProperties.put("hibernate.hbm2ddl.auto", env.getProperty
    ("hibernate.hbm2ddl.auto"));
    factory.setJpaProperties(jpaProperties);

    factory.afterPropertiesSet();
    factory.setLoadTimeWeaver(new InstrumentationLoadTimeWeaver());
    return factory;
}

@Bean
public HibernateExceptionTranslator hibernateExceptionTranslator()
{
    return new HibernateExceptionTranslator();
}

@Bean
public DataSource dataSource()
{
    BasicDataSource dataSource = new BasicDataSource();
    dataSource.setDriverClassName(env.getProperty("jdbc.driverClassName"));
    dataSource.setUrl(env.getProperty("jdbc.url"));
    dataSource.setUsername(env.getProperty("jdbc.username"));
    dataSource.setPassword(env.getProperty("jdbc.password"));
    return dataSource;
}

@Bean
public DataSourceInitializer dataSourceInitializer(DataSource dataSource)
{
    DataSourceInitializer dataSourceInitializer = new DataSourceInitializer();
    dataSourceInitializer.setDataSource(dataSource);
    ResourceDatabasePopulator databasePopulator = new ResourceDatabasePopulator();
    databasePopulator.addScript(new ClassPathResource(env.getProperty("init-scripts")));
    dataSourceInitializer.setDatabasePopulator(databasePopulator);
```

```
        dataSourceInitializer.setEnabled(Boolean.parseBoolean(env.getProperty("init-db",
        "false")));
        return dataSourceInitializer;
    }
}
```

In the `AppConfig.java` configuration class, we did the following:

- Marked it as a Spring `Configuration` class using the `@Configuration` annotation.

- Enabled Annotation-based transaction management using `@EnableTransactionManagement`.

- Configured `@EnableJpaRepositories` to indicate where to look for Spring Data JPA repositories.

- Configured the `PropertyPlaceHolder` bean using the `@PropertySource` annotation and `PropertySourcesPlaceholderConfigurer` bean definition, which loads properties from the `application.properties` file.

- Defined beans for `DataSource`, JPA `EntityManagerFactory`, and `JpaTransactionManager`.

- Configured the `DataSourceInitializer` bean to initialize the database by executing the `data.sql` script on application start-up.

1. Now configure the property placeholder values in `application.properties`, as shown in Listing 1-6.

Listing 1-6. The src/main/resources/application.properties File

```
jdbc.driverClassName=com.mysql.jdbc.Driver
jdbc.url=jdbc:mysql://localhost:3306/test
jdbc.username=root
jdbc.password=admin
init-db=true
init-scripts=data.sql
hibernate.dialect=org.hibernate.dialect.MySQLDialect
hibernate.show_sql=true
hibernate.hbm2ddl.auto=update
packages-to-scan=com.apress.demo
```

2. Create a simple SQL script called `data.sql` to populate sample data into the USER table, as shown in Listing 1-7.

Listing 1-7. The src/main/resources/data.sql File

```
delete from user;
insert into user(id, name) values(1,'John');
insert into user(id, name) values(2,'Smith');
insert into user(id, name) values(3,'Siva');
```

3. Create the `log4j.properties` file with a basic configuration, as shown in
    Listing 1-8.

Listing 1-8. The src/main/resources/log4j.properties File

```
log4j.rootCategory=INFO, stdout
log4j.appender.stdout=org.apache.log4j.ConsoleAppender
log4j.appender.stdout.layout=org.apache.log4j.PatternLayout
log4j.appender.stdout.layout.ConversionPattern=%5p %t %c{2}:%L - %m%n
log4j.category.com.apress=DEBUG
log4j.category.org.springframework=INFO
```

4. Now configure the Spring MVC web layer beans such as `ThymeleafViewResolver`,
    static `ResourceHandlers`, and `MessageSource` for i18n, as shown in Listing 1-9.

Listing 1-9. The com.apress.demo.config.WebMvcConfig.java File

```java
package com.apress.demo.config;

import org.springframework.context.MessageSource;
import org.springframework.context.annotation.Bean;
import org.springframework.context.annotation.ComponentScan;
import org.springframework.context.annotation.Configuration;
import org.springframework.context.support.ReloadableResourceBundleMessageSource;
import org.springframework.web.servlet.config.annotation.DefaultServletHandlerConfigurer;
import org.springframework.web.servlet.config.annotation.EnableWebMvc;
import org.springframework.web.servlet.config.annotation.ResourceHandlerRegistry;
import org.springframework.web.servlet.config.annotation.WebMvcConfigurerAdapter;
import org.thymeleaf.spring4.SpringTemplateEngine;
import org.thymeleaf.spring4.view.ThymeleafViewResolver;
import org.thymeleaf.templateresolver.ServletContextTemplateResolver;
import org.thymeleaf.templateresolver.TemplateResolver;

@Configuration
@ComponentScan(basePackages = { "com.apress.demo.web"})
@EnableWebMvc
public class WebMvcConfig extends WebMvcConfigurerAdapter
{

    @Bean
    public TemplateResolver templateResolver() {
        TemplateResolver templateResolver = new ServletContextTemplateResolver();
        templateResolver.setPrefix("/WEB-INF/views/");
        templateResolver.setSuffix(".html");
        templateResolver.setTemplateMode("HTML5");
        templateResolver.setCacheable(false);
        return templateResolver;
    }
```

```java
@Bean
public SpringTemplateEngine templateEngine() {
    SpringTemplateEngine templateEngine = new SpringTemplateEngine();
    templateEngine.setTemplateResolver(templateResolver());
    return templateEngine;
}

@Bean
public ThymeleafViewResolver viewResolver() {
    ThymeleafViewResolver thymeleafViewResolver = new ThymeleafViewResolver();
    thymeleafViewResolver.setTemplateEngine(templateEngine());
    thymeleafViewResolver.setCharacterEncoding("UTF-8");
    return thymeleafViewResolver;
}

@Override
public void addResourceHandlers(ResourceHandlerRegistry registry)
{
    registry.addResourceHandler("/resources/**").addResourceLocations("/resources/");
}

@Override
public void configureDefaultServletHandling(DefaultServletHandlerConfigurer configurer)
{
    configurer.enable();
}

@Bean(name = "messageSource")
public MessageSource messageSource()
{
    ReloadableResourceBundleMessageSource messageSource = new
    ReloadableResourceBundleMessageSource();
    messageSource.setBasename("classpath:messages");
    messageSource.setCacheSeconds(5);
    messageSource.setDefaultEncoding("UTF-8");
    return messageSource;
}
}
```

In the `WebMvcConfig.java` configuration class, we did the following:

- Marked it as a Spring `Configuration` class using `@Configuration` annotation.

- Enabled Annotation-based Spring MVC configuration using `@EnableWebMvc`.

- Configured `ThymeleafViewResolver` by registering the `TemplateResolver`, `SpringTemplateEngine`, and `ThymeleafViewResolver` beans.

- Registered the `ResourceHandlers` bean to indicate requests for static resources. The URI `/resources/**` will be served from the `/resources/` directory.

- Configured `MessageSource` bean to load i18n messages from ResourceBundle `messages_{country-code}.properties` from the classpath.

5. Create the `messages.properties` file in the `src/main/resources` folder and add the following property:

```
app.title=SpringMVC JPA Demo (Without SpringBoot)
```

6. Next, you are going to register the Spring MVC `FrontController` servlet `DispatcherServlet`.

■ **Note** Prior to Servlet 3.x specification, you have to register servlets/filters in `web.xml`. Since the Servlet 3.x specification, you can register servlets/filters programmatically using `ServletContainerInitializer`. Spring MVC provides a convenient class called `AbstractAnnotationConfigDispatcherServletInitializer` to register `DispatcherServlet`.

Listing 1-10. The com.apress.demo.config.SpringWebAppInitializer.java File

```java
package com.apress.demo.config;

import javax.servlet.Filter;

import org.springframework.orm.jpa.support.OpenEntityManagerInViewFilter;
import org.springframework.web.servlet.support.
AbstractAnnotationConfigDispatcherServletInitializer;

public class SpringWebAppInitializer extends
AbstractAnnotationConfigDispatcherServletInitializer
{
    @Override
    protected Class<?>[] getRootConfigClasses()
    {
        return new Class<?>[] { AppConfig.class};
    }

    @Override
    protected Class<?>[] getServletConfigClasses()
    {
        return new Class<?>[] { WebMvcConfig.class };
    }

    @Override
    protected String[] getServletMappings()
    {
        return new String[] { "/" };
    }
```

```
    @Override
    protected Filter[] getServletFilters()
    {
        return new Filter[]{ new OpenEntityManagerInViewFilter() };
    }
}
```

In the `SpringWebAppInitializer.java` configuration class, we did the following:

- Configured `AppConfig.class` as `RootConfirationClasses`, which will become the parent `ApplicationContext` that contains bean definitions shared by all child (`DispatcherServlet`) contexts.

- Configured `WebMvcConfig.class` as `ServletConfigClasses`, which is the child `ApplicationContext` that contains WebMvc bean definitions.

- Configured / as `ServletMapping`, which means that all the requests will be handled by `DispatcherServlet`.

- Registered `OpenEntityManagerInViewFilter` as a servlet filter so that we can lazy-load the JPA entity lazy collections while rendering the view.

7. Create a JPA entity user and its Spring Data JPA Repository interface `UserRepository`. Create a JPA entity called `User.java`, as shown in Listing 1-11, and a Spring Data JPA repository called `UserRepository.java`, as shown in Listing 1-12.

Listing 1-11. The com.apress.demo.domain.User.java File

```
package com.apress.demo.domain;

import javax.persistence.*;

@Entity
public class User
{
    @Id @GeneratedValue(strategy=GenerationType.AUTO)
    private Integer id;
    private String name;

    public User()
    {
    }

    public User(Integer id, String name)
    {
        this.id = id;
        this.name = name;
    }

    public Integer getId()
    {
        return id;
    }
```

```
    public void setId(Integer id)
    {
        this.id = id;
    }

    public String getName()
    {
        return name;
    }

    public void setName(String name)
    {
        this.name = name;
    }
}
```

Listing 1-12. The com.apress.demo.repositories.UserRepository.java File

```
package com.apress.demo.repositories;

import org.springframework.data.jpa.repository.JpaRepository;
import com.apress.demo.domain.User;

public interface UserRepository extends JpaRepository<User, Integer>
{

}
```

If you don't understand what JpaRepository is, don't worry. You will learn more about Spring Data JPA in future chapters.

8. Create a SpringMVC controller to handle URL /, which renders a list of users. See Listing 1-13.

Listing 1-13. The com.apress.demo.web.controllers.HomeController.java File

```
package com.apress.demo.web.controllers;

import org.springframework.beans.factory.annotation.Autowired;
import org.springframework.stereotype.Controller;
import org.springframework.ui.Model;
import org.springframework.web.bind.annotation.RequestMapping;

import com.apress.demo.repositories.UserRepository;

@Controller
public class HomeController
{
    @Autowired
    private UserRepository userRepo;
```

```java
@RequestMapping("/")
public String home(Model model)
{
    model.addAttribute("users", userRepo.findAll());
    return "index";
}
}
```

9. Create a Thymeleaf view called `index.html` in the `/WEB-INF/views/` folder to render a list of users, as shown in Listing 1-14.

Listing 1-14. The src/main/webapp/WEB-INF/views/index.html File

```html
<!DOCTYPE html>
<html xmlns="http://www.w3.org/1999/xhtml"
      xmlns:th="http://www.thymeleaf.org">
    <head>
        <meta charset="utf-8"/>
        <title>Home</title>
    </head>
    <body>
        <h2 th:text="#{app.title}">App Title</h2>
        <table>
            <thead>
                <tr>
                    <th>Id</th>
                    <th>Name</th>
                </tr>
            </thead>
            <tbody>
                <tr th:each="user : ${users}">
                    <td th:text="${user.id}">Id</td>
                    <td th:text="${user.name}">Name</td>
                </tr>
            </tbody>
        </table>
    </body>
</html>
```

You are all set now to run the application. But before that, you need to download and configure a server like Tomcat, Jetty, or Wildflyetc in your IDE. You can download Tomcat 8 and configure your favorite IDE, run the application, and point your browser to `http://localhost:8080/springmvcjpa-demo`. If you do, you should see the list of user details in a table, as shown in Figure 1-1.

Figure 1-1. *Showing a list of users*

Yay...you did it. But wait, isn't it too much work to just show a list of user details pulled from a database table?

Let's be honest and fair. All this configuration is not just for this one use-case. This configuration becomes the basis for the rest of the application. Again, this is too much work to do if you want to quickly get up and running. Another problem with it is, assume that you want to develop another SpringMVC application with a similar technical stack. You could copy and paste the configuration and tweak it. Right?

Remember one thing: if you have to do the same thing again and again, you should find an automated way to do it.

Apart from writing the same configuration again and again, do you see any other problems here? Let's take a look at the problems I am seeing here.

- You need to hunt through all the compatible libraries for the specific Spring version and configure them.

- Most of the time, you'll configure the `DataSource`, `EntitymanagerFactory`, `TransactionManager`, etc. beans the same way. Wouldn't it be great if Spring could do it for you automatically?

- Similarly, you configure the SpringMVC beans like `ViewResolver`, `MessageSource`, etc. the same way most of the time. If Spring can automatically do it for you, that would be awesome.

What if Spring is capable of configuring beans automatically? What if you can customize the automatic configuration using simple customizable properties?

For example, instead of mapping the `DispatcherServlet url-pattern` to /, you want to map it to /app/. Instead of putting Thymeleaf views in the `/WEB-INF/views` folder, you want to place them in the `/WEB-INF/templates/` folder.

So basically you want Spring to do things automatically, yet provide the flexibility to override the default configuration in a simpler way. You are about to enter the world of Spring Boot, where your dreams can come true!

A Quick Taste of Spring Boot

Welcome to Spring Boot! Spring Boot will configure application components automatically for you, but allows you to override the defaults if you want to.

Instead of explaining this in theory, I prefer to explain by example. In this section, you'll see how to implement the same application, this time using Spring Boot.

1. Create a Maven-based Spring Boot project and configure the dependencies in the pom.xml file, as shown in Listing 1-15.

Listing 1-15. The pom.xml File

```xml
<?xml version="1.0" encoding="UTF-8"?>
<project xmlns="http://maven.apache.org/POM/4.0.0"
        xmlns:xsi="http://www.w3.org/2001/XMLSchema-instance"
        xsi:schemaLocation="http://maven.apache.org/POM/4.0.0
        http://maven.apache.org/maven-v4_0_0.xsd">
    <modelVersion>4.0.0</modelVersion>
    <groupId>com.apress</groupId>
    <artifactId>hello-springboot</artifactId>
    <packaging>jar</packaging>
    <version>1.0-SNAPSHOT</version>
    <name>hello-springboot</name>
    <parent>
        <groupId>org.springframework.boot</groupId>
        <artifactId>spring-boot-starter-parent</artifactId>
        <version>2.0.0.RELEASE</version>
    </parent>
    <properties>
        <project.build.sourceEncoding>UTF-8</project.build.sourceEncoding>
        <java.version>1.8</java.version>
    </properties>
    <dependencies>
        <dependency>
            <groupId>org.springframework.boot</groupId>
            <artifactId>spring-boot-starter-data-jpa</artifactId>
        </dependency>
        <dependency>
            <groupId>org.springframework.boot</groupId>
            <artifactId>spring-boot-starter-web</artifactId>
        </dependency>
        <dependency>
            <groupId>org.springframework.boot</groupId>
            <artifactId>spring-boot-starter-thymeleaf</artifactId>
        </dependency>
        <dependency>
            <groupId>mysql</groupId>
            <artifactId>mysql-connector-java</artifactId>
        </dependency>
```

```
        </dependencies>
        <build>
            <plugins>
                <plugin>
                    <groupId>org.springframework.boot</groupId>
                    <artifactId>spring-boot-maven-plugin</artifactId>
                </plugin>
            </plugins>
        </build>
</project>
```

Wow, this pom.xml file suddenly become so small!

Note   Don't worry if this configuration doesn't make sense at this point in time. You have plenty more to learn in coming chapters.

If you want to use any the MILESTONE or SNAPSHOT version of Spring Boot, you need to configure the following milestone/snapshot repositories in pom.xml.

```
<parent>
    <groupId>org.springframework.boot</groupId>
    <artifactId>spring-boot-starter-parent</artifactId>
    <version>2.0.0.BUILD-SNAPSHOT</version>
</parent>

<repositories>
    <repository>
        <id>spring-snapshots</id>
        <name>Spring Snapshots</name>
        <url>https://repo.spring.io/snapshot</url>
        <snapshots>
            <enabled>true</enabled>
        </snapshots>
    </repository>
    <repository>
        <id>spring-milestones</id>
        <name>Spring Milestones</name>
        <url>https://repo.spring.io/milestone</url>
        <snapshots>
            <enabled>false</enabled>
        </snapshots>
    </repository>
</repositories>

<pluginRepositories>
    <pluginRepository>
        <id>spring-snapshots</id>
        <name>Spring Snapshots</name>
```

```
        <url>https://repo.spring.io/snapshot</url>
        <snapshots>
            <enabled>true</enabled>
        </snapshots>
    </pluginRepository>
    <pluginRepository>
        <id>spring-milestones</id>
        <name>Spring Milestones</name>
        <url>https://repo.spring.io/milestone</url>
        <snapshots>
            <enabled>false</enabled>
        </snapshots>
    </pluginRepository>
</pluginRepositories>
```

2. Configure datasource/JPA properties in `src/main/resources/application.properties`, as shown in Listing 1-16.

Listing 1-16. The src/main/resources/application.properties File

```
spring.datasource.driver-class-name=com.mysql.jdbc.Driver
spring.datasource.url=jdbc:mysql://localhost:3306/test
spring.datasource.username=root
spring.datasource.password=admin
spring.datasource.initialize=true
spring.jpa.hibernate.ddl-auto=update
spring.jpa.show-sql=true
```

Copy the same `data.sql` file into the `src/main/resources` folder.

3. Create a JPA Entity called `User.java`, Spring Data JPA Repository Interface called `UserRepository.java`, and controller called `HomeController.java`, as shown in the previous `springmvc-jpa-demo` application.

4. Create a Thymeleaf view to show the list of users. You can copy `/WEB-INF/views/index.html`, which you created in the `springmvc-jpa-demo` application, into the `src/main/resources/templates` folder of this new project.

5. Create a Spring Boot EntryPointclass `Application.java` file with the main method, as shown in Listing 1-17.

Listing 1-17. The com.apress.demo.Application.java File

```
package com.apress.demo;

import org.springframework.boot.SpringApplication;
import org.springframework.boot.autoconfigure.SpringBootApplication;

@SpringBootApplication
public class Application
{
```

```
    public static void main(String[] args)
    {
        SpringApplication.run(Application.class, args);
    }
}
```

Now run `Application.java` as a Java application and point your browser to `http://localhost:8080/`. You should see the list of users in a table format.

By you might be scratching your head, thinking "What is going on?". The next section explains what just happened.

Easy Dependency Management

The first thing to note is the use of the dependencies named `spring-boot-starter-*`. Remember that I said, "Most of the time, you use the same configuration". So when you add the `springboot-starter-web` dependency, it will by default pull all the commonly used libraries while developing Spring MVC applications, such as `spring-webmvc`, `jackson-json`, `validation-api`, and `tomcat`.

We added the `spring-boot-starter-data-jpa` dependency. This pulls all the `spring-data-jpa` dependencies and adds Hibernate libraries because most applications use Hibernate as a JPA implementation.

Autoconfiguration

Not only does the `spring-boot-starter-web` add all these libraries but it also configures the commonly registered beans like `DispatcherServlet`, `ResourceHandlers`, `MessageSource`, etc. with sensible defaults.

We also added `spring-boot-starter-thymeleaf`, which not only adds the Thymeleaf library dependencies but also configures the `ThymeleafViewResolver` beans automatically.

We haven't defined any of the `DataSource`, `EntityManagerFactory`, or `TransactionManager` beans, but they are automatically created. How?

If you have any in-memory database drivers like H2 or HSQL in the classpath, then Spring Boot will automatically create an in-memory datasource and will register the `EntityManagerFactory` and `TransactionManager` beans automatically with sensible defaults.

But you are using MySQL, so you need to explicitly provide MySQL connection details. You have configured those MySQL connection details in the `application.properties` file and Spring Boot creates a `DataSource` using those properties.

Embedded Servlet Container Support

The most important and surprising thing is that we created a simple Java class annotated with some magical annotation (`@SpringApplication`), which has a `main()` method. By running that `main()` method, we are able to run the application and access it at `http://localhost:8080/`. Where does the servlet container come from?

We added `spring-boot-starter-web`, which pulls `spring-boot-starter-tomcat` automatically. When we run the `main()` method, it starts tomcat as an embedded container so that we don't have to deploy our application on any externally installed tomcat server. What if we want to use a Jetty server instead of Tomcat? You simply exclude `spring-boot-starter-tomcat` from `spring-boot-starter-web` and include `spring-boot-starter-jetty`. That's it.

But this looks magical! I can imagine what you are thinking. You are thinking like Spring Boot looks cool and it is doing a lot of things automatically for you. You still do not fully understand how it is all working behind the scenes. Right?

I can understand. Watching a magic show is fun, but mystery is not so fun with software development. Don't worry, we will be looking at each of these things and explaining in detail what's happening behind the scenes. I don't want to overwhelm you by dumping everything on you in this first chapter.

Summary

This chapter was a quick overview of various Spring configuration styles. The goal was to show you the complexity of configuring Spring applications. Also, you had a quick look at Spring Boot by creating a simple web application.

The next chapter takes a more detailed look at Spring Boot and shows how you can create Spring Boot applications in different ways.

CHAPTER 2

Getting Started with Spring Boot

This chapter takes a more detailed look at Spring Boot and its features. Then the chapter looks at various options of creating a Spring Boot application, such as the Spring Initializr, Spring Tool Suite, Intellij IDEA, etc. Finally, the chapter explores the generated code and looks at how to run an application.

What Is Spring Boot?

Spring Boot is an opinionated framework that helps developers build Spring-based applications quickly and easily. The main goal of Spring Boot is to quickly create Spring-based applications without requiring developers to write the same boilerplate configuration again and again. The key Spring Boot features include:

- Spring Boot starters

- Spring Boot autoconfiguration

- Elegant configuration management

- Spring Boot actuator

- Easy-to-use embedded servlet container support

Spring Boot Starters

Spring Boot offers many starter modules to get started quickly with many of the commonly used technologies, like SpringMVC, JPA, MongoDB, Spring Batch, SpringSecurity, Solr, ElasticSearch, etc. These starters are pre-configured with the most commonly used library dependencies so you don't have to search for the compatible library versions and configure them manually.

For example, the `spring-boot-starter-data-jpa` starter module includes all the dependencies required to use Spring Data JPA, along with Hibernate library dependencies, as Hibernate is the most commonly used JPA implementation.

Note   You can find a list of all the Spring Boot starters that come out-of-the-box in the official documentation at: `http://docs.spring.io/spring-boot/docs/current/reference/htmlsingle/` `#using-boot-starter-poms`.

© K. Siva Prasad Reddy 2017

K. S. Prasad Reddy, *Beginning Spring Boot 2*, DOI 10.1007/978-1-4842-2931-6_2

Spring Boot Autoconfiguration

Spring Boot addresses the problem that Spring applications need complex configuration by eliminating the need to manually set up the boilerplate configuration.

Spring Boot takes an opinionated view of the application and configures various components automatically, by registering beans based on various criteria. The criteria can be:

- Availability of a particular class in a classpath

- Presence or absence of a Spring bean

- Presence of a system property

- Absence of a configuration file

For example, if you have the `spring-webmvc` dependency in your classpath, Spring Boot assumes you are trying to build a SpringMVC-based web application and automatically tries to register `DispatcherServlet` if it is not already registered.

If you have any embedded database drivers in the classpath, such as H2 or HSQL, and if you haven't configured a `DataSource` bean explicitly, then Spring Boot will automatically register a `DataSource` bean using in-memory database settings. You will learn more about the autoconfiguration in Chapter 3.

Elegant Configuration Management

Spring supports externalizing configurable properties using the `@PropertySource` configuration. Spring Boot takes it even further by using the sensible defaults and powerful type-safe property binding to bean properties. Spring Boot supports having separate configuration files for different profiles without requiring much configuration.

Spring Boot Actuator

Being able to get the various details of an application running in production is crucial to many applications. The Spring Boot actuator provides a wide variety of such production-ready features without requiring developers to write much code. Some of the Spring actuator features are:

- Can view the application bean configuration details

- Can view the application URL mappings, environment details, and configuration parameter values

- Can view the registered health check metrics

Easy-to-Use Embedded Servlet Container Support

Traditionally, while building web applications, you need to create WAR type modules and then deploy them on external servers like Tomcat, WildFly, etc. But by using Spring Boot, you can create a JAR type module and embed the servlet container in the application very easily so that the application will be a self-contained deployment unit. Also, during development, you can easily run the Spring Boot JAR type module as a Java application from the IDE or from the command-line using a build tool like Maven or Gradle.

You will learn more about these features and how to use them effectively in the following chapters.

Your First Spring Boot Application

There are many ways to create a Spring Boot application. The simplest way is to use Spring Initializr at http://start.spring.io/, which is an online Spring Boot application generator. In this section, you'll see how to create a simple Spring Boot web application serving a simple HTML page and explore various aspects of a typical Spring Boot application.

Using Spring Initializr

You can point your browser to http://start.spring.io/ and see the project details, as shown in Figure 2-1.

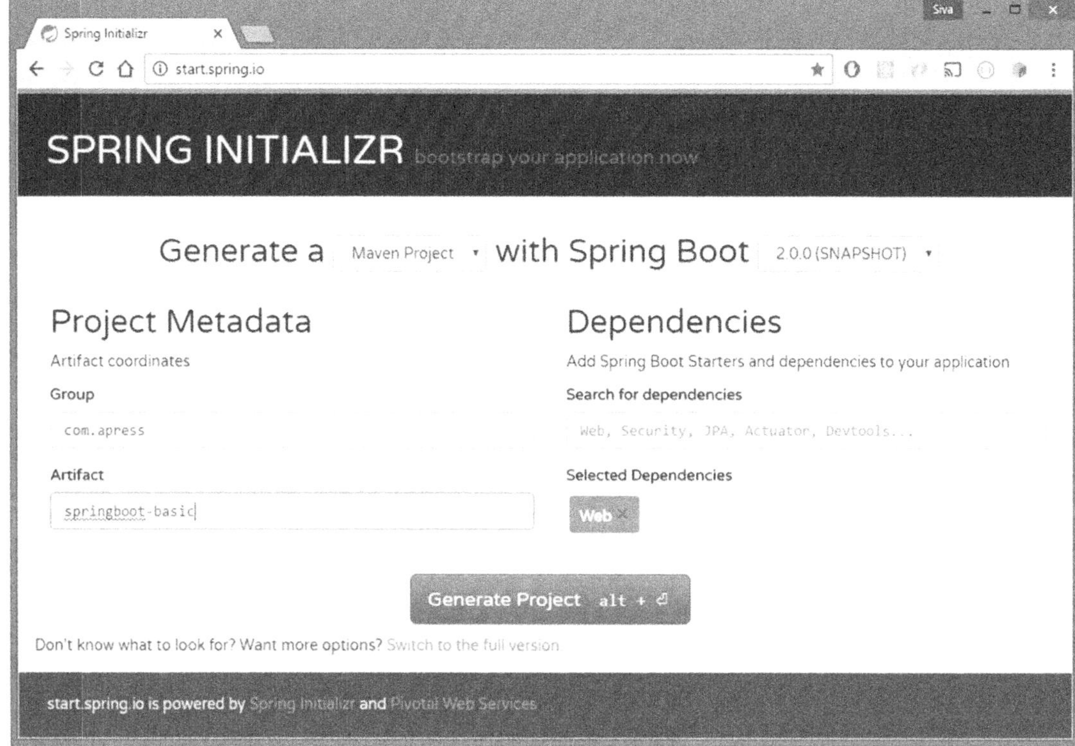

Figure 2-1. *Spring Initializr*

1. Select Maven Project and Spring Boot version (as of writing this book, the latest version is 2.0.0—SNAPSHOT).

2. Enter the Maven project details as follows:

    - Group: com.apress

    - Artifact: springboot-basic

    - Name: springboot-basic

    - Package Name: com.apress.demo

- Packaging: JAR

- Java version: 1.8

- Language: Java

3. You can search for the starters if you are already familiar with their names or click on the Switch to the Full Version link to see all the available starters. You'll see many starter modules organized into various categories, like Core, Web, Data, etc. Select the Web checkbox from the Web category.

4. Click on the Generate Project button.

Now you can extract the downloaded ZIP file and import it into your favorite IDE.

Using the Spring Tool Suite

The Spring Tool Suite (STS: `https://spring.io/tools/sts`) is an extension of the Eclipse IDE with lots of Spring framework related plugins. You can easily create a Spring Boot application from STS by selecting File ➤ New ➤ Other ➤ Spring ➤ Spring Starter Project ➤ Next. You will see the wizard, which looks similar to the Spring Initializr (Figure 2-2).

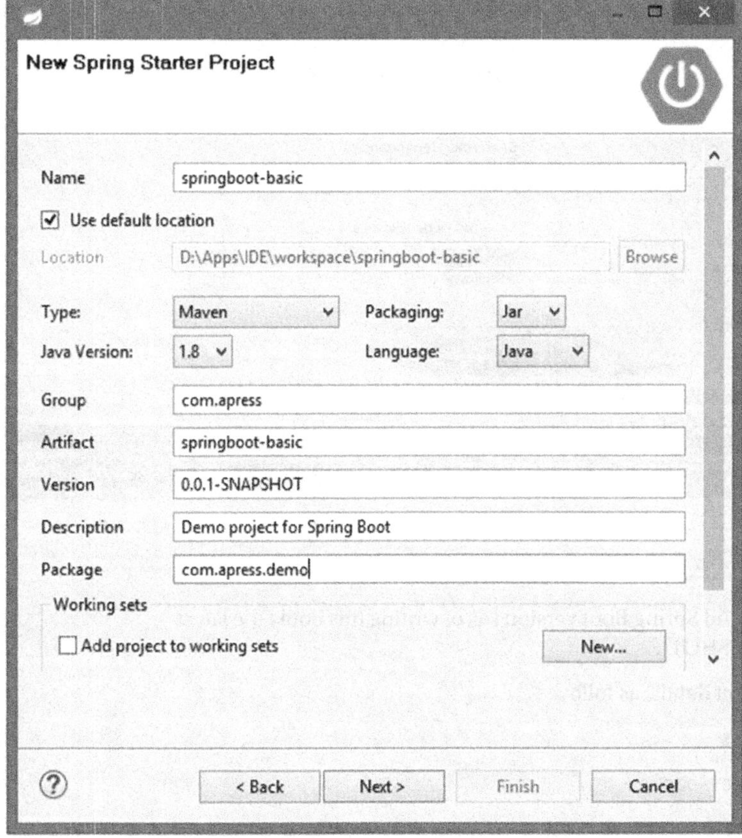

Figure 2-2. STS New Spring Starter Project wizard

Enter the project details and click Next. Then select the latest Spring Boot Version and Web starter (Figure 2-3) and click Finish.

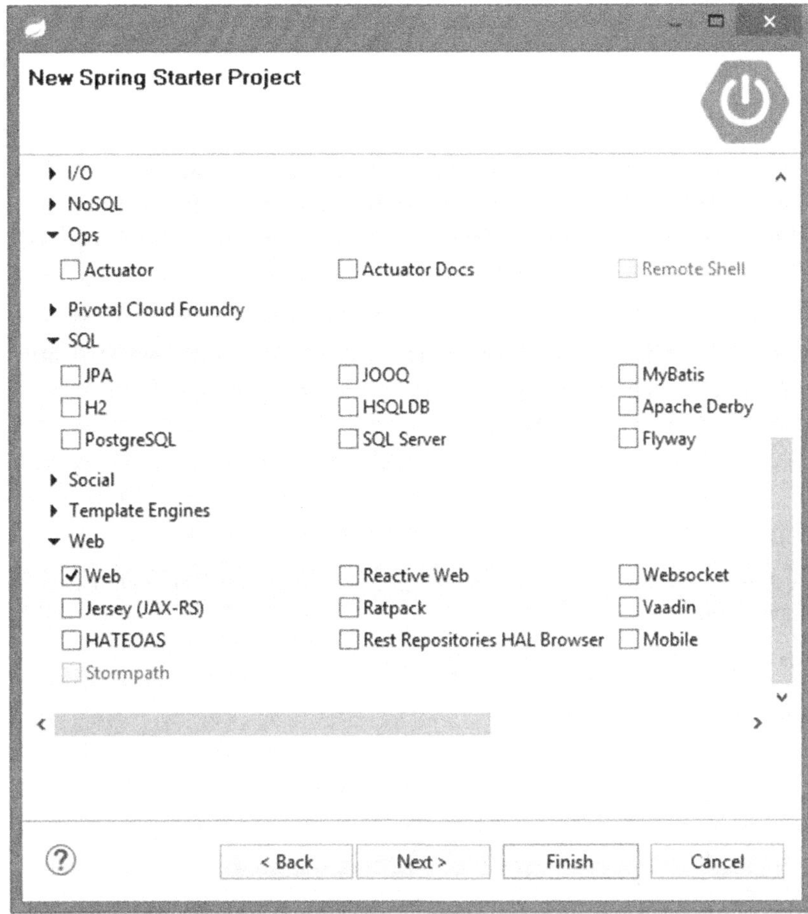

Figure 2-3. *STS Spring Starters selection wizard*

The Spring Boot project will be created and automatically imported into the STS IDE.

Using Intellij IDEA

Intellij IDEA is a powerful commercial IDE with great features, including support for Spring Boot. You can create a Spring Boot project from Intellij IDEA by selecting File ➤ New ➤ Project ➤ Spring Initializr ➤ Next. Enter the project details and click Next. Then select the starters and click Next. Finally, enter the project name and click Finish.

■ **Note** Spring framework support comes only with the commercial Intellij IDEA Ultimate Edition, not with the Community Edition, which is free. If you want to use the Intellij IDEA Community Edition, you can generate the project using Spring Initializr and import it into Intellij IDEA as a Maven/Gradle project.

Using NetBeans IDE

The NetBeans IDE is another popular IDE for developing Java applications. As of now, there is no out-of- the-box support for creating Spring Boot projects in NetBeans, but the community built the NB Spring Boot plugin (see `https://github.com/AlexFalappa/nb-springboot`), which supports creating Spring Boot applications directly from the IDE.

■ **Note** There are some other options for quickly using Spring Boot, by using Spring Boot CLI and SDKMAN. You can find more details at "Installing Spring Boot" at: `http://docs.spring.io/spring-boot/docs/ current/reference/htmlsingle/#getting-started-installing-spring-boot`.

Exploring the Project

Now that you created a Spring Boot Maven-based project with the web starter, you're ready to explore what is contained in the generated application.

1. First, take a look at the pom.xml file, as shown in Listing 2-1.

Listing 2-1. The pom.xml File

```xml
<?xml version="1.0" encoding="UTF-8"?>
<project xmlns="http://maven.apache.org/POM/4.0.0"
        xmlns:xsi="http://www.w3.org/2001/XMLSchema-instance"
        xsi:schemaLocation="http://maven.apache.org/POM/4.0.0
    http://maven.apache.org/xsd/maven-4.0.0.xsd">
    <modelVersion>4.0.0</modelVersion>
    <groupId>com.apress</groupId>
    <artifactId>springboot-basic</artifactId>
    <version>0.0.1-SNAPSHOT</version>
    <packaging>jar</packaging>
    <name>springboot-basic</name>
    <description>Demo project for Spring Boot</description>
    <parent>
        <groupId>org.springframework.boot</groupId>
        <artifactId>spring-boot-starter-parent</artifactId>
        <version>2.0.0.BUILD-SNAPSHOT</version>
        <relativePath/>
    </parent>
```

```xml
<properties>
    <project.build.sourceEncoding>UTF-8</project.build.sourceEncoding>
    <project.reporting.outputEncoding>UTF-8</project.reporting.outputEncoding>
    <java.version>1.8</java.version>
</properties>
<repositories>
    <repository>
        <id>spring-snapshots</id>
        <name>Spring Snapshots</name>
        <url>https://repo.spring.io/snapshot</url>
        <snapshots>
            <enabled>true</enabled>
        </snapshots>
    </repository>
    <repository>
        <id>spring-milestones</id>
        <name>Spring Milestones</name>
        <url>https://repo.spring.io/milestone</url>
        <snapshots>
            <enabled>false</enabled>
        </snapshots>
    </repository>
</repositories>
<pluginRepositories>
    <pluginRepository>
        <id>spring-snapshots</id>
        <name>Spring Snapshots</name>
        <url>https://repo.spring.io/snapshot</url>
        <snapshots>
            <enabled>true</enabled>
        </snapshots>
    </pluginRepository>
    <pluginRepository>
        <id>spring-milestones</id>
        <name>Spring Milestones</name>
        <url>https://repo.spring.io/milestone</url>
        <snapshots>
            <enabled>false</enabled>
        </snapshots>
    </pluginRepository>
</pluginRepositories>
<dependencies>
    <dependency>
        <groupId>org.springframework.boot</groupId>
        <artifactId>spring-boot-starter-web</artifactId>
    </dependency>
```

```
    <dependency>
        <groupId>org.springframework.boot</groupId>
        <artifactId>spring-boot-starter-test</artifactId>
        <scope>test</scope>
    </dependency>
</dependencies>
<build>
    <plugins>
        <plugin>
            <groupId>org.springframework.boot</groupId>
            <artifactId>spring-boot-maven-plugin</artifactId>
        </plugin>
    </plugins>
</build>
</project>
```

The first thing to note here is that the `springboot-basic` Maven module is inheriting from the `springboot-starter-parent` module. By inheriting from `spring-boot-starter-parent`, this new module will automatically have the following benefits:

- You only need to specify the Spring Boot version once in the parent module configuration. You don't need to specify the version for all the starter dependencies and other supporting libraries. To see the list of supporting libraries, check out the `pom.xml` file of the `org.springframework.boot:springboot-dependencies:{version}` Maven module.

- The parent module `spring-boot-starter-parent` already includes the most commonly used plugins, such as `maven-jar-plugin`, `maven-surefire-plugin`, `maven-war-plugin`, `exec-maven-plugin`, and `maven-resources-plugin`, with sensible defaults.

- In addition to the previously mentioned plugins, the `spring-boot-starter-parent` module also configures the `spring-boot-maven-plugin`, which will be used to build fat JARs. We cover the `spring-boot-maven-plugin` in more detail later in this chapter.

This example selects only `web` starter, but `test` starter is also included by default. We selected 1.8 as the Java version, hence the property `<java.version>1.8</java.version>` is included. This `java.version` value will be used to configure the JDK version for the Maven compiler in the `spring-boot-starter-parent` module.

```
<maven.compiler.source>${java.version}</maven.compiler.source>
<maven.compiler.target>${java.version}</maven.compiler.target>
```

2. The generated Spring Boot JAR type module will have an application entry point Java class called `SpringbootBasicApplication.java` with the `public static void main(String[] args)` method, which you can run to start the application. See Listing 2-2.

Listing 2-2. com.apress.demo.SpringbootBasicApplication.java

```java
package com.apress.demo;
import org.springframework.boot.SpringApplication;
import org.springframework.boot.autoconfigure.SpringBootApplication;

@SpringBootApplication
public class SpringbootBasicApplication
{
    public static void main(String[] args)
    {
        SpringApplication.run(SpringbootBasicApplication.class, args);
    }
}
```

Here, the `SpringbootBasicApplication` class is annotated with the `@SpringBootApplication` annotation, which is a composed annotation.

```java
@Target(ElementType.TYPE)
@Retention(RetentionPolicy.RUNTIME)
@Documented
@Inherited
@SpringBootConfiguration
@EnableAutoConfiguration
@ComponentScan(excludeFilters = {
                @Filter(type = FilterType.CUSTOM, classes = TypeExcludeFilter.class),
                @Filter(type = FilterType.CUSTOM, classes = AutoConfigurationExcludeFilter.
                class) })
public @interface SpringBootApplication {

    ....
    ....
}
```

The `@SpringBootConfiguration` is another composed annotation with the `@Configuration` annotation.

```java
@Target(ElementType.TYPE)
@Retention(RetentionPolicy.RUNTIME)
@Documented
@Configuration
public @interface SpringBootConfiguration {

}
```

Here are the meanings of these annotations:

- `@Configuration` indicates that this class is a Spring configuration class.

- `@ComponentScan` enables component scanning for Spring beans in the package in which the current class is defined.

- `@EnableAutoConfiguration` triggers Spring Boot's autoconfiguration mechanisms.

You are bootstrapping the application by calling `SpringApplication.run(SpringbootBasicApplication.class, args)` in the `main()` method. You can pass one or more Spring configuration classes the `SpringApplication.run()` method. But if you have your application entry point class in a root package, it is sufficient to pass the application entry class only, which takes care of scanning other Spring configuration classes in all the sub-packages.

3. Now create a simple SpringMVC controller, called `HomeController.java`, as shown in Listing 2-3.

Listing 2-3. HomeController.java

```
package com.apress.demo;

import org.springframework.stereotype.Controller;
import org.springframework.ui.Model;
import org.springframework.web.bind.annotation.RequestMapping;

@Controller
public class HomeController
{
    @RequestMapping("/")
    public String home(Model model) {
        return "index.html";
    }
}
```

This is a simple SpringMVC controller with one request handler method for URL /, which returns the view named `index.html`.

4. Create a HTML view called `index.html`.

By default, Spring Boot serves the static content from the `src/main/public/` and `src/main/static/` directories. So create `index.html` in `src/main/public/`, as shown in Listing 2-4.

Listing 2-4. src/main/public/index.html

```
<!DOCTYPE html>
<html>
<head>
<meta charset="utf-8"/>
<title>Home</title>
</head>
<body>
<h2>Hello World!!</h2>
</body>
</html>
```

Now, from your IDE, run the `SpringbootBasicApplication.main()` method as a standalone Java class that will start the embedded Tomcat server on port 8080 and point the browser to `http://localhost:8080/`. You should be able to see the response: `Hello World!!`.

You can also run the Spring Boot application using `spring-boot-maven-plugin`, as follows:

```
mvn spring-boot:run
```

The Application Entry Point Class

Spring Boot applications should have an entry point class with the `public static void main(String[]` `args)` method, which is usually annotated with the `@SpringBootApplication` annotation and will be used to bootstrap the application (Listing 2-5).

Listing 2-5. Main Class com.mycompany.myproject.Application.java in the Root Package

```
package com.mycompany.myproject;

import org.springframework.boot.SpringApplication;
import org.springframework.boot.autoconfigure.SpringBootApplication;

@SpringBootApplication
public class Application
{
    public static void main(String[] args)
    {
        SpringApplication.run(Application.class, args);
    }
}
```

It is highly recommended that you put the main entry point class in the root package, say in `com.mycompany.myproject`, so that the `@EnableAutoConfiguration` and `@ComponentScan` annotations will scan for Spring beans, JPA entities, etc., in the root and all of its sub-packages automatically.

If you have an entry point class in a nested package, you might need to specify the `basePackages` to scan for Spring components explicitly (Listing 2-6).

Listing 2-6. Main Class com.mycompany.myproject.config.Application.java in a Non-Root Package

```
package com.mycompany.myproject.config;

@Configuration
@EnableAutoConfiguration
@ComponentScan(basePackages = "com.mycompany.myproject")
@EntityScan(basePackageClasses=Person.class)
public class Application
{
    public static void main(String[] args)
    {
        SpringApplication.run(Application.class, args);
    }
}
```

Here, the `Application.java` main class is in the `com.mycompany.myproject.config` package, which is not the root package. So, you need to specify `@ComponentScan(basePackages = "com.mycompany.myproject")` so that Spring Boot will scan `com.mycompany.myproject` and all of its sub-packages for Spring components. Also, we specified `@EntityScan(basePackageClasses=Person.class)` so that Spring Boot will scan for JPA entities under the package where `Person.class` exists.

Fat JAR Using the Spring Boot Maven Plugin

You can run your application directly from the IDE or use Maven `spring-boot:run` during development, but ultimately you need to create a deployment unit that can be run in the production environment without any IDE support. You can use `spring-boot-maven-plugin` to create a single deployment unit (a fat JAR) by executing the following Maven goals.

```
mvn clean package
```

Now there are two interesting files in the `target` directory—`springboot-basic-1.0-SNAPSHOT.jar` and `springboot-basic-1.0-SNAPSHOT.jar.original`. The `springboot-basic-1.0-SNAPSHOT.jar.original` file will contain only the compiled classes and classpath resources.

But if you look at `springboot-basic-1.0-SNAPSHOT.jar`, you find the following:

- Compiled classes of your own source code in `src/main/java` and static resources from `src/main/resources` will be in the `BOOT-INF/classes` directory

- All the dependent JARs in the `BOOT-INF/lib` directory

- Classes in the `org.springframework.boot.loader` package that do the Spring Boot magic of running the Spring Boot application

You can create self-contained deployment units for JAR-type modules using plugins like `maven-shade-plugin`, which packages all the dependent JAR classes into a single JAR file. But Spring Boot follows a different approach and it allows you to nest JARs directly within your Spring Boot application JAR file. You can read more about at: `http://docs.spring.io/spring-boot/docs/current/reference/htmlsingle/#executable-jar`.

You can run the application using the following command:

```
java -jar springboot-basic-1.0-SNAPSHOT.jar
```

Spring Boot Using Gradle

Gradle is another popular build tool based on Groovy DSL. You can use Gradle instead of Maven to build Spring Boot applications. Gradle follows a similar project structure as Maven. For example, like the main Java source resides in `src/main/java`, the main resources reside in `src/main/resources`, and so on.

You can create a Gradle-based Spring Boot project by selecting Gradle as the build tool while creating the application through Spring Initializr or the IDEs. The generated `build.gradle` file will look like Listing 2-7.

Listing 2-7. build.gradle

```
buildscript {
    ext {
        springBootVersion = '2.0.0.BUILD-SNAPSHOT'
    }
    repositories {
        mavenCentral()
maven { url "https://repo.spring.io/snapshot" }
maven { url "https://repo.spring.io/milestone" }
    }
```

```
    dependencies {
        classpath("org.springframework.boot:spring-boot-gradle-plugin:${springBootVersion}")
    }
}

apply plugin: 'java'
apply plugin: 'eclipse'
apply plugin: 'org.springframework.boot'

version = '0.0.1-SNAPSHOT'
sourceCompatibility = 1.8

repositories {
    mavenCentral()
maven { url "https://repo.spring.io/snapshot" }
    maven { url "https://repo.spring.io/milestone" }
}

dependencies {
    compile('org.springframework.boot:spring-boot-starter-web')
    testCompile('org.springframework.boot:spring-boot-starter-test')
}
```

Now you can run the application by using the **gradle bootRun** command. You can also use the **gradle build** command, which generates the fat JAR in the build/libs directory.

Maven or Gradle?

In the Java world, Maven and Gradle are the two most popular build tools. Maven was released in 2004 and is used widely by many developers. Gradle was released in 2012 and it's more powerful and easy to customize.

As Maven is still the most commonly used build tool, it is used throughout the book. However, you can find the Gradle build scripts in the book's sample code for each of the modules. So you can use Maven or Gradle. The choice is yours!

Summary

This chapter quickly covered Spring Boot's features and discussed different ways to create Spring Boot applications. Now that you know how to create a simple Spring Boot application and run it, you probably want to understand how Spring Boot's autoconfiguration works. But before that, you should know about Spring's @Conditional feature, on which Spring Boot's autoconfiguration depends.

The next chapter explores the power of the @Conditional annotation feature and takes a detailed look at how Spring Boot autoconfiguration works.

CHAPTER 3

Spring Boot Autoconfiguration

The Spring Boot autoconfiguration mechanism heavily depends on the @Conditional feature. This chapter explores how you can conditionally register Spring beans by using the @Conditional annotation and create various types of Conditional implementations meeting certain criteria. Then you will look into how Spring Boot leverages the @Conditional feature to configure beans automatically based on certain criteria.

Exploring the Power of @Conditional

While developing Spring-based applications, you may come across a need to register beans conditionally. For example, you may want to register a DataSource bean pointing to the DEV database when running applications locally and point to a different PRODUCTION database when running in production.

You can externalize the database connection parameters into property files and use the file that's appropriate for the environment. But you must change the configuration whenever you need to point to a different environment and redeploy the application.

To address this issue, Spring 3.1 introduced the concept of *profiles*. You can register multiple beans of the same type and associate them with one or more profiles. When you run the application, you can activate the desired profile(s). That way, only the beans associated with the activated profiles will be registered.

```
@Configuration
public class AppConfig
{
    @Bean
    @Profile("DEV")
    public DataSource devDataSource() {
        ...
    }

    @Bean
    @Profile("PROD")
    public DataSource prodDataSource() {
        ...
    }
}
```

With this configuration, you can specify the active profile using the -Dspring.profiles.active=DEV system property. This approach works fine for simple cases, such as when you're enabling or disabling bean registrations based on activated profiles. But if you want to register beans based on some conditional logic, the profiles approach itself is not sufficient.

© K. Siva Prasad Reddy 2017
K. S. Prasad Reddy, *Beginning Spring Boot 2*, DOI 10.1007/978-1-4842-2931-6_3

To provide much more flexibility for registering Spring beans conditionally, Spring 4 introduced the concept of the @Conditional. Using the @Conditional approach, you can register a bean conditionally based on any arbitrary condition.

For example, you may want to register a bean when:

- A specific class is present in the classpath

- A Spring bean of a certain type isn't already registered in the ApplicationContext

- A specific file exists in a location

- A specific property value is configured in a configuration file

- A specific system property is present/absent

These are just a few examples and you can set up any condition you want. The next section looks at how Spring's @Conditional works.

Using @Conditional Based on System Properties

Suppose you have a UserDAO interface with methods to get data from a datastore. You have two implementations of UserDAO interface—JdbcUserDAO talks to the MySQL database and MongoUserDAO talks to MongoDB. You may want to enable only JdbcUserDAO or MongoUserDAO based on a specific system property, say dbType.

If the application is started using java -jar myapp.jar -DdbType=MySQL, then you want to enable JdbcUserDAO; otherwise, if the application is started using java -jar myapp.jar -DdbType=MONGO, you want to enable MongoUserDAO.

Suppose you have the UserDAO interface and the JdbcUserDAO and MongoUserDAO implementations, as shown in Listing 3-1.

Listing 3-1. UserDAO Interface and the JdbcUserDAO and MongoUserDAO Implementations

```
public interface UserDAO
{
    List<String> getAllUserNames();
}

public class JdbcUserDAO implements UserDAO
{
    @Override
    public List<String> getAllUserNames()
    {
        System.out.println("**** Getting usernames from RDBMS *****");
        return Arrays.asList("Jim","John","Rob");
    }
}

public class MongoUserDAO implements UserDAO
{
    @Override
    public List<String> getAllUserNames()
    {
        System.out.println("**** Getting usernames from MongoDB *****");
        return Arrays.asList("Bond","James","Bond");
    }
}
```

You can implement the `MySQLDatabaseTypeCondition` condition to check whether the dbType system property is `MYSQL`, as shown in Listing 3-2.

Listing 3-2. MySQLDatabaseTypeCondition.java

```java
public class MySQLDatabaseTypeCondition implements Condition
{
    @Override
    public boolean matches(ConditionContext conditionContext, AnnotatedTypeMetadata metadata)
    {
        String enabledDBType = System.getProperty("dbType");
        return (enabledDBType != null &&
        enabledDBType.equalsIgnoreCase("MYSQL"));
    }
}
```

You can implement the `MongoDBDatabaseTypeCondition` condition to check whether the dbType system property is `MONGODB`, as shown in Listing 3-3.

Listing 3-3. MongoDBDatabaseTypeCondition.java

```java
public class MongoDBDatabaseTypeCondition implements Condition
{
    @Override
    public boolean matches(ConditionContext conditionContext, AnnotatedTypeMetadata metadata)
    {
        String enabledDBType = System.getProperty("dbType");
        return (enabledDBType != null && enabledDBType.equalsIgnoreCase("MONGODB"));
    }
}
```

Now you can configure both the `JdbcUserDAO` and `MongoUserDAO` beans conditionally using @ `Conditional`, as shown in Listing 3-4.

Listing 3-4. AppConfig.java

```java
@Configuration
public class AppConfig
{
    @Bean
    @Conditional(MySQLDatabaseTypeCondition.class)
    public UserDAO jdbcUserDAO(){
        return new JdbcUserDAO();
    }

    @Bean
    @Conditional(MongoDBDatabaseTypeCondition.class)
    public UserDAO mongoUserDAO(){
        return new MongoUserDAO();
    }
}
```

If you run the application, such as `java -jar myapp.jar -DdbType=MYSQL`, only the `JdbcUserDAO` bean will be registered. But if you set the system property to `-DdbType=MONGODB`, the `MongoUserDAO` bean will be registered. This is how you conditionally register a bean based on a system property.

Using @Conditional Based on the Presence/Absence of a Java Class

Suppose you want to register the `MongoUserDAO` bean only when the MongoDB Java driver class called `com.mongodb.Server` is available on the classpath. Otherwise, you want to register the `JdbcUserDAO` bean.

To accomplish this, you can create conditions to check the presence or absence of the MongoDB driver class called `com.mongodb.Server`, as shown in Listing 3-5.

Listing 3-5. MongoDriverPresentsCondition.java and MongoDriverNotPresentsCondition.java

```
public class MongoDriverPresentsCondition implements Condition
{
    @Override
    public boolean matches(ConditionContext conditionContext, AnnotatedType
    Metadata metadata)
    {
        try {
            Class.forName("com.mongodb.Server");
            return true;
        } catch (ClassNotFoundException e) {
            return false;
        }
    }
}

public class MongoDriverNotPresentsCondition implements Condition
{
    @Override
    public boolean matches(ConditionContext conditionContext, AnnotatedType
    Metadata metadata)
    {
        try {
            Class.forName("com.mongodb.Server");
            return false;
        } catch (ClassNotFoundException e) {
            return true;
        }
    }
}
```

This is how you register beans conditionally based on the presence or absence of a class in the classpath.

Using @Conditional Based on the Configured Spring Beans

What if you want to register the `MongoUserDAO` bean only when no other Spring bean of type `UserDAO` are already registered?

You can create a condition to check if there are any existing beans of a certain type, as shown in Listing 3-6.

Listing 3-6. UserDAOBeanNotPresentsCondition.java

```java
public class UserDAOBeanNotPresentsCondition implements Condition
{
    @Override
    public boolean matches(ConditionContext conditionContext, AnnotatedTypeMetadata metadata)
    {
        UserDAO userDAO = conditionContext.getBeanFactory().getBean(UserDAO.class);
        return (userDAO == null);
    }
}
```

Using @Conditional Based on a Property's Configuration

What if you want to register the MongoUserDAO bean only if the app.dbType=MONGO property is set in the property's placeholder configuration file? You can implement that condition, as shown in Listing 3-7.

Listing 3-7. MongoDbTypePropertyCondition.java

```java
public class MongoDbTypePropertyCondition implements Condition
{
    @Override
    public boolean matches(ConditionContext conditionContext, AnnotatedType
    Metadata metadata)
    {
        String dbType = conditionContext.getEnvironment().getProperty("app.dbType");
        return "MONGO".equalsIgnoreCase(dbType);
    }
}
```

You have seen how to implement various types of conditions. But there is an even more elegant way to implement conditions using annotations.

Instead of creating a condition implementation for MYSQL and MongoDB, you can create a DatabaseType annotation as follows:

```java
@Target({ ElementType.TYPE, ElementType.METHOD })
@Retention(RetentionPolicy.RUNTIME)
@Conditional(DatabaseTypeCondition.class)
public @interface DatabaseType
{
    String value();
}
```

Then you implement DatabaseTypeCondition to use the DatabaseType value to determine whether to enable or disable bean registration, as follows:

```java
public class DatabaseTypeCondition implements Condition
{
    @Override
    public boolean matches(ConditionContext conditionContext, AnnotatedType
    Metadata metadata)
    {
        Map<String, Object> attributes = metadata.getAnnotationAttributes(Database
        Type.class.getName());
        String type = (String) attributes.get("value");
        String enabledDBType = System.getProperty("dbType","MYSQL");
        return (enabledDBType != null && type != null && enabledDBType.equals
        IgnoreCase(type));
    }
}
```

Now you can use the @DatabaseType annotation on the bean definitions, as follows:

```java
@Configuration
@ComponentScan
public class AppConfig
{
    @DatabaseType("MYSQL")
    public UserDAO jdbcUserDAO(){
        return new JdbcUserDAO();
    }

    @Bean
    @DatabaseType("MONGO")
    public UserDAO mongoUserDAO(){
        return new MongoUserDAO();
    }
}
```

Here, you are getting the metadata from DatabaseType annotation and checking against the dbType system property value to determine whether to enable or disable the bean registration.

You have seen a good number of examples of how you can register beans conditionally using the @Conditional annotation. Spring Boot extensively uses the @Conditional feature to register beans conditionally based on various criteria.

Spring Boot's Built-In @Conditional Annotations

Spring Boot provides many custom @Conditional annotations to meet developers' autoconfiguration needs based on various criteria. Table 3-1 lists the @Conditional annotations provided by Spring Boot out-of-the-box.

Table 3-1. *Spring Boot @Conditional Annotations*

Annotation	Description
@ConditionalOnBean	Matches when the specified bean classes and/or names are already registered.
@ConditionalOnMissingBean	Matches when the specified bean classes and/or names are not already registered.
@ConditionalOnClass	Matches when the specified classes are on the classpath.
@ConditionalOnMissingClass	Matches when the specified classes are not on the classpath.
@ConditionalOnProperty	Matches when the specified properties have a specific value.
@ConditionalOnResource	Matches when the specified resources are on the classpath.
@ConditionalOnWebApplication	Matches when the application context is a web application context.

Spring Boot provides implementations for these annotations to verify whether the condition is matching or not. For example, look at the source code of the @ConditionalOnClass annotation and OnClassCondition.java in the Spring Boot source code.

```java
@Target({ ElementType.TYPE, ElementType.METHOD })
@Retention(RetentionPolicy.RUNTIME)
@Documented
@Conditional(OnClassCondition.class)
public @interface ConditionalOnClass {

    /**
     * The classes that must be present. Since this annotation parsed by loading class
     * bytecode it is safe to specify classes here that may ultimately not be on the
     * classpath.
     * @return the classes that must be present
     */
    Class<?>[] value() default {};

    /**
     * The classes names that must be present.
     * @return the class names that must be present.
     */
    String[] name() default {};

}

@Order(Ordered.HIGHEST_PRECEDENCE)
class OnClassCondition extends SpringBootCondition
        implements AutoConfigurationImportFilter, BeanFactoryAware, BeanClassLoaderAware {

    private BeanFactory beanFactory;

    private ClassLoader beanClassLoader;

    @Override
    public boolean[] match(String[] autoConfigurationClasses,
```

```
        AutoConfigurationMetadata autoConfigurationMetadata) {
    ConditionEvaluationReport report = getConditionEvaluationReport();
    ConditionOutcome[] outcomes = getOutcomes(autoConfigurationClasses,
            autoConfigurationMetadata);
    boolean[] match = new boolean[outcomes.length];
    for (int i = 0; i < outcomes.length; i++) {
        match[i] = (outcomes[i] == null || outcomes[i].isMatch());
        if (!match[i] && outcomes[i] != null) {
            logOutcome(autoConfigurationClasses[i], outcomes[i]);
            if (report != null) {
                report.recordConditionEvaluation(autoConfigurationClasses[i], this,
                        outcomes[i]);
            }
        }
    }
    return match;
}

...
...
...
}
```

You can see how Spring Boot is using the @ConditionalOnClass annotation and OnClassCondition.
class to check whether a given class is present or not. Similarly, you can find various other conditional
annotations from Spring Boot, such as @ConditionalOnBean, @ConditionalOnMissingBean, @Conditiona
lOnResource, @ConditionalOnProperty, etc.

■ **Note**   You can find various condition implementations that Spring Boot uses in the org.springframework.
boot.autoconfigure.condition package of spring-boot-autoconfigure-{version}.jar.

Now that you know how Spring Boot uses the @Conditional feature to conditionally check whether to
register a bean, you might wonder what exactly triggers the autoconfiguration mechanism. This is what the
next section covers.

How Spring Boot Autoconfiguration Works

The key to Spring Boot's autoconfiguration is its @EnableAutoConfiguration annotation. Typically, you
annotate the application entry point class with @SpringBootApplication or, if you want to customize the
defaults, you can use the following annotations:

```
@Configuration
@EnableAutoConfiguration
@ComponentScan
public class Application
{
}
```

The @EnableAutoConfiguration annotation enables the autoconfiguration of Spring ApplicationContext by scanning the classpath components and registering the beans that match various conditions. Spring Boot provides various autoconfiguration classes in spring-boot-autoconfigure-{version}.jar, and they are responsible for registering various components.

Autoconfiguration classes are typically annotated with @Configuration to mark it as a Spring configuration class and annotated with @EnableConfigurationProperties to bind the customization properties and one or more conditional bean registration methods.

For example, consider the org.springframework.boot.autoconfigure.jdbc. DataSourceAutoConfiguration class.

```java
@Configuration
@ConditionalOnClass({ DataSource.class, EmbeddedDatabaseType.class })
@EnableConfigurationProperties(DataSourceProperties.class)
@Import({ Registrar.class, DataSourcePoolMetadataProvidersConfiguration.class })
public class DataSourceAutoConfiguration {
    ...
    ...
    @Bean
    @ConditionalOnMissingBean
    public DataSourceInitializer dataSourceInitializer(DataSourceProperties properties,
            ApplicationContext applicationContext) {
        return new DataSourceInitializer(properties, applicationContext);
    }

    ...
    ...

    @Conditional(EmbeddedDatabaseCondition.class)
    @ConditionalOnMissingBean({ DataSource.class, XADataSource.class })
    @Import(EmbeddedDataSourceConfiguration.class)
    protected static class EmbeddedDatabaseConfiguration {

    }

    @Configuration
    @Conditional(PooledDataSourceCondition.class)
    @ConditionalOnMissingBean({ DataSource.class, XADataSource.class })
    @Import({ DataSourceConfiguration.Tomcat.class, DataSourceConfiguration.Hikari.class,
            DataSourceConfiguration.Dbcp2.class, DataSourceConfiguration.Generic.class })
    protected static class PooledDataSourceConfiguration {

    }
    ...
    ...
```

```
@Configuration
@ConditionalOnProperty(prefix = "spring.datasource", name = "jmx-enabled")
@ConditionalOnClass(name = "org.apache.tomcat.jdbc.pool.DataSourceProxy")
@Conditional(DataSourceAutoConfiguration.DataSourceAvailableCondition.class)
@ConditionalOnMissingBean(name = "dataSourceMBean")
protected static class TomcatDataSourceJmxConfiguration {

    ...
    ...
}
...
...
}
```

Here, DataSourceAutoConfiguration is annotated with @ConditionalOnClass({ DataSource.
class, EmbeddedDatabaseType.class }), which means that the autoconfiguration of beans
defined in DataSourceAutoConfiguration will be considered only if the DataSource.class and
EmbeddedDatabaseType.class classes are available on the classpath.

The class is also annotated with @EnableConfigurationProperties(DataSourceProperties.
class), which enables binding the properties in application.properties to the properties of the
DataSourceProperties class automatically.

```
@ConfigurationProperties(prefix = DataSourceProperties.PREFIX)
public class DataSourceProperties implements BeanClassLoaderAware, EnvironmentAware,
InitializingBean {
    public static final String PREFIX = "spring.datasource";
    ...
    ...
    private String driverClassName;
    private String url;
    private String username;
    private String password;
    ...
    //setters and getters
}
```

With this configuration, all the properties that start with spring.datasource.* will be automatically
bound to the DataSourceProperties object.

```
spring.datasource.url=jdbc:mysql://localhost:3306/test
spring.datasource.username=root
spring.datasource.password=secret
spring.datasource.driver-class-name=com.mysql.jdbc.Driver
```

You can also see some inner classes and bean definition methods that are annotated with Spring
Boot's conditional annotations, such as @ConditionalOnMissingBean, @ConditionalOnClass, and @
ConditionalOnProperty. These bean definitions will be registered in ApplicationContext only if those
conditions match.

You can also explore many other AutoConfiguration classes in spring-boot-autoconfigure-{version}.jar, such as:

- org.springframework.boot.autoconfigure.web.Dispatcher ServletAutoConfiguration

- org.springframework.boot.autoconfigure.orm.jpa.Hibernate JpaAutoConfiguration

- org.springframework.boot.autoconfigure.data.jpa.JpaRepositories AutoConfiguration

- org.springframework.boot.autoconfigure.jackson.JacksonAutoConfiguration

You should now have a basic understanding of how Spring Boot autoconfiguration works, by using various autoconfiguration classes along with @Conditional features.

Summary

This chapter explained how to register Spring beans conditionally using the @Conditional annotation and how Spring Boot leverages @Conditional and @EnableAutoConfiguration annotations to autoconfigure beans based on various criteria.

The next chapter looks at some of the cool features of Spring Boot that help increase developer productivity.

CHAPTER 4

Spring Boot Essentials

The primary goal of Spring Boot is to make it easy to develop Spring-based applications. Spring Boot provides several features to implement commonly used features, such as logging and externalizing configuration properties in a much easier way. This chapter covers configuring logging, externalizing configuration properties, and configuring profile specific properties. Then it explores how to use the Spring Boot developer tools to automatically restart the server on code changes, which will improve developer productivity.

Logging

Logging is a very important part of any application and it helps with debugging issues. Spring Boot, by default, includes `spring-boot-starter-logging` as a transitive dependency for the `spring-boot-starter` module. By default, Spring Boot includes SLF4J along with Logback implementations. Spring Boot has a `LoggingSystem` abstraction that automatically configures logging based on the logging configuration files available in the classpath.

If Logback is available, Spring Boot will choose it as the logging handler. You can easily configure logging levels within the `application.properties` file without having to create logging provider specific configuration files such as `logback.xml` or `log4j.properties`.

```
logging.level.org.springframework.web=INFO
logging.level.org.hibernate=ERROR
logging.level.com.apress=DEBUG
```

If you want to log the data into a file in addition to the console, specify the filename as follows:

```
logging.path=/var/logs/app.log
```

or

```
logging.file=myapp.log
```

If you want to have more control over the logging configuration, create the logging provider specific configuration files in their default locations, which Spring Boot will automatically use.

© K. Siva Prasad Reddy 2017
K. S. Prasad Reddy, *Beginning Spring Boot 2*, DOI 10.1007/978-1-4842-2931-6_4

For example, if you place the `logback.xml` file in the root classpath, Spring Boot will automatically use it to configure the logging system. See Listing 4-1.

Listing 4-1. The logback.xml File

```xml
<configuration>
    <appender name="STDOUT" class="ch.qos.logback.core.ConsoleAppender">
        <encoder>
            <pattern>%d{HH:mm:ss.SSS} [%thread] %-5level %logger{36} - %msg%n</pattern>
        </encoder>
    </appender>
    <appender name="FILE" class="ch.qos.logback.core.FileAppender">
        <file>app.log</file>
        <encoder>
            <pattern>%date %level [%thread] %logger{10} [%file:%line] %msg%n </pattern>
        </encoder>
    </appender>
    <logger name="com.apress" level="DEBUG" additivity="false">
        <appender-ref ref="STDOUT" />
        <appender-ref ref="FILE" />
    </logger>
    <root level="INFO">
        <appender-ref ref="STDOUT" />
        <appender-ref ref="FILE" />
    </root>
</configuration>
```

If you want to use other logging libraries, such as Log4J or Log4j2, instead of Logback, you can exclude `spring-boot-starter-logging` and include the respective logging starter, as follows:

```xml
<dependency>
    <groupId>org.springframework.boot</groupId>
    <artifactId>spring-boot-starter</artifactId>
    <exclusions>
        <exclusion>
            <groupId>org.springframework.boot</groupId>
            <artifactId>spring-boot-starter-logging</artifactId>
        </exclusion>
    </exclusions>
</dependency>

<dependency>
    <groupId>org.springframework.boot</groupId>
    <artifactId>spring-boot-starter-log4j</artifactId>
</dependency>
```

Now you can add the `log4j.properties` file to the root classpath, which Spring Boot will automatically use for logging.

Externalizing Configuration Properties

Typically you will want to externalize configuration parameters into separate properties or XML files instead of burying them inside code so that you can easily change them based on the environment of the application. Spring provides the @PropertySource annotation to specify the list of configuration files.

Spring Boot takes it one step further by automatically registering a PropertyPlaceHolderConfigurer bean using the application.properties file in the root classpath by default. You can also create profile specific configuration files using the filename as application-{profile}.properties.

For example, you can have application.properties, which contains the default properties values, application-dev.properties, which contains the dev profile configuration, and application-prod. properties, which contains the production profile configuration values. If you want to configure properties that are common for all the profiles, you can configure them in application-default.properties.

■ **Note**   You can also use YAML (.yml) files as an alternative to .properties. See the "Using YAML Instead of Properties" section of the Spring Boot reference documentation at: http://docs.spring.io/spring-boot/docs/current/reference/htmlsingle/#boot-features-external-config-yaml.

Type-Safe Configuration Properties

Spring provides the @Value annotation to bind any property value to a bean property. Suppose you had the following application.properties file:

```
jdbc.driver=com.mysql.jdbc.Driver
jdbc.url=jdbc:mysql://localhost:3306/test
jdbc.username=root
jdbc.password=secret
```

You can bind these property values into bean properties using @Value as follows:

```
@Configuration
public class AppConfig
{
    @Value("${jdbc.driver}")
    private String driver;

    @Value("${jdbc.url}")
    private String url;

    @Value("${jdbc.username}")
    private String username;

    @Value("${jdbc.password}")
    private String password;

    ...
    ...
}
```

But binding each property using @Value is a tedious process. So, Spring Boot introduced a mechanism to bind a set of properties to a bean's properties automatically in a type-safe manner.

Suppose you have the previous JDBC parameters and a DataSourceConfig class as follows:

```
public class DataSourceConfig
{
    private String driver;
    private String url;
    private String username;
    private String password;

    //setters and getters
}
```

Now you can simply annotate DataSourceConfig with @ConfigurationProperties(prefix="jdbc") to automatically bind the properties that start with jdbc.*.

```
@Component
@ConfigurationProperties(prefix="jdbc")
public class DataSourceConfig
{
...
...
}
```

Now you can inject the DataSourceConfig bean into other Spring beans and access the properties using getters.

Relaxed Binding

The bean property names need not be exactly the same as the property key names. Spring Boot supports relaxed binding, where the bean property driverClassName will be mapped from any of these: driverClassName, driver-class-name, or DRIVER_CLASS_NAME.

Validating Properties with the Bean Validation API

You can use Bean Validation API annotations such as @NotNull, @Min, @Max, etc., to validate the property's values.

```
@Component
@ConfigurationProperties(prefix="support")
public class Support
{
    @NotNull
    private String applicationName;

    @NotNull
    @Email
    private String email;
```

```
@Min(1) @Max(5)
private Integer severity;

//setters and getters
}
```

If you configured any property values that are invalid as per the configured validation annotations, an exception will thrown at the application startup time. For more details on externalizing properties, see "Externalized Configuration" at: `http://docs.spring.io/spring-boot/docs/current/reference/htmlsingle/#boot-features-external-config`.

Developer Tools

During development, you may need to change the code often and restart the server for those code changes to take effect. Spring Boot provides developer tools (the `spring-boot-devtools` module) that include support for quick application restarts whenever the application classpath content changes.

When you include the `spring-boot-devtools` module during development, the caching of the view templates (Thymeleaf, Velocity, and Freemarkeretc) will be disabled automatically so that you can see the changes immediately. You can see the list of configured properties at `org.springframework.boot.devtools.env.DevToolsPropertyDefaultsPostProcessor`.

```
<dependency>
<groupId>org.springframework.boot</groupId>
<artifactId>spring-boot-devtools</artifactId>
<optional>true</optional>
</dependency>
```

Note that this specifies `spring-boot-devtools` as **optional** by using `<optional>true</optional>` so that it won't be packaged in a fat JAR.

The Spring Boot developer tools trigger application restarts automatically whenever there is a change to the classpath content.

■ **Note** In Eclipse or STS, as soon as you change the classpath resources and save them, devtools will restart the server. In IntelliJ IDEA, you need to run Make Project to trigger a restart.

Whenever you change the class or properties files in the classpath, Spring Boot will automatically restart the server. You won't typically need to restart the server when static content, such as CSS, JS, and HTMLs, changes. So by default Spring Boot excludes these static resource locations from the file change watch list.

```
@ConfigurationProperties(prefix = "spring.devtools")
public class DevToolsProperties {
    ....
    ....
    public static class Restart {

        private static final String DEFAULT_RESTART_EXCLUDES =
        "META-INF/maven/**,"
        + "META-INF/resources/**,resources/**,"
        + "static/**,public/**,templates/**,"
        + "**/*Test.class,**/*Tests.class,git.properties, META-INF/build-info.properties ";
```

```
    /**
     * Patterns that should be excluded from triggering a full restart.
     */
    private String exclude = DEFAULT_RESTART_EXCLUDES;
    ....

    ....
  }
}
```

You can override this default exclusion list by configuring the `spring.devtools.restart.exclude` property.

```
spring.devtools.restart.exclude=assets/**,resources/**
```

If you want to add locations to the restart exclude/include paths, use the following properties.

```
spring.devtools.restart.additional-exclude=assets/**,setup-instructions/**
spring.devtools.restart.additional-paths=D:/global-overrides/
```

Spring Boot's restart mechanism helps increase developer productivity by automatically restarting the server after code changes. But at times, you may need to change multiple classes to implement some feature and it would be annoying if the server kept restarting after every file change. In this case, you can use the `spring.devtools.restart.trigger-file` property to configure a file path to watch for changes. That way, the server will restart only when the `trigger-file` has changed.

```
spring.devtools.restart.trigger-file=restart.txt
```

■ **Note** Once you configure `spring.devtools.restart.trigger-file` and update the trigger file, the server will restart only if there are modifications to the files being watched. Otherwise, the server won't be restarted.

The restart mechanism works by using two classloaders—one (the base classloader) to load classes that don't change (such as classes in third-party jars) and the other (the restart classloader) to load classes that frequently change (such as classes from your application code). When the application restarts, only the classes in the restart classloader will be recreated. This will yield faster restarts.

You can disable restarting by setting the `spring.devtools.restart.enabled = false` property. This will still use two classloaders but the restart classloader won't watch for file changes. If you want to completely turn off the restart mechanism, set the `spring.devtools.restart.enabled=false` property as the system property, as follows.

```
java -jar -Dspring.devtools.restart.enabled=false app.jar
```

If you are developing a bunch of Spring Boot applications and want to apply the same devtools settings to all of them, you can configure global settings by creating a `.spring-bootdevtools.properties` file in the HOME directory.

On Windows OS, it is `C:\Users\<username>\.spring-boot-devtools.properties` and on Linux/ MacOS, it is `/home/<username>/.spring-boot-devtools.properties`.

You can read more about the Spring Boot developer tools at `http://docs.spring.io/spring-boot/ docs/current/reference/htmlsingle/#using-boot-devtools`.

Summary

This chapter looked at some of the cool features of Spring Boot that help developers increase productivity. The next chapter covers how to work with relational databases using Spring Boot.

CHAPTER 5

Working with JdbcTemplate

Data persistence is a crucial part of software systems. Most software applications use relational databases as datastores but recently NoSQL data stores like MongoDB, Redis, Cassandra are getting popular too. Java provides JDBC API to talk to the database, but it is a low-level API that requires lots of boilerplate coding. The JavaEE platform provides the Java Persistence API (JPA) specification, which is an Object Relational Mapping (ORM) framework. Hibernate and EclipseLink are the most popular JPA implementations. There are other popular persistence frameworks, such as MyBatis and JOOQ, that are more SQL focused.

Spring provides a nice abstraction on top of the JDBC API, using JdbcTemplate, and provides great transaction management capabilities using an annotation-based approach. Spring Data is an umbrella project that provides support for integration with most of the popular data access technologies, such as JPA, MongoDB, Redis, Cassandra, Solr, ElasticSearch, etc. Spring Boot makes it easier to work with these persistence technologies by automatically configuring required beans based on various criteria.

This chapter takes a look at how you can use JdbcTemplate without Spring Boot and how Spring Boot makes it easy to use JdbcTemplate without much coding or configuration. You will also learn about the performing database migration using Flyway.

Using JdbcTemplate Without SpringBoot

First, let's take a quick look at how you can generally use Spring's JdbcTemplate (without Spring Boot) by registering the DataSource, TransactionManager, and JdbcTemplate beans. You can also register the DataSourceInitializer bean to initialize the database.

```
@Configuration
@ComponentScan
@EnableTransactionManagement
@PropertySource(value = { "classpath:application.properties" })
public class AppConfig {

    @Autowired
    private Environment env;

    @Bean
    public static PropertySourcesPlaceholderConfigurer placeHolderConfigurer()
    {
        return new PropertySourcesPlaceholderConfigurer();
    }
```

© K. Siva Prasad Reddy 2017
K. S. Prasad Reddy, *Beginning Spring Boot 2*, DOI 10.1007/978-1-4842-2931-6_5

```java
@Value("${init-db:false}")
private String initDatabase;

@Bean
public JdbcTemplate jdbcTemplate(DataSource dataSource)
{
    return new JdbcTemplate(dataSource);
}

@Bean
public PlatformTransactionManager transactionManager(DataSource dataSource)
{
    return new DataSourceTransactionManager(dataSource);
}

@Bean
public DataSource dataSource()
{
    BasicDataSource dataSource = new BasicDataSource();
    dataSource.setDriverClassName(env.getProperty("jdbc.driverClassName"));
    dataSource.setUrl(env.getProperty("jdbc.url"));
    dataSource.setUsername(env.getProperty("jdbc.username"));
    dataSource.setPassword(env.getProperty("jdbc.password"));
    return dataSource;
}

@Bean
public DataSourceInitializer dataSourceInitializer(DataSource dataSource)
{
    DataSourceInitializer dataSourceInitializer = new DataSourceInitializer();
    dataSourceInitializer.setDataSource(dataSource);
    ResourceDatabasePopulator databasePopulator = new ResourceDatabasePopulator();
    databasePopulator.addScript(new ClassPathResource("data.sql"));
    dataSourceInitializer.setDatabasePopulator(databasePopulator);
    dataSourceInitializer.setEnabled(Boolean.parseBoolean(initDatabase));
    return dataSourceInitializer;
}
}
```

You should configure the JDBC connection parameters in src/main/resources/application.
properties, as follows.

```
jdbc.driverClassName=com.mysql.jdbc.Driver
jdbc.url=jdbc:mysql://localhost:3306/test
jdbc.username=root
jdbc.password=admin
```

You can then create a database setup script called data.sql in src/main/resources, as follows:

```
DROP TABLE IF EXISTS USERS;

CREATE TABLE users (
  id int(11) NOT NULL AUTO_INCREMENT,
  name varchar(100) NOT NULL,
  email varchar(100) DEFAULT NULL,
  PRIMARY KEY (id)
);

insert into users(id, name, email) values(1,'John','john@gmail.com');
insert into users(id, name, email) values(2,'Rod','rod@gmail.com');
insert into users(id, name, email) values(3,'Mike','mike@gmail.com');
```

If you prefer to keep the schema generation script and seed data insertion script separate, you can put them in separate files and add them as follows:

```
databasePopulator.addScripts(new ClassPathResource("schema.sql"),
                             new ClassPathResource("seed-data.sql") );
```

With this configuration in place, you can inject JdbcTemplate into the data access components to interact with the databases.

```
public class User
{
    private Integer id;
    private String name;
    private String email;

    // setters & getters
}


@Repository
public class UserRepository
{
    @Autowired
    private JdbcTemplate jdbcTemplate;

    @Transactional(readOnly=true)
    public List<User> findAll() {
        return jdbcTemplate.query("select * from users", new UserRowMapper());
    }
}


class UserRowMapper implements RowMapper<User>
{
    @Override
    public User mapRow(ResultSet rs, int rowNum) throws SQLException {
        User user = new User();
        user.setId(rs.getInt("id"));
```

```
        user.setName(rs.getString("name"));
        user.setEmail(rs.getString("email"));

        return user;
    }
}
```

You might have observed that most of the time, you'll use this similar type of configuration in your applications.

The next section shows you how to use `JdbcTemplate` without having to configure all these beans manually, by using Spring Boot.

Using JdbcTemplate with Spring Boot

If you use Spring Boot's autoconfiguration feature, you don't have to configure beans manually. To start, create a Spring Boot Maven-based project and add the `spring-boot-starter-jdbc` module.

```
<dependency>
    <groupId>org.springframework.boot</groupId>
    <artifactId>spring-boot-starter-jdbc</artifactId>
</dependency>
```

By adding the `spring-boot-starter-jdbc` module, you get the following autoconfiguration features:

- The `spring-boot-starter-jdbc` module transitively pulls `tomcat-jdbc-{version}.jar`, which is used to configure the `DataSource` bean.

- If you have not defined a `DataSource` bean explicitly and if you have any embedded database drivers in the classpath, such as H2, HSQL, or Derby, then Spring Boot will automatically register the `DataSource` bean using the in-memory database settings.

- If you haven't registered any of the following beans, then Spring Boot will register them automatically.

    - `PlatformTransactionManager` (`DataSourceTransactionManager`)

    - `JdbcTemplate`

    - `NamedParameterJdbcTemplate`

- You can have the `schema.sql` and `data.sql` files in the root classpath, which Spring Boot will automatically use to initialize the database.

Initializing the Database

Spring Boot uses the `spring.datasource.initialize` property value, which is true by default, to determine whether to initialize the database. If the `spring.datasource.initialize` property is set to `true`, Spring Boot will use the `schema.sql` and `data.sql` files in the root classpath to initialize the database.

In addition to `schema.sql` and `data.sql`, Spring Boot will load the `schema-${platform}.sql` and `data-${platform}.sql` files if they are available in the root classpath. Here, the platform value is the value of the `spring.datasource.platform` property, which can be `hsqldb`, `h2`, `oracle`, `mysql`, `postgresql`, etc.

You can customize the default names of the scripts using the following properties:

```
spring.datasource.schema=create-db.sql
spring.datasource.data=seed-data.sql
```

If you want to turn off the database initialization, you can set spring.datasource.initialize=false. If there are any errors in executing the scripts, the application will fail to start. If you want to continue, you can set spring.datasource.continueOnError=true.

To add the H2 database driver to the pom.xml file, you use the following:

```
<dependency>
    <groupId>com.h2database</groupId>
    <artifactId>h2</artifactId>
</dependency>
```

Create schema.sql in src/main/resources, as follows:

```
CREATE TABLE users
(
    id int(11) NOT NULL AUTO_INCREMENT,
    name varchar(100) NOT NULL,
    email varchar(100) DEFAULT NULL,
    PRIMARY KEY (id)
);
```

Create data.sql in src/main/resources, as follows:

```
insert into users(id, name, email) values(1,'John','john@gmail.com');
insert into users(id, name, email) values(2,'Rod','rod@gmail.com');
insert into users(id, name, email) values(3,'Mike','mike@gmail.com');
```

Now you can inject JdbcTemplate into UserRepository, as shown in Listing 5-1.

Listing 5-1. UserRepository.java

```
@Repository
public class UserRepository
{
    @Autowired
    private JdbcTemplate jdbcTemplate;

    @Transactional(readOnly=true)
    public List<User> findAll() {
        return jdbcTemplate.query("select * from users",
                                new UserRowMapper());
    }

    @Transactional(readOnly=true)
    public User findUserById(int id) {
        return jdbcTemplate.queryForObject("select * from users where id=?",
                                new Object[]{id}, new UserRowMapper());
    }
```

```java
    public User create(final User user) {
        final String sql = "insert into users(name,email) values(?,?)";

        KeyHolder holder = new GeneratedKeyHolder();

        jdbcTemplate.update(new PreparedStatementCreator() {

                @Override
                public PreparedStatement createPreparedStatement(Connection connection)
                        throws SQLException {
                    PreparedStatement ps = connection
                            .prepareStatement(sql, Statement.RETURN_GENERATED_KEYS);
                    ps.setString(1, user.getName());
                    ps.setString(2, user.getEmail());
                    return ps;
                }
            }, holder);

        int newUserId = holder.getKey().intValue();
        user.setId(newUserId);
        return user;
    }
}


class UserRowMapper implements RowMapper<User>
{

    @Override
    public User mapRow(ResultSet rs, int rowNum) throws SQLException {
        User user = new User();
        user.setId(rs.getInt("id"));
        user.setName(rs.getString("name"));
        user.setEmail(rs.getString("email"));

        return user;
    }
}
```

Create the entry point called `SpringbootJdbcDemoApplication.java`, as shown in Listing 5-2.

Listing 5-2. SpringbootJdbcDemoApplication.java

```java
@SpringBootApplication
public class SpringbootJdbcDemoApplication
{
    public static void main(String[] args)
    {
        SpringApplication.run(SpringbootJdbcDemoApplication.class, args);
    }
}
```

Now you can create a JUnit test class to test the UserRepository methods, as shown in Listing 5-3.

Listing 5-3. SpringbootJdbcDemoApplicationTests.java

```java
@RunWith(SpringRunner.class)
@SpringBootTest(SpringbootJdbcDemoApplication.class)
public class SpringbootJdbcDemoApplicationTests
{
    @Autowired
    private UserRepository userRepository;

    @Test
    public void findAllUsers()  {
        List<User> users = userRepository.findAll();
        assertNotNull(users);
        assertTrue(!users.isEmpty());
    }

    @Test
    public void findUserById()  {
        User user = userRepository.findUserById(1);
        assertNotNull(user);
    }

    @Test
    public void createUser() {
        User user = new User(0, "Johnson", "johnson@gmail.com");
        User savedUser = userRepository.create(user);
        User newUser = userRepository.findUserById(savedUser.getId());
        assertNotNull(newUser);
        assertEquals("Johnson", newUser.getName());
        assertEquals("johnson@gmail.com", newUser.getEmail());
    }
}
```

Note   By default, the Spring Boot features such as external properties, logging, etc., are available in the `ApplicationContext` only if you use `SpringApplication`. So, Spring Boot provides the `@SpringBootTest` annotation to configure the `ApplicationContext` for tests that use `SpringApplication` behind the scenes.

You have learned how to get started quickly with embedded databases. But what if you want to use non-embedded databases like MySQL, Oracle, and PostgreSQL?

You can configure the database properties in the `application.properties` file so that Spring Boot will use those JDBC parameters to configure the `DataSource` bean.

```
spring.datasource.driver-class-name=com.mysql.jdbc.Driver
spring.datasource.url=jdbc:mysql://localhost:3306/test
spring.datasource.username=root
spring.datasource.password=admin
```

For any reason if you want to have more control and configure the DataSource bean by yourself, you can configure it in a configuration class. If you register the DataSource bean, Spring Boot will not configure it automatically using autoconfiguration.

Using Other Connection Pooling Libraries

Spring Boot, by default, pulls in tomcat-jdbc-{version}.jar and uses org.apache.tomcat.jdbc.pool. DataSource to configure the DataSource bean.

Spring Boot checks the availability of the following classes and uses the first one that is available in the classpath.

- org.apache.tomcat.jdbc.pool.DataSource

- com.zaxxer.hikari.HikariDataSource

- org.apache.commons.dbcp.BasicDataSource

- org.apache.commons.dbcp2.BasicDataSource

If you want to use HikariDataSource, you can exclude tomcat-jdbc and add the HikariCP dependency as follows:

```
<dependency>
    <groupId>org.springframework.boot</groupId>
    <artifactId>spring-boot-starter-jdbc</artifactId>
    <exclusions>
        <exclusion>
            <groupId>org.apache.tomcat</groupId>
            <artifactId>tomcat-jdbc</artifactId>
        </exclusion>
    </exclusions>
</dependency>

<dependency>
    <groupId>com.zaxxer</groupId>
    <artifactId>HikariCP</artifactId>
</dependency>
```

You can configure specific settings for the connection pool library as follows:

```
spring.datasource.tomcat.*= # Tomcat Datasource specific settings
spring.datasource.hikari.*= # Hikari DataSource specific settings
spring.datasource.dbcp2.*= # Commons DBCP2 specific settings
```

For example, you can set the HikariCP connection pool settings as follows:

```
spring.datasource.hikari.allow-pool-suspension=true
spring.datasource.hikari.connection-test-query=SELECT 1
spring.datasource.hikari.transaction-isolation=TRANSACTION_READ_COMMITTED
spring.datasource.hikari.connection-timeout=45000
```

Database Migration with Flyway

Having a proper database migration plan for enterprise applications is crucial. The new versions of the application may be released with new features or enhancements that involve changes to the database schema. It is strongly recommended that you have versioned database scripts so that you can track which database changes were introduced in which release and can restore the database to a particular version if required.

This section looks at one of the popular database migration tools, called Flyway, which Spring Boot supports out of the box.

You can create your database migration scripts as `.sql` files following a specific naming pattern so that Flyway can run these scripts in order based on the current schema version. Flyway creates a database table called `schema_version` that keeps track of the current schema version so that it will run any pending migration scripts while performing the migration operation (Figure 5-1).

	installed_rank	version	description	type	script	checksum	installed_by	installed_on	executi...	success
☐	1	1.1	init	SQL	V1_1__init.sql	72970307	root	2017-03-26 09:01	300	1
☐	2	1.2	Add Col Dob	SQL	V1_2__Add_Col_Dob.sql	487040151	root	2017-03-26 09:01	583	1
*	(NULL)	(NULL)	(NULL)	(NULL)	(NULL)	(NULL)	(NULL)	CURRENT_TIMESTAM	(NULL)	(NULL)

Figure 5-1. *Flyway schema_version table*

You should follow the naming convention when naming the migration scripts so that the scripts will run in the correct order.

```
V{Version}__{Description}.sql
```

Here, {Version} is the version number and can contain dots (.) and underscores (_). The {Description} can contain text describing the migration changes. {Version} and {Description} should be separated by a separator; the default is two consecutive underscores (__), but this option is configurable.

Examples:

```
V1__Init.sql
V1.1_CreatePersonTable.sql
V1_2__UpdatePersonTable.sql
V2.1.0__CreateSecurityTables.sql
V2_1_1__AddAuditingTables.sql
```

To add Flyway migration support to a Spring Boot application, you just need to add the `flyway-core` dependency and place the migration scripts in the `db/migration` directory in the classpath.

```xml
<dependency>
    <groupId>org.flywaydb</groupId>
    <artifactId>flyway-core</artifactId>
</dependency>
```

Now create the two migration scripts shown in Listings 5-4 and 5-5 in the `src/main/resources/db/migration` directory.

Listing 5-4. V1.0__Init.sql

```
CREATE TABLE users
(
  id int(11) NOT NULL AUTO_INCREMENT,
  name varchar(100) NOT NULL,
  email varchar(100) DEFAULT NULL,
  PRIMARY KEY (id)
);

insert into users(id, name, email) values(1,'John','john@gmail.com');
insert into users(id, name, email) values(2,'Rod','rod@gmail.com');
insert into users(id, name, email) values(3,'Renold','renold@gmail.com');
```

Listing 5-5. V1.1__Add_DOB_Column.sql

```
ALTER TABLE USERS ADD COLUMN DOB DATE DEFAULT NULL;
```

Now, when you start the application, it will check the current schema version number (maximum of the `schema_version.version` column value) and run if there are any pending migration scripts with a higher version value.

If you already have an existing database with tables, you can take the dump of the existing database structure and make it the baseline script so that you can clean the database and start from scratch. If you don't want to take a dump and re-run the initial script (which is common in production environments), you can set `flyway.baseline-on-migrate=true`, which will insert a baseline record in the `schema_version` table with the version set to 1. Now you can add migration scripts with version numbers higher than 1—say 1.1, 1_2, etc.

For more information about Flyway migrations, see `https://flywaydb.org/`.

Summary

In this chapter, you learned how to use `JdbcTemplate` easily in Spring Boot and how to connect to databases like H2 and MySQL. The chapter also covered how to initialize a database using SQL scripts. You also learned how to use various connection pooling libraries. The next chapter explains how to use MyBatis with Spring Boot.

CHAPTER 6

Working with MyBatis

MyBatis is an open source Java persistence framework that abstracts JDBC boilerplate code and provides a simple and easy-to-use API to interact with the database.

Unlike Hibernate, which is a full-blown ORM framework, MyBatis is a SQL mapping framework. It automates the process of populating the SQL resultset into Java objects and it persists data into tables by extracting the data from the Java objects.

This chapter covers how to use the Spring Boot MyBatis starter, how to execute database queries using MyBatis XML, and how to use annotation-based mappers.

Using the Spring Boot MyBatis Starter

The MyBatis community built the Spring Boot starter for MyBatis, which you can use while creating the Spring Boot project from the Spring Initializer or from the IDE. You can explore the source code on GitHub at: `https://github.com/mybatis/mybatis-spring-boot`.

Next you learn how to use the Spring Boot MyBatis starter to use MyBatis in SpringBoot applications quickly.

1. Create a Spring Boot Maven project and configure the MyBatis Starter dependency and H2/MySQL driver dependencies.

```xml
<dependency>
    <groupId>org.mybatis.spring.boot</groupId>
    <artifactId>mybatis-spring-boot-starter</artifactId>
    <version>1.3.0</version>
</dependency>

<dependency>
    <groupId>com.h2database</groupId>
    <artifactId>h2</artifactId>
</dependency>

<dependency>
    <groupId>mysql</groupId>
    <artifactId>mysql-connector-java</artifactId>
</dependency>
```

This example reuses the `User.java`, `schema.sql`, and `data.sql` files created in the previous chapter.

2. Create the MyBatis SQL Mapper interface called `UserMapper.java` with a few database operations, as shown in Listing 6-1.

Listing 6-1. com.apress.demo.mappers.UserMapper.java

```
package com.apress.demo.mappers;

public interface UserMapper
{
    void insertUser(User user);
    User findUserById(Integer id);
    List<User> findAllUsers();
}
```

3. You now need to create mapper XML files to define the queries for the SQL statements mapped to the corresponding mapper interface methods. Create the UserMapper.xml file in the src/main/resources/com/apress/demo/mappers/ directory, as shown in Listing 6-2.

Listing 6-2. src/main/resources/com/apress/demo/mappers/UserMapper.xml

```
<!DOCTYPE mapper
    PUBLIC "-//mybatis.org//DTD Mapper 3.0//EN"
    "http://mybatis.org/dtd/mybatis-3-mapper.dtd">

<mapper namespace="com.apress.demo.mappers.UserMapper">

<resultMap id="UserResultMap" type="User">
    <id column="id"  property="id"  />
    <result column="name"  property="name"  />
    <result column="email"  property="email"  />
</resultMap>

<select id="findAllUsers" resultMap="UserResultMap">
        select id, name, email from users
</select>

<select id="findUserById" resultMap="UserResultMap">
        select id, name, email from users WHERE id=#{id}
</select>

<insert id="insertUser" parameterType="User" useGeneratedKeys="true"
        keyProperty="id">
        insert into users(name,email) values(#{name},#{email})
</insert>

</mapper>
```

A few things to observe here are:

*   The namespace in the mapper XML should be the same as the Fully Qualified Name (FQN) of the mapper interface.

- The statement id values should be the same as the mapper interface method names.

- If the query result column names are different from the bean property names, you can use the <resultMap> configuration to provide mapping between column names and their corresponding bean property names.

4. MyBatis also provides annotation-based query configurations without requiring mapper XMLs. You can create the UserMapper.java interface and configure the mapped SQLs using annotations, as shown in Listing 6-3.

Listing 6-3. com.apress.demo.mappers.UserMapper.java

```java
public interface UserMapper
{
    @Insert("insert into users(name,email) values(#{name},#{email})")
    @SelectKey(statement="call identity()", keyProperty="id",
                before=false, resultType=Integer.class)
    void insertUser(User user);

    @Select("select id, name, email from users WHERE id=#{id}")
    User findUserById(Integer id);

    @Select("select id, name, email from users")
    List<User> findAllUsers();

}
```

5. Next, you have to configure the starter configuration parameters. Configure the type-aliases-package and mapper-locations parameters in application. properties as follows.

```
mybatis.type-aliases-package=com.apress.demo.domain
mybatis.mapper-locations=classpath*:/mappers/*.xml
```

6. Create the entry point class called SpringbootMyBatisDemoApplication.java, as shown in Listing 6-4.

Listing 6-4. com.apress.demo.SpringbootMyBatisDemoApplication.java

```java
@SpringBootApplication
@MapperScan("com.apress.demo.mappers")
public class SpringbootMyBatisDemoApplication
{
    public static void main(String[] args)
    {
        SpringApplication.run(SpringbootMyBatisDemoApplication.class, args);
    }
}
```

■ **Note**   This example uses the `@MapperScan("com.apress.demo.mappers")` annotation to specify where to look for the mapper interfaces. Instead of using `@MapperScan`, you could also annotate mapper interfaces with the new `@Mapper` annotation that shipped with MyBatis 3.4.0.

7. Create a JUnit test class and test the `UserMapper` methods, as shown in Listing 6-5.

Listing 6-5. com.apress.demo.SpringbootMyBatisDemoApplicationTests.java

```java
@RunWith(SpringRunner.class)
@SpringBootTest
public class SpringbootMyBatisDemoApplicationTests
{

    @Autowired
    private UserMapper userMapper;

    @Test
    public void findAllUsers()  {
        List<User> users = userMapper.findAllUsers();
        assertNotNull(users);
        assertTrue(!users.isEmpty());

    }

    @Test
    public void findUserById()  {
        User user = userMapper.findUserById(1);
        assertNotNull(user);
    }

    @Test
    public void createUser() {
        User user = new User(0, "george", "george@gmail.com");
        userMapper.insertUser(user);
        User newUser = userMapper.findUserById(user.getId());
        assertEquals("george", newUser.getName());
        assertEquals("george@gmail.com", newUser.getEmail());
    }
}
```

The Spring Boot MyBatis starter provides the following MyBatis configuration parameters, which you can use to customize your MyBatis settings.

```
mybatis.config-location =  #mybatis config filename
mybatis.check-config-location=  # Indicates whether to perform presence check of the MyBatis
xml config file
mybatis.mapper-locations =  #mappers file locations
mybatis.type-aliases-package =  #domain object's package
```

```
mybatis.type-handlers-package =  #handler's package
mybatis.check-config-location =  #check the mybatis configuration exists
mybatis.executor-type =  #mode of execution. Default is SIMPLE
mybatis.configuration-properties=  #externalized properties for mybatis configuration
```

You can read more about MyBatis at `http://blog.mybatis.org/p/products.html`.

Summary

In this chapter, you learned how to work with MyBatis in Spring Boot applications. The next chapter covers how to use another popular Java persistence framework with Spring Boot, called JOOQ.

CHAPTER 7

Working with JOOQ

JOOQ (Java Object Oriented Querying) is a persistence framework that embraces SQL. JOOQ provides the following features:

- Typesafe SQL using DSL API

- Typesafe database object referencing using code generation

- Easy-to-use API for querying and data fetching

- SQL logging and debugging

This chapter covers using the Spring Boot JOOQ Starter, using the JOOQ Maven Codegen plugin to generate code from the database schema, and performing various types of database operations.

Introduction to JOOQ

JOOQ is a Java persistence framework that provides typesafe QueryDSL so that you can implement the persistence layer of your application in a typesafe manner. JOOQ provides code generation tools to generate code based on the database schema and you can use that generated code to build typesafe queries.

You'll first see how you can use JOOQ to query a database table.

Create a configuration file named jooq-config.xml, as shown in Listing 7-1.

Listing 7-1. The jooq-config.xml File

```
<?xml version="1.0" encoding="UTF-8" standalone="yes"?>
<configuration xmlns="http://www.jooq.org/xsd/jooq-codegen-3.9.2.xsd">

  <jdbc>
    <driver>com.mysql.jdbc.Driver</driver>
    <url>jdbc:mysql://localhost:3306/test</url>
    <user>root</user>
    <password>admin</password>
  </jdbc>

  <generator>
    <name>org.jooq.util.JavaGenerator</name>
    <database>
      <name>org.jooq.util.mysql.MySQLDatabase</name>
      <inputSchema>test</inputSchema>
      <includes>.*</includes>
    </database>
```

```
  <target>
    <packageName>org.mycompany.myproj.jooq.model</packageName>
    <directory>C:/projects/myproject/src/main/java</directory>
  </target>
</generator>

</configuration>
```

Now you can run the following command to generate JOOQ code based on the configuration:

```
java -classpath jooq-3.9.3.jar;jooq-meta-3.9.3.jar;jooq-codegen-3.9.3.jar;mysql-connector-
java-5.1.18-bin.jar;. org.jooq.util.GenerationTool jooq-config.xml
```

Assume that you have a POST table in your database. JOOQ will generate a POST class based on the POST table's metadata. Now you can use JOOQ to query the POST table and fetch data, as shown in Listing 7-2.

Listing 7-2. Using the JOOQ DSL API

```
String userName = "root";
String password = "admin";
String url = "jdbc:mysql://localhost:3306/test";
Class.forName('com.mysql.jdbc.Driver');
Connection conn = DriverManager.getConnection(url, userName, password);

DSLContext jooq = DSL.using(conn, SQLDialect.MYSQL);
Result<Record> result = jooq.select().from(POST).fetch();

for (Record r : result)
{
    Integer id = r.getValue(POST.ID);
    String title = r.getValue(POST.TITLE);
    String content = r.getValue(POST.CONTENT);

    System.out.println("Id: " + id + " title: " + title + " content: " + content);
}
```

This example creates a database `Connection` and instantiates the `DSLContext` object, which is the entry point for using JOOQ QueryDSL. Using the `DSLContext` object, it is querying the POST table and iterating through the resultset.

You can integrate JOOQ with the Spring framework so that you don't have to create `Connection` and instantiate `DSLContext` manually. See `https://www.jooq.org/doc/3.9/manual-single-page/#jooq-with-spring` to learn how to integrate Spring with JOOQ.

Spring Boot provides JOOQ Starter so that you can quickly get up and running with JOOQ. You do this by leveraging its autoconfiguration mechanism.

Using Spring Boot's JOOQ Starter

Spring Boot provides a starter, called `spring-boot-starter-jooq`, which allows you to quickly integrate with JOOQ. This section shows you how to use `spring-boot-starter-jooq` using a step-by-step approach.

Configure Spring Boot JOOQ Starter

Create a Spring Boot Maven-based project and add the `spring-boot-starter-jooq` dependency along with H2 and MySQL driver dependencies.

```xml
<dependency>
    <groupId>org.springframework.boot</groupId>
    <artifactId>spring-boot-starter-jooq</artifactId>
</dependency>

<dependency>
    <groupId>org.springframework.boot</groupId>
    <artifactId>spring-boot-starter-test</artifactId>
    <scope>test</scope>
</dependency>

<dependency>
    <groupId>com.h2database</groupId>
    <artifactId>h2</artifactId>
</dependency>

<dependency>
    <groupId>mysql</groupId>
    <artifactId>mysql-connector-java</artifactId>
</dependency>
```

This example uses the H2 in-memory database first, and later you will see how to use MySQL.

Database Schema

Create a simple database with two tables—POSTS and COMMENTS. Create the database creation script called `src/main/resources/schema.sql`, as shown in Listing 7-3.

Listing 7-3. The src/main/resources/schema.sql File

```sql
DROP TABLE IF EXISTS POSTS;

 CREATE TABLE POSTS
(
  ID int(11) NOT NULL AUTO_INCREMENT,
  TITLE VARCHAR(200) NOT NULL,
  CONTENT LONGTEXT DEFAULT NULL,
  CREATED_ON DATETIME DEFAULT NULL,
  PRIMARY KEY (ID)
);

DROP TABLE IF EXISTS COMMENTS;

CREATE TABLE COMMENTS
(
  ID INT(11) NOT NULL AUTO_INCREMENT,
  POST_ID INT(11) NOT NULL,
  NAME VARCHAR(200) NOT NULL,
  EMAIL VARCHAR(200) NOT NULL,
```

```
CONTENT LONGTEXT DEFAULT NULL,
CREATED_ON DATETIME DEFAULT NULL,
PRIMARY KEY (ID),
FOREIGN KEY (POST_ID) REFERENCES POSTS(ID)
);
```

Now populate some sample data using the src/main/resources/data.sql script, as shown in Listing 7-4.

Listing 7-4. The src/main/resources/data.sql File

```
insert into posts(id, title, content, created_on)
values(1, 'Post 1', 'This is post 1', '2017-01-03');

insert into posts(id, title, content, created_on)
values(2, 'Post 2', 'This is post 2', '2017-01-05');

insert into posts(id, title, content, created_on)
values(3, 'Post 3', 'This is post 3', '2017-01-07');

insert into comments(id, post_id, name, email, content, created_on)
values(1, 1, 'User1', 'user1@gmail.com', 'This is comment 1 on post 1', '2017-01-07');

insert into comments(id, post_id, name, email, content, created_on)
values(2, 1, 'User2', 'user2@gmail.com', 'This is comment 2 on post 1', '2017-01-07');

insert into comments(id, post_id, name, email, content, created_on)
values(3, 2, 'User1', 'user1@gmail.com', 'This is comment 1 on post 2', '2017-01-07');
```

Code Generation Using the JOOQ Maven Codegen Plugin

JOOQ provides the JOOQ Maven Codegen plugin to generate database artifacts using Maven goals. In this section, you see how to use Maven profiles to configure the jooq-codegen-maven configuration properties based on database type. See Listing 7-5.

Listing 7-5. The jooq-codegen-maven Plugin Configuration in the pom.xml File

```
<profiles>
    <profile>
        <id>h2</id>
        <build>
            <plugins>
                <plugin>
                    <groupId>org.jooq</groupId>
                    <artifactId>jooq-codegen-maven</artifactId>
                    <executions>
                        <execution>
                            <goals>
                                <goal>generate</goal>
                            </goals>
                        </execution>
                    </executions>
```

```xml
                <dependencies>
                    <dependency>
                        <groupId>com.h2database</groupId>
                        <artifactId>h2</artifactId>
                        <version>${h2.version}</version>
                    </dependency>
                </dependencies>
                <configuration>
                    <jdbc>
                        <driver>org.h2.Driver</driver>
                        <url>jdbc:h2:~/springbootjooq</url>
                    </jdbc>
                    <generator>
                        <name>org.jooq.util.DefaultGenerator</name>
                        <database>
                            <name>org.jooq.util.h2.H2Database</name>
                            <includes>.*</includes>
                            <excludes />
                            <inputSchema>PUBLIC</inputSchema>
                        </database>
                        <target>
                            <packageName>com.apress.demo.jooq.domain</packageName>
                            <directory>gensrc/main/java</directory>
                        </target>
                    </generator>
                </configuration>
            </plugin>
        </plugins>
    </build>
</profile>
<profile>
    <id>mysql</id>
    <build>
        <plugins>
            <plugin>
                <groupId>org.jooq</groupId>
                <artifactId>jooq-codegen-maven</artifactId>
                <executions>
                    <execution>
                        <goals>
                            <goal>generate</goal>
                        </goals>
                    </execution>
                </executions>
                <dependencies>
                    <dependency>
                        <groupId>mysql</groupId>
                        <artifactId>mysql-connector-java</artifactId>
                        <version>${mysql.version}</version>
                    </dependency>
                </dependencies>
                <configuration>
```

```xml
                    <jdbc>
                        <driver>com.mysql.jdbc.Driver</driver>
                        <url>jdbc:mysql://localhost:3306/test</url>
                        <user>root</user>
                        <password>admin</password>
                    </jdbc>
                    <generator>
                        <name>org.jooq.util.DefaultGenerator</name>
                        <database>
                            <name>org.jooq.util.mysql.MySQLDatabase</name>
                            <includes>.*</includes>
                            <excludes />
                            <inputSchema>test</inputSchema>
                        </database>
                        <target>
                            <packageName>com.apress.demo.jooq.domain</packageName>
                            <directory>gensrc/main/java</directory>
                        </target>
                    </generator>
                </configuration>
            </plugin>
        </plugins>
    </build>
</profile>
</profiles>
```

This example configures two profiles (h2 and mysql) with the appropriate JDBC configuration parameters. It generates the code artifacts and places them in the com.apress.demo.jooq.domain package within the gensrc/main/java directory.

You can run the Maven build that activates the h2 or mysql profile, as follows:

```
mvn clean install -P h2 (or) mvn clean install -P mysql
```

Add JOOQ Generated Code as a Source Folder

Next, you have to configure build-helper-maven-plugin so that Maven will add the JOOQ generated code to the gensrc/main/java directory as a source folder.

```xml
<plugin>
    <groupId>org.codehaus.mojo</groupId>
    <artifactId>build-helper-maven-plugin</artifactId>
    <executions>
        <execution>
            <phase>generate-sources</phase>
            <goals>
                <goal>add-source</goal>
            </goals>
            <configuration>
                <sources>
                    <source>gensrc/main/java</source>
                </sources>
```

```
        </configuration>
      </execution>
    </executions>
</plugin>
```

Domain Objects

This section shows how to create the following domain objects, which can be used to pass data across the layers. It uses only JOOQ generated database artifacts to talk to the database. See Listing 7-6.

Listing 7-6. Domain Objects Post.java and Comment.java

```java
package com.apress.demo.entities;

public class Post
{
    private Integer id;
    private String title;
    private String content;
    private Timestamp createdOn;
    private List<Comment> comments = new ArrayList<>();
    //setters & getters

}


package com.apress.demo.entities;

public class Comment
{
    private Integer id;
    private Integer postId;
    private String name;
    private String email;
    private String content;
    private Timestamp createdOn;
    //setters & getters
}
```

Using JOOQ DSL

DSLContext is the main entry point for the JOOQ DSL API. You will see how to implement the data persistence methods using the JOOQ DSL API.

First, you create the PostService class with the DSLContext object autowired, as shown in Listing 7-7.

Listing 7-7. com.apress.demo.services.PostService.java

```java
package com.apress.demo.services;

import java.sql.Timestamp;
import java.util.ArrayList;
import java.util.List;
```

```java
import org.jooq.DSLContext;
import org.jooq.Record;
import org.jooq.Result;
import org.springframework.beans.factory.annotation.Autowired;
import org.springframework.stereotype.Service;
import org.springframework.transaction.annotation.Transactional;

import com.apress.demo.entities.Comment;
import com.apress.demo.entities.Post;

import static com.apress.demo.jooq.domain.tables.Posts.POSTS;
import static com.apress.demo.jooq.domain.tables.Comments.COMMENTS;
import com.apress.demo.jooq.domain.tables.records.CommentsRecord;
import com.apress.demo.jooq.domain.tables.records.PostsRecord;

@Service
@Transactional
public class PostService
{
    @Autowired
    private DSLContext dsl;


    ...
    ...
}
```

When you query the database using JOOQ, you will get a record from which you can extract the data.
The example is going to query the POSTS and COMMENTS tables, so you'll create two utility methods that extract
post and comment information from the Record object.

```java
@Service
@Transactional
public class PostService
{
    ...
    ...

    private Post getPostEntity(Record r)
    {
        Integer id = r.getValue(POSTS.ID, Integer.class);
        String title = r.getValue(POSTS.TITLE, String.class);
        String content = r.getValue(POSTS.CONTENT, String.class);
        Timestamp createdOn = r.getValue(POSTS.CREATED_ON, Timestamp.class);
        return new Post(id, title, content, createdOn);
    }

    private Comment getCommentEntity(Record r)
    {
        Integer id = r.getValue(COMMENTS.ID, Integer.class);
        Integer postId = r.getValue(COMMENTS.POST_ID, Integer.class);
        String name = r.getValue(COMMENTS.NAME, String.class);
```

```
            String email = r.getValue(COMMENTS.EMAIL, String.class);
            String content = r.getValue(COMMENTS.CONTENT, String.class);
            Timestamp createdOn = r.getValue(COMMENTS.CREATED_ON, Timestamp.class);
            return new Comment(id, postId, name, email, content, createdOn);
    }
}
```

Now implement the methods to insert a new Post and Comment in PostService.java as follows:

```
public Post createPost(Post post)
{
    PostsRecord postsRecord = dsl.insertInto(POSTS)
            .set(POSTS.TITLE, post.getTitle())
            .set(POSTS.CONTENT, post.getContent())
            .set(POSTS.CREATED_ON, post.getCreatedOn())
            .returning(POSTS.ID)
            .fetchOne();

    post.setId(postsRecord.getId());
    return post;
}

public Comment createComment(Comment comment)
{
    CommentsRecord commentsRecord = dsl.insertInto(COMMENTS)
            .set(COMMENTS.POST_ID, comment.getPostId())
            .set(COMMENTS.NAME, comment.getName())
            .set(COMMENTS.EMAIL, comment.getEmail())
            .set(COMMENTS.CONTENT, comment.getContent())
            .set(COMMENTS.CREATED_ON, comment.getCreatedOn())
            .returning(COMMENTS.ID)
            .fetchOne();

    comment.setId(commentsRecord.getId());
    return comment;
}
```

The example uses the dsl.insertInto() method to insert a new record and specifies the returning() method to return the auto-generated primary key column value. It also calls the fetchOne() method to return the newly inserted record.

Now implement fetching a list of Posts using JOOQ DSL, as follows:

```
public List<Post> getAllPosts()
{
    List<Post> posts = new ArrayList<>();
    Result<Record> result = dsl.select().from(POSTS).fetch();
    for (Record r : result) {
        posts.add(getPostEntity(r));
    }
    return posts ;
}
```

It is fetching all rows from the POSTS table using dsl.select().from(), which returns Result<Record>. The example loops through Result<Record> and converts the record into a Post domain object using the getPostEntity() utility method that you created earlier.

Now you'll fetch a Post record for a given post ID along with the comments associated with that post.

```java
publicxr postId)
{
    Record record = dsl.select()
                        .from(POSTS)
                        .where(POSTS.ID.eq(postId))
                        .fetchOne();
    if(record != null)
    {
        Post post = getPostEntity(record);

        Result<Record> commentRecords = dsl.select()
                                    .from(COMMENTS)
                                    .where(COMMENTS.POST_ID.eq(postId))
                                    .fetch();

        for (Record r : commentRecords) {
            post.addComment(getCommentEntity(r));
        }
        return post;
    }
    return null;
}
```

Finally, you'll implement the method to delete a comment:

```java
public void deleteComment(Integer commentId)
{
        dsl.deleteFrom(COMMENTS)
                .where(COMMENTS.ID.equal(commentId))
                .execute();
}
```

You have learned how to perform various operations, like inserting new records and querying and deleting records using JOOQ DSL.

Now you'll create an entry point class called SpringbootJooqDemoApplication.java, as shown in Listing 7-8.

Listing 7-8. com.apress.demo.SpringbootJooqDemoApplication.java

```java
@SpringBootApplication
public class SpringbootJooqDemoApplication
{
    public static void main(String[] args) {
        SpringApplication.run(SpringbootJooqDemoApplication.class, args);
    }
}
```

Next, you write JUnit tests for PostService methods, as shown in Listing 7-9.

Listing 7-9. SpringbootJooqDemoApplicationTests.java

```java
@RunWith(SpringRunner.class)
@SpringBootTest
public class SpringbootJooqDemoApplicationTests
{

    @Autowired
    private PostService postService;

    @Test
    public void findAllPosts()  {
        List<Post> posts = postService.getAllPosts();
        assertNotNull(posts);
        assertTrue(!posts.isEmpty());
        for (Post post : posts)
        {
            System.err.println(post);
        }
    }

    @Test
    public void findPostById()  {
        Post post = postService.getPost(1);
        assertNotNull(post);
        System.out.println(post);
        List<Comment> comments = post.getComments();
        System.out.println(comments);

    }

    @Test
    public void createPost() {
        Post post = new Post(0, "My new Post",
                            "This is my new test post",
                            new Timestamp(System.currentTimeMillis()));
        Post savedPost = postService.createPost(post);
        Post newPost = postService.getPost(savedPost.getId());
        assertEquals("My new Post", newPost.getTitle());
        assertEquals("This is my new test post", newPost.getContent());
    }

    @Test
    public void createComment() {
        Integer postId = 1;
        Comment comment = new Comment(0, postId, "User4",
                                "user4@gmail.com", "This is my new comment on post1",
                                new Timestamp(System.currentTimeMillis()));
        Comment savedComment = postService.createComment(comment);
        Post post = postService.getPost(postId);
```

```
        List<Comment> comments = post.getComments();
        assertNotNull(comments);
        for (Comment comm : comments)
        {
            if(savedComment.getId() == comm.getId()){
                assertEquals("User4", comm.getName());
                assertEquals("user4@gmail.com", comm.getEmail());
                assertEquals("This is my new comment on post1", comm.getContent());
            }
        }

    }

}
```

You have created the JUnit test class to test for `PostService` methods. You are performing various operations and asserting the response based on the same data you inserted using `data.sql`.

Assuming you have generated code using the H2 profile, you can run the JUnit test without any further configuration. But if you have generated code using the `mysql` profile, you will have to configure the following properties in `application.properties`:

```
spring.datasource.driver-class-name=com.mysql.jdbc.Driver
spring.datasource.url=jdbc:mysql://localhost:3306/test
spring.datasource.username=root
spring.datasource.password=admin
spring.jooq.sql-dialect=MYSQL
```

■ **Note** You should use the correct SQL dialect for the database; otherwise, you may get SQL syntax errors at runtime.

For more info on JOOQ, visit `http://www.jooq.org/learn/`.

Summary

This chapter explained how to use the JOOQ framework by using the Spring Boot JOOQ Starter. The next chapter explains how to work with JPA (with the Hibernate implementation) in your Spring Boot applications.

CHAPTER 8

Working with JPA

The Java Persistence API (JPA) is an Object Relational Mapping (ORM) framework that's part of the Java EE platform. JPA simplifies the implementation of the data access layer by letting developers work with an object oriented API instead of writing SQL queries by hand. The most popular JPA implementations are Hibernate, EclipseLink, and OpenJPA.

The Spring framework provides a Spring ORM module to integrate easily with ORM frameworks. You can also use Spring's declarative transaction management capabilities with JPA. In addition to the Spring ORM module, the Spring data portfolio project provides a consistent, Spring-based programming model for data access to relational and NoSQL datastores.

Spring Data integrates with most of the popular data access technologies, including JPA, MongoDB, Redis, Cassandra, Solr, ElasticSearch, etc.

This chapter explores the Spring Data JPA, explains how to use it with Spring Boot, and looks into how you can work with multiple databases in the same Spring Boot application.

Introducing the Spring Data JPA

Chapter 1 discussed how to develop a web application using SpringMVC and JPA without using Spring Boot. Without using Spring Boot, you need to configure various beans like `DataSource`, `TransactionManager`, `LocalContainerEntityManagerFactoryBean`, etc. by yourself. You can use the Spring Boot JPA Starter `spring-boot-starter-data-jpa` to quickly get up and running with JPA. Before getting into how to use `spring-boot-starter-data-jpa`, let's first look at Spring Data JPA.

As noted in Chapter 5, Spring Data is an umbrella project that provides data access support for most of the popular data access technologies—including JPA, MongoDB, Redis, Cassandra, Solr, and ElasticSearch—in a consistent programming model. Spring Data JPA is one of the modules for working with relational databases using JPA.

At times, you may need to implement the data management applications to store, edit, and delete data. For those applications, you just need to implement CRUD (Create, Read, Update, Delete) operations for entities. Instead of implementing the same CRUD operations again and again or rolling out your own generic CRUD DAO implementation, Spring Data provides various repository abstractions, such as `CrudRepository`, `PagingAndSortingRepository`, `JpaRepository`, etc. They provide out-of-the-box support for CRUD operations, as well as pagination and sorting. See Figure 8-1.

Figure 8-1. *JpaRepository methods*

As shown in Figure 8-1, `JpaRepository` provides several methods for CRUD operations, along with the following interesting methods:

- `long count();`—Returns the total number of entities available.

- `boolean existsById(ID id);`—Returns whether an entity with the given ID exists.

- `List<T> findAll(Sort sort);`—Returns all entities sorted by the given options.

- `Page<T> findAll(Pageable pageable);`—Returns a page of entities meeting the paging restriction provided in the `Pageable` object.

Spring Data JPA not only provides CRUD operations out-of-the-box, but it also supports dynamic query generation based on the method names.

For example:

- By defining a User findByEmail(String email) method, Spring Data will automatically generate the query with a where clause, as in "where email = ?1".

- By defining a User findByEmailAndPassword(String email, String password) method, Spring Data will automatically generate the query with a where clause, as in "where email = ?1 and password=?2".

■ **Note** You can also use other operators such as OR, LIKE, Between, LessThan, LessThanEqual, and so on. Refer to http://docs.spring.io/spring-data/jpa/docs/current/reference/html/#jpa.query-methods. query-creation for a complete list of supporting operations.

But sometimes you may not be able to express your criteria using method names or the method names look ugly. Spring Data provides flexibility to configure the query explicitly using the @Query annotation.

```
@Query("select u from User u where u.email=?1 and u.password=?2 and u.enabled=true")
User findByEmailAndPassword(String email, String password);
```

You can also perform data update operations using @Modifying and @Query, as follows:

```
@Modifying
@Query("update User u set u.enabled=:status")
int updateUserStatus(@Param("status") boolean status)
```

Note that this example uses the named parameter :status instead of the positional parameter ?1.

Using Spring Data JPA with Spring Boot

Now that you've had a glimpse of what Spring Data JPA is and what kind of features it provides, this section shows you how to put it into action.

1. Create a Spring Boot Maven project and add the following dependencies.

```
<dependencies>
    <dependency>
        <groupId>org.springframework.boot</groupId>
        <artifactId>spring-boot-starter-data-jpa</artifactId>
    </dependency>
    <dependency>
        <groupId>com.h2database</groupId>
        <artifactId>h2</artifactId>
    </dependency>
```

```xml
<dependency>
    <groupId>org.springframework.boot</groupId>
    <artifactId>spring-boot-starter-test</artifactId>
    <scope>test</scope>
</dependency>
</dependencies>
```

2. Create a JPA entity called User and a JPA repository interface called UserRepository.

3. Create a user JPA entity, as shown in Listing 8-1.

Listing 8-1. JPA Entity User.java

```java
@Entity
@Table(name="USERS")
public class User
{

    @Id @GeneratedValue(strategy=GenerationType.AUTO)
    private Integer id;
    @Column(nullable=false)
    private String name;
    @Column(nullable=false, unique=true)
    private String email;
    private boolean disabled;

    //setters and getters
}
```

4. Create the UserRepository interface by extending the JpaRepository interface, as shown in Listing 8-2.

Listing 8-2. JPA Repository Interface UserRepository.java

```java
public interface UserRepository extends JpaRepository<User, Integer>
{

}
```

5. You can now populate some sample data using the SQL script src/main/resources/data.sql:

```sql
insert into users(id, name, email,disabled)
values(1,'John','john@gmail.com', false);

insert into users(id, name, email,disabled)
values(2,'Rod','rod@gmail.com', false);

insert into users(id, name, email,disabled)
values(3,'Becky','becky@gmail.com', true);
```

Since you configured the in-memory database (H2) driver, Spring Boot automatically registers a DataSource. Since you added the spring-boot-starter-data-jpa dependency, Spring Boot autoconfiguration takes care of creating the JPA related beans like LocalContainerEntityManagerFactoryBean, TransactionManager, etc., automatically with sensible defaults.

6. Create a Spring Boot entry point class called SpringbootJPADemoApplication. java, as shown in Listing 8-3.

Listing 8-3. SpringbootJPADemoApplication.java

```java
@SpringBootApplication
public class SpringbootJPADemoApplication
{
    public static void main(String[] args)
    {
        SpringApplication.run(SpringbootJPADemoApplication.class, args);
    }
}
```

7. Create a JUnit test class for testing the UserRepository methods, as shown in Listing 8-4.

Listing 8-4. SpringbootJPADemoApplicationTests.java

```java
@RunWith(SpringRunner.class)
@SpringBootTest
public class SpringbootJPADemoApplicationTests
{

    @Autowired
    private UserRepository userRepository;

    @Test
    public void findAllUsers()  {
        List<User> users = userRepository.findAll();
        assertNotNull(users);
        assertTrue(!users.isEmpty());

    }

    @Test
    public void findUserById()  {
Optional<User> user = userRepository.getById(1);
        assertNotNull(user.get());
    }

    @Test
    public void createUser() {
        User user = new User(null, "Paul", "paul@gmail.com");
        User savedUser = userRepository.save(user);
```

```
        User newUser = userRepository.findById(savedUser.getId()).get();
        assertEquals("SivaPrasad", newUser.getName());
        assertEquals("sivaprasad@gmail.com", newUser.getEmail());
    }
}
```

Add Dynamic Query Methods

Now you'll add some finder methods to see how dynamic query generation based on method names works.

To get a user by name, use this:

```
User findByName(String name)
```

To search for users by name, use this:

```
List<User> findByNameLike(String name)
```

The preceding method generates a where clause like `where u.name like ?1`.

Suppose you want to do a wildcard search, such as `where u.name like %?1%`. You can use @Query as follows:

```
@Query("select u from User u where u.name like %?1%")
List<User> searchByName(String name)
```

Using the Sort and Pagination Features

Suppose you want to get all users by their names in ascending order. You can use the `findAll(Sort sort)` method as follows:

```
Sort sort = new Sort(Direction.ASC, "name");
List<User> users = userRepository.findAll(sort);
```

You can also apply sorting on multiple properties, as follows:

```
Order order1 = new Order(Direction.ASC, "name");
Order order2 = new Order(Direction.DESC, "id");
Sort sort = Sort.by(order1, order2);
List<User> users = userRepository.findAll(sort);
```

The users will be ordered first by name in ascending order and then by ID in descending order.

In many web applications, you'll want to show data in a page-by-page manner. Spring Data makes it very easy to load data in the pagination style. Suppose you want to load the first 25 users on one page. We can use Pageable and PageRequest to get results by page, as follows:

```
int size = 25;
int page = 0; //zero-based page index.
Pageable pageable = PageRequest.of(page, size);
Page<User> usersPage = userRepository.findAll(pageable);
```

The usersPage will contain the first 25 user records only. You can get additional details, like the total number of pages, the current page number, whether there is a next page, whether there is a previous page, and more.

- usersPage.getTotalElements();—Returns the total amount of elements.

- usersPage.getTotalPages();—Returns the total number of pages.

- usersPage.hasNext();

- usersPage.hasPrevious();

- List<User> usersList = usersPage.getContent();

You can also apply pagination along with sorting as follows:

```
Sort sort = new Sort(Direction.ASC, "name");
Pageable pageable = PageRequest.of(page, size, sort);
Page<User> usersPage = userRepository.findAll(pageable);
```

Working with Multiple Databases

Spring Boot autoconfiguration works out-of-the-box if you have single database to work with and provides plenty of customization options through its properties.

But if your application demands more control over the application configuration, you can turn off specific autoconfigurations and configure the components by yourself.

For example, you might want to use multiple databases in the same application. If you need to connect to multiple databases, you need to configure various Spring beans like DataSources, TransactionManagers, EntityManagerFactoryBeans, DataSourceInitializers, etc., explicitly.

Suppose you have an application where the security data has been stored in one database/schema and order-related data has been stored in another database/schema.

If you add the spring-boot-starter-data-jpa starter and just define the DataSource beans only, then Spring Boot will try to automatically create some beans (for example, TransactionManager), assuming there will be only one data source. It will fail.

Now you'll see how you can work with multiple databases in Spring Boot and use the Spring Data JPA based application.

1. Create a Spring Boot application with the data-jpa starter. Configure the following dependencies in pom.xml:

```
<dependency>
    <groupId>org.springframework.boot</groupId>
    <artifactId>spring-boot-starter-data-jpa</artifactId>
</dependency>

<dependency>
    <groupId>mysql</groupId>
    <artifactId>mysql-connector-java</artifactId>
</dependency>
```

2. Turn off the DataSource/JPA autoconfiguration. As you are going to configure the database related beans explicitly, you will turn off the DataSource/JPA autoconfiguration by excluding the AutoConfiguration classes, as shown in Listing 8-5.

Listing 8-5. SpringbootMultipleDSDemoApplication.java

```
@SpringBootApplication(
        exclude = { DataSourceAutoConfiguration.class,
                    HibernateJpaAutoConfiguration.class,
                    DataSourceTransactionManagerAutoConfiguration.class})
@EnableTransactionManagement
public class SpringbootMultipleDSDemoApplication
{
    public static void main(String[] args)
    {
        SpringApplication.run(SpringbootMultipleDSDemoApplication.class, args);
    }
}
```

As you have turned off AutoConfigurations, you are enabling TransactionManagement explicitly by using the @EnableTransactionManagement annotation.

3. Configure the datasource properties. Configure the Security and Orders database connection parameters in the application.properties file.

```
datasource.security.driver-class-name=com.mysql.jdbc.Driver
datasource.security.url=jdbc:mysql://localhost:3306/security
datasource.security.username=root
datasource.security.password=admin

datasource.security.initialize=true

datasource.orders.driver-class-name=com.mysql.jdbc.Driver
datasource.orders.url=jdbc:mysql://localhost:3306/orders
datasource.orders.username=root
datasource.orders.password=admin

datasource.orders.initialize=true

hibernate.hbm2ddl.auto=update
hibernate.show-sql=true
```

Here, you have used custom property keys to configure the two datasource properties.

4. Create a security related JPA entity and a JPA repository. Then create a User entity, as follows:

```
package com.apress.demo.security.entities;

@Entity
@Table(name="USERS")
public class User
{
    @Id @GeneratedValue(strategy=GenerationType.AUTO)
    private Integer id;
```

```
    @Column(nullable=false)
    private String name;

    @Column(nullable=false, unique=true)
    private String email;

    private boolean disabled;

    //setters & getters
}
```

5.   Create UserRepository as follows:

```
package com.apress.demo.security.repositories;

public interface UserRepository extends JpaRepository<User, Integer>
{

}
```

Note that you have created User.java and UserRepository.java in the com.apress.demo.security sub-packages.

6.   Create an orders-related JPA entity and JPA repository. Create an Order entity as follows:

```
package com.apress.demo.orders.entities;

@Entity
@Table(name="ORDERS")
public class Order
{
    @Id @GeneratedValue(strategy=GenerationType.AUTO)
    private Integer id;

    @Column(nullable=false, name="cust_name")
    private String customerName;

    @Column(nullable=false, name="cust_email")
    private String customerEmail;

    //setters & getters
}
```

Create the OrderRepository as follows:

```
package com.apress.demo.orders.repositories;

public interface OrderRepository extends JpaRepository<Order, Integer>
{

}
```

Note that you have created Order.java and OrderRepository.java in the com.apress.demo.orders sub-packages.

7. Create SQL scripts to initialize sample data. Create the security-data.sql script in the src/main/resources folder to initialize the USERS table with sample data.

```
delete from users;

insert into users(id, name, email,disabled)
values(1,'John','john@gmail.com', false);

insert into users(id, name, email,disabled)
values(2,'Rob','rob@gmail.com', false);

insert into users(id, name, email,disabled)
values(3,'Remo','remo@gmail.com', true);
```

Create the orders-data.sql script in the src/main/resources folder to initialize the ORDERS table with sample data.

```
delete from orders;

insert into orders(id, cust_name, cust_email)
values(1,'Andrew','andrew@gmail.com');

insert into orders(id, cust_name, cust_email)
values(2,'Paul','paul@gmail.com');

insert into orders(id, cust_name, cust_email)
values(3,'Jimmy','jimmy@gmail.com');
```

8. Create the SecurityDBConfig.java configuration class. You will configure the Spring beans such as DataSource, TransactionManager, EntityManagerFactoryBean, and DataSourceInitializer by connecting to the Security database in SecurityDBConfig.java, as shown in Listing 8-6.

Listing 8-6. SecurityDBConfig.java

```
package com.apress.demo.config;

@Configuration
@EnableJpaRepositories(
        basePackages = "com.apress.demo.security.repositories",
        entityManagerFactoryRef = "securityEntityManagerFactory",
        transactionManagerRef = "securityTransactionManager"
)
public class SecurityDBConfig
{
    @Autowired
    private Environment env;
```

```java
@Bean
@ConfigurationProperties(prefix="datasource.security")
public DataSourceProperties securityDataSourceProperties()
{
    return new DataSourceProperties();
}

@Bean
public DataSource securityDataSource()
{
    DataSourceProperties securityDataSourceProperties = securityDataSourceProperties();
    return DataSourceBuilder.create()
            .driverClassName(securityDataSourceProperties.getDriverClassName())
            .url(securityDataSourceProperties.getUrl())
            .username(securityDataSourceProperties.getUsername())
            .password(securityDataSourceProperties.getPassword())
            .build();
}

@Bean
public PlatformTransactionManager securityTransactionManager()
{
    EntityManagerFactory factory = securityEntityManagerFactory().getObject();
    return new JpaTransactionManager(factory);
}

@Bean
public LocalContainerEntityManagerFactoryBean securityEntityManagerFactory()
{
    LocalContainerEntityManagerFactoryBean factory =
            new LocalContainerEntityManagerFactoryBean();
    factory.setDataSource(securityDataSource());
    factory.setPackagesToScan("com.apress.demo.security.entities");
    factory.setJpaVendorAdapter(new HibernateJpaVendorAdapter());

    Properties jpaProperties = new Properties();
    jpaProperties.put("hibernate.hbm2ddl.auto", env.getProperty("hibernate.hbm2ddl.
auto"));
    jpaProperties.put("hibernate.show-sql", env.getProperty("hibernate.show-sql"));
    factory.setJpaProperties(jpaProperties);

    return factory;
}

@Bean
public DataSourceInitializer securityDataSourceInitializer()
{
    DataSourceInitializer dsInitializer = new DataSourceInitializer();
    dsInitializer.setDataSource(securityDataSource());
    ResourceDatabasePopulator dbPopulator = new ResourceDatabasePopulator();
    dbPopulator.addScript(new ClassPathResource("security-data.sql"));
```

```
        dsInitializer.setDatabasePopulator(dbPopulator);
        dsInitializer.setEnabled(env.getProperty("datasource.security.initialize",
                            Boolean.class, false) );
        return dsInitializer;
    }

}
```

Observe that you have populated the datasource.security.* properties into DataSourceProperties by using @ConfigurationProperties(prefix="dataso urce.security") and DataSourceBuilder fluent API to create the DataSource bean.

While creating the LocalContainerEntityManagerFactoryBean bean, you have configured the package called com.apress.demo.security.entities to scan for JPA entities. You have configured the DataSourceInitializer bean to initialize the sample data from security-data.sql.

Finally, you enabled Spring Data JPA support by using the @ EnableJpaRepositories annotation. As you are going to have multiple EntityManagerFactory and TransactionManager beans, you configured the bean IDs for entityManagerFactoryRef and transactionManagerRef by pointing to the respective bean names. You also configured the basePackages property to indicate where to look for the Spring Data JPA repositories (the packages).

9. Create the OrdersDBConfig.java configuration class. Similar to SecurityDBConfig.java, you will create OrdersDBConfig.java but point it to the Orders database. See Listing 8-7.

Listing 8-7. OrdersDBConfig.java

```
package com.apress.demo.config;

@Configuration
@EnableJpaRepositories(
        basePackages = "com.apress.demo.orders.repositories",
        entityManagerFactoryRef = "ordersEntityManagerFactory",
        transactionManagerRef = "ordersTransactionManager"
)
public class OrdersDBConfig
{

    @Autowired
    private Environment env;

    @Bean
    @ConfigurationProperties(prefix="datasource.orders")
    public DataSourceProperties ordersDataSourceProperties()
    {
        return new DataSourceProperties();
    }
```

```
@Bean
public DataSource ordersDataSource()
{
    DataSourceProperties primaryDataSourceProperties = ordersDataSourceProperties();
    return DataSourceBuilder.create()
            .driverClassName(primaryDataSourceProperties.getDriverClassName())
            .url(primaryDataSourceProperties.getUrl())
            .username(primaryDataSourceProperties.getUsername())
            .password(primaryDataSourceProperties.getPassword())
            .build();
}

@Bean
public PlatformTransactionManager ordersTransactionManager()
{
    EntityManagerFactory factory = ordersEntityManagerFactory().getObject();
    return new JpaTransactionManager(factory);
}

@Bean
public LocalContainerEntityManagerFactoryBean ordersEntityManagerFactory()
{
    LocalContainerEntityManagerFactoryBean factory = new
    LocalContainerEntityManagerFactoryBean();
    factory.setDataSource(ordersDataSource());
    factory.setPackagesToScan("com.apress.demo.orders.entities");
    factory.setJpaVendorAdapter(new HibernateJpaVendorAdapter());

    Properties jpaProperties = new Properties();
    jpaProperties.put("hibernate.hbm2ddl.auto",env.getProperty("hibernate.hbm2ddl.
    auto"));
    jpaProperties.put("hibernate.show-sql", env.getProperty("hibernate.show-sql"));
    factory.setJpaProperties(jpaProperties);

    return factory;

}

@Bean
public DataSourceInitializer ordersDataSourceInitializer()
{
    DataSourceInitializer dsInitializer = new DataSourceInitializer();
    dsInitializer.setDataSource(ordersDataSource());
    ResourceDatabasePopulator dbPopulator = new ResourceDatabasePopulator();
    dbPopulator.addScript(new ClassPathResource("orders-data.sql"));
    dsInitializer.setDatabasePopulator(dbPopulator);
    dsInitializer.setEnabled(env.getProperty("datasource.orders.initialize",
                            Boolean.class, false));
    return dsInitializer;
}

}
```

Note that you have used `datasource.orders.*` properties to create the DataSource bean, configured the `com.apress.demo.orders.entities` package to scan for JPA entities, and configured the `DataSourceInitializer` bean to initialize the database with sample data from `orders-data.sql`.

10. Now you'll create a JUnit test class that invokes the JPA repository methods, as shown in Listing 8-8.

Listing 8-8. SpringbootMultipleDSDemoApplicationTests.java

```java
@RunWith(SpringRunner.class)
@SpringBootTest
public class SpringbootMultipleDSDemoApplicationTests
{
    @Autowired
    private UserRepository userRepository;

    @Autowired
    private OrderRepository orderRepository;

    @Test
    public void findAllUsers()
    {
        List<User> users = userRepository.findAll();
        assertNotNull(users);
        assertTrue(!users.isEmpty());
    }

    @Test
    public void findAllOrders()
    {
        List<Order> orders = orderRepository.findAll();
        assertNotNull(orders);
        assertTrue(!orders.isEmpty());
    }
}
```

Use OpenEntityManagerInViewFilter for Multiple Data Sources

If you have multiple database configuration set up as described in previous section in web applications, and want to use `OpenEntityManagerInViewFilter` to enable lazy loading of JPA entity LAZY associated collections while rendering the view, you need to register the `OpenEntityManagerInViewFilter` beans, as shown in Listing 8-9.

Listing 8-9. WebMvcConfig.java

```java
@Configuration
public class WebMvcConfig
{

    @Bean
    public OpenEntityManagerInViewFilter primaryOpenEntityManagerInViewFilter()
```

```
{
    OpenEntityManagerInViewFilter osivFilter =
                    new OpenEntityManagerInViewFilter();
    osivFilter.setEntityManagerFactoryBeanName
                    ("primaryEntityManagerFactory");
    return osivFilter;
}

@Bean
public OpenEntityManagerInViewFilter reportingOpenEntityManagerInViewFilter()
{
    OpenEntityManagerInViewFilter osivFilter =
                    new OpenEntityManagerInViewFilter();
    osivFilter.setEntityManagerFactoryBeanName
                    ("reportingEntityManagerFactory");
    return osivFilter;
}
}
```

This code configures two OpenEntityManagerInViewFilter beans by setting the two
EntityManagerFactory bean names—primaryEntityManagerFactory and reportingEntityManagerFactory.

Note   To learn more about Spring Data JPA, visit the official Spring Data JPA Documentation at:
`http://docs.spring.io/spring-data/jpa/docs/current/reference/html`.

Summary

This chapter covered Spring Data JPA and covered how to use it with Spring Boot. The next chapter explains
how to work with MongoDB in your Spring Boot applications.

CHAPTER 9

Working with MongoDB

MongoDB is one of the most popular document-oriented NoSQL databases. Spring Data MongoDB provides support for working with MongoDB with a consistent Spring-based programming model similar to Spring Data JPA. Spring Boot provides a starter for Spring Data Mongo, which makes it even easier to use by implementing its autoconfiguring mechanism.

This chapter discusses MongoDB, including how to install a MongoDB server on various platforms like Windows, MacOS, and Linux. The chapter explains how to perform various database operations from the Mongo Shell. Then you will explore how to use Spring Data Mongo features by using Spring Boot's `spring-boot-starter-data-mongodb` starter.

Introducing MongoDB

MongoDB is an open-source document-oriented NoSQL database. MongoDB uses a document storage and data interchange format called BSON, which provides a binary representation of JSON-like documents. MongoDB stores documents in collections. *Collections* are analogous to tables in relational databases. Unlike a table, however, a collection does not require its documents to have the same schema. See Listing 9-1.

Listing 9-1. A Sample Blog Post Document in a MongoDB Collection

```
{
    "_id" : ObjectId("13f345492b7c8eb21818bd09"),
    "title" : "Working with MongoDB in SpringBoot app",
    "url": "http://localhost:8080/blog/working-with-mongodb",
    "created_on" : ISODate("2016-10-01T00:00:00Z"),
    "tags" : ["NoSQL","MongoDB","SpringBoot"],
    "content" : "Long Blog post content goes here",
    "comments": [
        {
            "name" : "John",
            "email": "john@gmail.com",
            "message": "Nice tutorial",
            "created_on" : ISODate("2016-10-01T00:00:00Z"),
        },
        {
            "name" : "Remo",
            "email": "remo@gmail.com",
```

```
            "message": "Thanks for the tutorial",
            "created_on" : ISODate("2016-10-04T00:00:00Z"),
        }
    ]
}
```

Installing MongoDB

MongoDB supports a wide variety of platforms, including the Windows, Linux, and MacOS operating systems. To get a complete list of supported platforms, see `https://docs.mongodb.com/manual/installation/#supported-platforms`.

■ **Note**   We use the MongoDB Community Server in this book.

Installing MongoDB on Windows

Download the latest version of MongoDB from `https://www.mongodb.com/download-center`. Run the MSI installer and choose an installation directory, say `C:\Apps`. In that case, MongoDB server will be installed at `C:\Apps\MongoDB\Server\3.4`.

MongoDB requires a data directory to store its files. The default location for the MongoDB data folder on Windows is `C:\data\db`. You can either create the data directory structure `C:\data\db` or pass a custom location of the data directory as an argument, as follows:

```
C:\Apps\MongoDB\Server\3.4\bin>mongod.exe --dbpath " C:\Apps\MongoDB\Server\3.4\data"
```

After you run this command, MongoDB should start on default port 27017. Instead of running this command and passing all the configuration options every time, you can create a config file and batch script to start MongoDB.

For example, you could create `mongod.cfg` in the `C:\Apps\MongoDB\Server\3.4` directory with the content shown in Listing 9-2.

Listing 9-2. MongoDB Server Configuration File Called `mongod.cfg`

```
systemLog:
    destination: file
    path: C:/Apps/MongoDB/Server/3.4/logs/mongo.log
storage:
    dbPath: C:/Apps/MongoDB/Server/3.4/data/db
net:
    bindIp: 127.0.0.1
    port: 27017
```

You create `start-mongo.bat` in the `C:\Apps\MongoDB\Server\3.4` directory as follows:

```
bin\mongod.exe --config C:\Apps\MongoDB\Server\3.4\mongod.cfg
```

Now you can simply start the MongoDB server as follows:

```
C:\Apps\MongoDB\Server\3.4>start-mongo.bat
```

■ **Note**   Make sure that the data and logs directories are already created before starting MongoDB.

You can learn more about the MongoDB server configuration options at `https://docs.mongodb.com/manual/reference/configuration-options/`.

Installing MongoDB on MacOS

The easiest way to install the MongoDB server on MacOS is by using Homebrew. See `https://brew.sh/` on how to install Homebrew. Once Homebrew is installed, you need to update Homebrew's package database and install the MongoDB package as follows:

```
> brew update
> brew install mongodb
```

On MacOS, the default data directory is /data/db. Make sure that the data directory has read-write permission. You can start the Mongo server without specifying the dbpath, which means it will use the default data directory, or you can pass a custom data directory location as follows:

```
> mongod --dbpath /Users/username/mongodb/data
```

For alternative options for installing MongoDB on MacOS, see `https://docs.mongodb.com/manual/tutorial/install-mongodb-on-os-x/`.

Installing MongoDB on Linux

MongoDB provides packages for most of the popular Linux distributions. For installation instructions of your specific Linux distribution, refer to `https://docs.mongodb.com/manual/administration/install-on-linux/`.

Getting Started with MongoDB Using the Mongo Shell

Once the MongoDB server is started, you can connect to the MongoDB server by starting the Mongo Shell. Open another command prompt and run `C:\Apps\MongoDB\Server\3.4\bin\mongo.exe`. If you have connected to the server successfully, it will print the MongoDB Shell version and the message connecting to: test.

```
C:\Apps\MongoDB\Server\3.4\bin> mongo.exe
MongoDB shell version: 3.2.1
connecting to: test
Welcome to the MongoDB shell.
For interactive help, type "help".
For more comprehensive documentation, see
        http://docs.mongodb.org/
Questions? Try the support group
        http://groups.google.com/group/mongodb-user
>
```

You can use the show dbs command to check the list of available databases:

```
> show dbs
```

By default, you are connected to the default database called test. You can use the use db_name command to switch to another database.

```
> use users
switched to db users
```

You can insert a user document into the users collection as follows:

```
> db.users.insert({"username": "siva","password": "secret" })
```

If the collection does not exist, it will be created automatically.
You can query the database to return all the documents as follows:

```
> db.users.find()
```

You can also apply filters to a query as follows:

```
> db.users.find({"name": "siva" })
```

You can also get the count of number of documents as follows:

```
> db.users.count()
```

■ **Note**   Covering MongoDB in-depth is out of the scope of this book. Visit the official documentation at: https://docs.mongodb.com/manual/ to learn more about MongoDB.

Introducing Spring Data MongoDB

The Spring Data umbrella project provides the Spring Data Mongo module, which provides support for performing CRUD (Create, Read, Update, Delete) operations and dynamic queries based on method names similar to Spring Data JPA.

The Spring Data MongoDB module provides the MongoTemplate, which provides higher level abstraction over MongoDB Java driver API com.mongodb.Mongo.

If you are not using Spring Boot, you need to configure the MongoDB components using JavaConfig, as shown in Listing 9-3.

Listing 9-3. MongoDB Components Configuration Using JavaConfig

```
@Configuration
public class MongoConfiguration
{
  @Bean
  public MongoDbFactory mongoDbFactory() throws Exception {
    return new SimpleMongoDbFactory(new Mongo(), "database");
  }
```

```
  @Bean
  public MongoTemplate mongoTemplate() throws Exception {
    return new MongoTemplate(mongoDbFactory());
  }
}
```

Spring Boot provides the `spring-boot-starter-data-mongodb` starter to easily work with MongoDB by autoconfiguring the MongoDB components without requiring the manual configuration.

```
<dependency>
    <groupId>org.springframework.boot</groupId>
    <artifactId>spring-boot-starter-data-mongodb</artifactId>
</dependency>
```

By adding the `spring-boot-starter-data-mongodb` dependency, Spring Boot will autoconfigure `MongoClient`, `MongoDbFactory`, `MongoTemplate`, etc. and connect to the local MongoDB server at `mongodb://localhost/test`.

You can customize the mongodb server URL by configuring the `spring.data.mongodb.uri` property in the `application.properties` file.

```
spring.data.mongodb.uri=mongodb://remoteserver:27017/blog
```

You can also use `MongoTemplate` to save, update, and delete domain objects that internally take care of mapping domain objects to documents in MongoDB.

First, you create the `User` class as follows:

```
public class User
{
    private String id;
    private String name;
    private String email;
    private boolean disabled;
    //setters and getters
}
```

You can then inject `MongoTemplate` and perform various operations on MongoDB, as shown in Listing 9-4.

Listing 9-4. Performing Database Operations Using MongoTemplate

```
@Service
public class MongoUserService
{
    @Autowired
    private MongoTemplate mongoTemplate;

    public List<User> getUsers()
    {
        return mongoTemplate.findAll(User.class, "users");
    }
```

```
    public User getUser(String id)
    {
        Query query = Query.query(Criteria.where("id").is(id));
        return mongoTemplate.findOne(query, User.class);
    }

    public void createUser(User user)
    {
        mongoTemplate.save(user, "users");
    }
}
```

In addition to using MongoTemplate, you can also create repositories that extend the MongoRepository interface and provide CRUD operations out-of-the-box.

You can map a domain object to a particular MongoDB collection name using the @Document annotation.

```
@Document(collection="users")
public class User
{
    @Id
    private String id;
    private String name;
    private String email;
    private boolean disabled;
    //setters and getters
}
```

By default, MongoDB generates an ObjectId primary key called _id. But you can map any existing property to be used as the primary key, simply by using the @Id annotation.

Create the UserRepository interface by extending the MongoRepository interface, as shown in Listing 9-5.

Listing 9-5. UserRepository.java

```
public interface UserRepository extends MongoRepository<User, String>
{

}
```

Now you can perform various CRUD operations as follows:

```
List<User> users = userRepository.findAll();
Optional<User> user1 = userRepository.findById("1");

User user2 = new User("2", "Robert", "robert@gmail.com");
User savedUser = userRepository.save(user2);

// delete user by primary key
userRepository.deleteById("1");
```

```
// delete user by object
userRepository.delete(user);

// get total count of user documents in users collection
userRepository.count();
```

You can also perform sorting and pagination similar to Spring Data JPA repositories.

```
Sort sort = new Sort(Direction.ASC, "name");
List<User> users = userRepository.findAll(sort);
```

You can also express the query criteria using @Query as follows:

```
@Query("{ 'name' : ?0 }")
User findByUserName(String name);
```

Using Embedded Mongo for Testing

It would be more convenient to use an embedded MongoDB for testing purposes, especially in continuous integration environments.

You can use the following embedded Mongo (https://github.com/flapdoodle-oss/de.flapdoodle. embed.mongo) dependency, which Spring Boot can autoconfigure, so that you can run tests without setting up an actual MongoDB server.

```
<dependency>
    <groupId>de.flapdoodle.embed</groupId>
    <artifactId>de.flapdoodle.embed.mongo</artifactId>
</dependency>
```

You can also initialize sample data by implementing the CommandLineRunner interface, which executes the public void run(String… args) method upon application startup, as shown in Listing 9-6.

Listing 9-6. SpringbootMongodbDemoApplication.java

```
@SpringBootApplication
public class SpringbootMongodbDemoApplication implements CommandLineRunner
{
    @Autowired
    private UserRepository userRepository;

    public static void main(String[] args)
    {
        SpringApplication.run(SpringbootMongodbDemoApplication.class, args);
    }

    @Override
    public void run(String... args) throws Exception {
        userRepository.save(new User("1", "Robert","robert@gmail.com"));
        userRepository.save(new User("2", "Dan","dan@gmail.com"));
    }
}
```

Create the JUnit test to test the basic CRUD operations on UserRepository, as shown in Listing 9-7.

Listing 9-7. SpringbootMongodbDemoApplicationTests.java

```java
@RunWith(SpringRunner.class)
public class SpringbootMongodbDemoApplicationTests
{
    @Autowired
    private UserRepository userRepository;

    @Test
    public void findAllUsers()  {
        List<User> users = userRepository.findAll();
        assertNotNull(users);
        assertTrue(!users.isEmpty());

    }

    @Test
    public void findUserById()  {
        User user = userRepository.findById("1").get();
        assertNotNull(user);
    }

    @Test
    public void createUser() {
        User user = new User("3", "Joseph", "joseph@gmail.com");
        User savedUser = userRepository.save(user);
        User newUser = userRepository.findById(savedUser.getId()).get();
        assertEquals("Joseph", newUser.getName());
        assertEquals("joseph@gmail.com", newUser.getEmail());
    }
}
```

To learn more about the Spring Data Mongo features, see the Spring Data MongoDB reference documentation at: http://docs.spring.io/spring-data/data-mongo/docs/current/reference/html.

Summary

This chapter explained how to install and use the MongoDB server. It explored how to work with Spring Data MongoDB in Spring Boot applications. In the next chapter, you will start developing web applications using Spring Boot and SpringMVC.

CHAPTER 10

Web Applications with Spring Boot

Spring MVC is the most popular Java web framework based on the Model-View-Controller (MVC) design pattern. Since the Spring 3.0 version, Spring MVC has provided annotation based request mapping capabilities using `@Controller` and `@RequestMapping`. But configuring Spring MVC web application components such as `DispatcherServlet`, `ViewResolvers`, `MultiPartResolver`, and `ExceptionHandlers` is a repetitive and tedious process.

Spring Boot makes it very easy to get started with Spring MVC because the Spring Boot autoconfiguration mechanism configures most of the components such as `DispatcherServlet`, `ViewResolvers`, `ContentNegotiatingViewResolver`, `LocaleResolver`, `MessageCodesResolver`, etc., with default values and provides the options to customize them.

Traditionally JSPs are being used for view rendering, but there are many other view templating technologies emerged over the time such as Thymeleaf, Mustache, Groovy Templates, FreeMarker, etc. Spring Boot provides autoconfiguration for these view templating libraries as well.

Spring Boot provides embedded servlet container support so that you can build your applications as self-contained deployment units. Spring Boot supports Tomcat, Jetty, and Undertow servlet containers out-of-the-box and provides customization hooks to implement all server level customizations.

This chapter looks into how to develop Spring MVC based web applications using the Web starter with Tomcat, Jetty, and Undertow as embedded servlet containers. You will learn how to customize the default Spring MVC configuration and how to register servlets, filters, and listeners as Spring beans.

You will learn how to use Thymeleaf View templates, how to perform form validations, and how to upload files and use ResourceBundles for internationalization (i18n).

Finally, you will learn about various ways of handling exceptions using `@ExceptionHandler` and `@ControllerAdvice` annotations and how Spring Boot makes it even simpler to do so.

Introducing SpringMVC

Spring MVC is a powerful web framework built on MVC and front controller design patterns. Spring MVC provides `DispatcherServlet`, which acts as a front controller by receiving all the requests and delegates the processing to request handlers (controllers). Once the processing is done, `ViewResolver` will render a view based on the view name. Figure 10-1 shows this flow process.

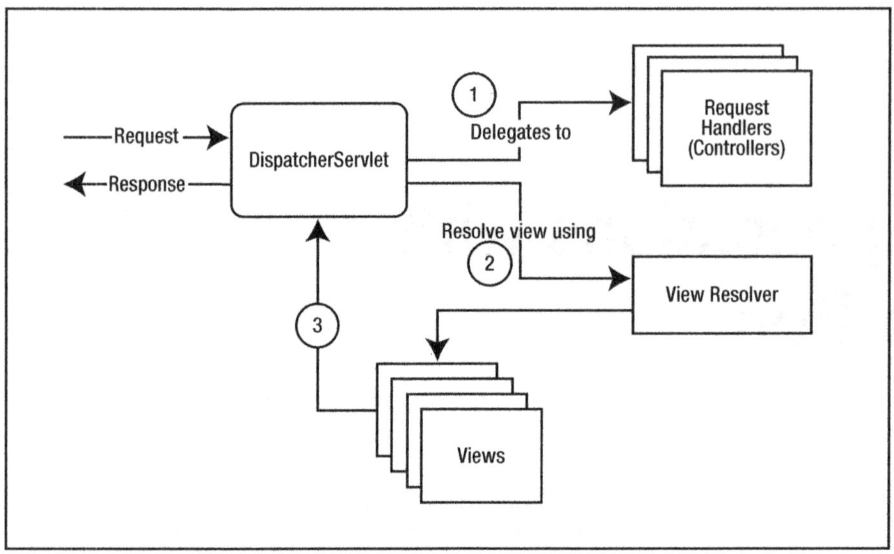

Figure 10-1. *SpringMVC request processing flow*

Spring MVC provides annotation-based mapping support to map request URL patterns to handler classes using @Controller and @RequestMapping annotations (Listing 10-1).

Listing 10-1. SpringMVC Annotation-Based Controller

```
@Controller
public class HomeController
{
    @RequestMapping(value="/home", method=RequestMethod.GET)
    public String home(Model model) {
        model.addAttribute("message", "Hello Spring MVC!!");
        return "home";
    }
}
```

The @Controller annotation on the HomeController class marks it as a request handler Spring component and the home() method will handle the GET requests to the /home URL. The ViewResolver will resolve the logical view name "home" to a view template, say /WEB-INF/views/home.html, and then render the view.

Spring 4.3 introduced @GetMapping, @PostMapping, @PutMapping, etc., annotations as convenient composed annotations so that you don't have to specify a method type in @RequestMapping(value="/url", method=RequestMethod.XXX). See Listing 10-2.

Listing 10-2. Using the @GetMapping and @PostMapping Annotations

```
@Controller
public class HomeController
{
```

```
@GetMapping("/home")
public String home(Model model) {
    model.addAttribute("message", "Hello Spring MVC!!");
    return "home";
}

@PostMapping("/users")
public String createUser(User user) {
    userRepository.save(user);
    return "users";
}
}
```

For SpringMVC-based web applications, we need to configure various web layer components like `DispatcherServlet`, `ViewResolvers`, `LocaleResolver`, `HandlerExceptionResolver`, etc. Spring Boot provides the Web starter, which autoconfigures all these commonly used web layer components, thus making web application development much easier.

Developing Web Application Using Spring Boot

Spring Boot provides the Web starter `spring-boot-starter-web` for developing web applications using Spring MVC. Spring Boot autoconfiguration registers the SpringMVC beans like `DispatcherServlet`, `ViewResolvers`, `ExceptionHandlers`, etc. You can develop a Spring Boot web application as a JAR type module using an embedded servlet container or as a WAR type module, which can be deployed on any external servlet container.

```
<dependency>
        <groupId>org.springframework.boot</groupId>
        <artifactId>spring-boot-starter-web</artifactId>
</dependency>
```

The `spring-boot-starter-web` starter by default configures `DispatcherServlet` to the URL pattern "/" and adds Tomcat as the embedded servlet container, which runs on port 8080.

Spring Boot by default serves the static resources (HTML, CSS, JS, images, etc.) from the following CLASSPATH locations:

- `/static`

- `/public`

- `/resources`

- `/META-INF/resources`

In addition to these locations, you can also use WebJars (`http://www.webjars.org/`) for serving static resources. Spring Boot automatically serves any request to the `/webjars/` path from the WebJars JAR files. You can override the static resource locations by configuring the `spring.resources.staticLocations` property in the `application.properties` file.

```
spring.resources.staticLocations=classpath:/assets/
```

Now you'll see how to create a Spring Boot Web project, display a simple HTML page, and use static resources like CSS and images. Bootstrap (http://getbootstrap.com/) is a popular CSS framework. This example adds Bootstrap CSS to the project using WebJars.

1. Create a Spring Boot Maven project with the Web starter and add the Bootstrap WebJars dependency.

```
<dependencies>

    <dependency>
        <groupId>org.springframework.boot</groupId>
        <artifactId>spring-boot-starter-web</artifactId>
    </dependency>

    <dependency>
        <groupId>org.webjars.bower</groupId>
        <artifactId>bootstrap</artifactId>
        <version>3.3.7</version>
    </dependency>

</dependencies>
```

2. Create the `styles.css` stylesheet in the `src/main/resources/static/css` folder.

```
body {
      background-color: #A7A5A4;
      padding-top: 50px;
}
```

3. Copy an image, such as `spring-boot.png`, into the `src/main/resources/static/images` folder.

4. Create the `index.html` file in the `src/main/resources/public` folder and add `bootstrap.css` to the `index.html` file. Use the Bootstrap navigation bar component.

```
<!DOCTYPE html>
<html>
<head>
<meta charset="utf-8" />
<title>Home</title>
<link rel="stylesheet" href="webjars/bootstrap/3.3.7 /css/bootstrap.css" />
<link rel="stylesheet" href="css/styles.css" />
</head>
<body>

    <nav class="navbar navbar-inverse navbar-fixed-top">
      <div class="container">
        <div class="navbar-header">
          <button type="button" class="navbar-toggle collapsed"
                  data-toggle="collapse" data-target="#navbar"
                  aria-expanded="false" aria-controls="navbar">
```

```html
      <span class="sr-only">Toggle navigation</span>
      <span class="icon-bar"></span>
      <span class="icon-bar"></span>
      <span class="icon-bar"></span>
    </button>
    <a class="navbar-brand" href="#">Project name</a>
  </div>
  <div id="navbar" class="collapse navbar-collapse">
    <ul class="nav navbar-nav">
      <li class="active"><a href="#">Home</a></li>
      <li><a href="#about">About</a></li>
      <li><a href="#contact">Contact</a></li>
    </ul>
  </div>
</div>
</nav>

<div class="container">
  <h2>Hello World!!</h2>
  <img alt="SpringBoot" src="images/spring-boot.png" />
</div>

</body>
</html>
```

   5.   Create an application entry point class.

```java
@SpringBootApplication
public class SpringbootWebDemoApplication
{
    public static void main(String[] args)
    {
        SpringApplication.run(SpringbootWebDemoApplication.class, args);
    }
}
```

Now run the SpringbootWebDemoApplication and navigate to http://localhost:8080/. You should be able to see the web page with the Bootstrap navigation bar, as shown in Figure 10-2.

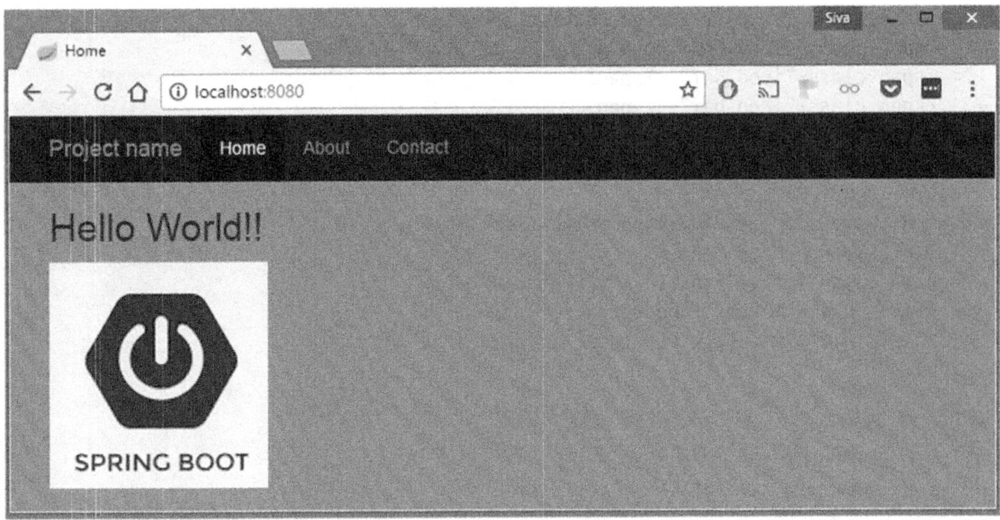

Figure 10-2. *Web page with bootstrap components using WebJars*

By default, the Spring Boot Web starter uses Tomcat as the embedded servlet container and runs on port 8080. However, you can customize the server properties using `server.*` in `application.properties`.

```
server.port=9090
server.servlet.context-path=/demo
server.servlet.path=/app
```

With these customizations, `DispatcherServlet` is configured to handle the URL pattern `/app`, the root `contextPath` will be `/demo`, and Tomcat now runs on port 9090. So, you would access the `index.html` file at `http://localhost:9090/demo/app/`.

Using the Tomcat, Jetty, and Undertow Embedded Servlet Containers

As mentioned, the Spring Boot Web starter includes Tomcat as the embedded servlet container by default. Instead of Tomcat, though, you can use other servlet containers like Jetty or Undertow.

To use Jetty as the embedded container, you simply need to exclude `spring-boot-starter-tomcat` and add `spring-boot-starter-jetty`.

```
<dependency>
    <groupId>org.springframework.boot</groupId>
    <artifactId>spring-boot-starter-web</artifactId>
    <exclusions>
        <exclusion>
            <groupId>org.springframework.boot</groupId>
            <artifactId>spring-boot-starter-tomcat</artifactId>
        </exclusion>
    </exclusions>
</dependency>
```

```
<dependency>
    <groupId>org.springframework.boot</groupId>
    <artifactId>spring-boot-starter-jetty</artifactId>
</dependency>
```

Undertow (http://undertow.io/) is a web server written in Java. It provides blocking and non-blocking APIs based on NIO. Spring Boot provides autoconfiguration support for the Undertow server as well. Similar to what you saw with Jetty, you can configure Spring Boot to use the Undertow embedded server instead of Tomcat as follows:

```
<dependency>
    <groupId>org.springframework.boot</groupId>
    <artifactId>spring-boot-starter-web</artifactId>
    <exclusions>
        <exclusion>
            <artifactId>spring-boot-starter-tomcat</artifactId>
            <groupId>org.springframework.boot</groupId>
        </exclusion>
    </exclusions>
</dependency>
<dependency>
    <groupId>org.springframework.boot</groupId>
    <artifactId>spring-boot-starter-undertow</artifactId>
</dependency>
```

You can customize various properties of the Tomcat, Jetty, and Undertow servlet containers using the server.tomcat.*, server.jetty.*, and server.undertow.* properties, respectively.

```
server.tomcat.accesslog.directory=logs # Directory in which log files are created.
server.tomcat.accesslog.enabled=false # Enable access log.
server.tomcat.accesslog.file-date-format=.yyyy-MM-dd # Date format to place in log file name.
server.tomcat.basedir= # Tomcat base directory. If not specified a temporary directory will
be used.
server.tomcat.max-connections= # Maximum number of connections that the server will accept
and process at any given time.
server.tomcat.max-http-header-size=0 # Maximum size in bytes of the HTTP message header.
server.tomcat.max-http-post-size=0 # Maximum size in bytes of the HTTP post content.
server.tomcat.max-threads=0 # Maximum amount of worker threads.
server.tomcat.min-spare-threads=0 # Minimum amount of worker threads.
server.tomcat.port-header=X-Forwarded-Port # Name of the HTTP header used to override the
original port value.

server.jetty.acceptors= # Number of acceptor threads to use.
server.jetty.accesslog.append=false # Append to log.
server.jetty.accesslog.date-format=dd/MMM/yyyy:HH:mm:ss Z
server.jetty.accesslog.enabled=false # Enable access log.
server.jetty.accesslog.filename= # Log filename. If not specified, logs will be redirected
to "System.err".
server.jetty.accesslog.log-cookies=false # Enable logging of the request cookies.
server.jetty.accesslog.log-latency=false # Enable logging of request processing time.
server.jetty.max-http-post-size=0 # Maximum size in bytes of the HTTP post or put content.
```

```
server.undertow.accesslog.dir= # Undertow access log directory.
server.undertow.accesslog.enabled=false # Enable access log.
server.undertow.accesslog.rotate=true # Enable access log rotation.
server.undertow.accesslog.suffix=log # Log file name suffix.
server.undertow.buffer-size= # Size of each buffer in bytes.
server.undertow.io-threads= # Number of I/O threads to create for the worker.
server.undertow.max-http-post-size=0 # Maximum size in bytes of the HTTP post content.
```

Use the `org.springframework.boot.autoconfigure.web.ServerProperties` class to see a complete list of server customization properties.

Customizing Embedded Servlet Containers

Spring Boot provides lot of customization options for configuring servlet containers using the `server.*` properties. You can customize the `port`, `connectionTimeout`, `contextPath`, and SSL configuration parameters, as well as the session configuration parameters by configuring these properties in `application.properties`.

But if you need more control, you can register embedded servlet containers programmatically by registering a bean of type `TomcatServletWebServerFactory`, `JettyServletWebServerFactory`, or `UndertowServletWebServerFactory` based on the embedded server you want to use.

One common scenario where you would want to register embedded servlet containers programmatically is to redirect the default HTTP request to the HTTPS protocol.

Suppose your application is running on `http://localhost:8080` and you want to use the HTTPS protocol. If anyone is accessing `http://localhost:8080`, you'll want to redirect the request to `https://localhost:8443`.

First, you generate a self-signed SSL certificate using the following command:

```
keytool -genkey -alias mydomain -keyalg RSA -keysize 2048 -keystore KeyStore.jks -validity
3650
```

After providing answers to questions that keytool asks, it will generate a `KeyStore.jks` file and copy it to the `src/main/resources` folder.

Now configure the SSL properties in the `application.properties` file as follows:

```
server.port=8443
server.ssl.key-store=classpath:KeyStore.jks
server.ssl.key-store-password=mysecret
server.ssl.keyStoreType=JKS
server.ssl.keyAlias=mydomain
```

If you are using the Tomcat embedded container, you can register `TomcatServletWebServerFactory` programmatically, as shown in Listing 10-3.

Listing 10-3. Registering the Tomcat Embedded Container Programmatically

```
@Configuration
public class TomcatConfiguration
{
    @LocalServerPort
    int serverPort;
```

```java
@Bean
public ServletWebServerFactory servletContainer() {
    TomcatServletWebServerFactory tomcat = new TomcatServletWebServerFactory() {
        @Override
        protected void postProcessContext(Context context) {
            SecurityConstraint securityConstraint = new SecurityConstraint();
            securityConstraint.setUserConstraint("CONFIDENTIAL");
            SecurityCollection collection = new SecurityCollection();
            collection.addPattern("/*");
            securityConstraint.addCollection(collection);
            context.addConstraint(securityConstraint);
        }
    };

    tomcat.addAdditionalTomcatConnectors(initiateHttpConnector());
    return tomcat;
}

private Connector initiateHttpConnector() {
    Connector connector = new Connector("org.apache.coyote.http11.Http11NioProtocol");
    connector.setScheme("http");
    connector.setPort(8080);
    connector.setSecure(false);
    connector.setRedirectPort(serverPort);
    return connector;
}
}
```

With this customization, the request to `http://localhost:8080/` will be automatically redirected to `https://localhost:8443/`.

Customizing SpringMVC Configuration

Most of the time, Spring Boot's default autoconfiguration, along with the customization properties, will be sufficient to tune your web application. But at times, you may need more control to configure the application components in a specific way to meet your application needs.

If you want to take advantage of Spring Boot's autoconfiguration and add some additional MVC configuration (interceptors, formatters, view controllers, etc.), then you can create a configuration class without the `@EnableWebMvc` annotation, which implements `WebMvcConfigurer` and supplies additional configuration. See Listing 10-4.

■ **Note** If you want complete control over the Spring MVC configuration, you can add your own configuration class annotated with `@EnableWebMvc`. Spring Boot's WebMVC autoconfiguration will be completely turned off if you create a configuration class with the `@Configuration` and `@EnableWebMvc` annotations.

Listing 10-4. Customizing the SpringMVC Configuration

```java
@Configuration
public class WebConfig implements WebMvcConfigurer
{
    @Override
    public void addViewControllers(ViewControllerRegistry registry){
        registry.addViewController("/login").setViewName("public/login");
        registry.addRedirectViewController("/", "/home");
    }

    @Override
    public void addInterceptors(InterceptorRegistry registry) {
        //Add additional interceptors here
    }

    @Override
    public void addResourceHandlers(ResourceHandlerRegistry registry) {
        registry.addResourceHandler("/assets/").addResourceLocations("/resources/assets/");
    }

    @Override
    public void configureDefaultServletHandling(DefaultServletHandlerConfigurer configurer) {
        configurer.enable();
    }

    @Override
    public void addFormatters(FormatterRegistry registry) {
        //Add additional formatters here
    }
}
```

SpringMVC provides `WebMvcConfigurerAdapter`, which is an implementation of the `WebMvcConfigurer` interface. But `WebMvcConfigurerAdapter` is deprecated as of Spring 5.0, because `WebMvcConfigurer` has default method implementations and uses Java 8 default method support.

Registering Servlets, Filters, and Listeners as Spring Beans

You can register servlets, filters, listeners by using the `ServletRegistrationBean`, `FilterRegistrationBean`, and `ServletListenerRegistrationBean` bean definitions.

Suppose you created the servlet shown in Listing 10-5 and marked it as a Spring bean using the `@Component` annotation.

Listing 10-5. MyServlet Defined as a Spring Bean Using the @Component Annotation

```java
@Component
public class MyServlet extends HttpServlet
{
    @Autowired
    private UserService userService;
```

```
    @Override
    protected void doGet(HttpServletRequest req, HttpServletResponse resp)
                                    throws ServletException, IOException {
        resp.getWriter().write(userService.getMessage());
    }
}
```

Now you can register `MyServlet` using `ServletRegistrationBean` and map it to the URL pattern `/myServlet`, as shown in Listing 10-6.

Listing 10-6. Registering MyServlet Using ServletRegistrationBean

```
@Configuration
public class WebMvcConfig implements WebMvcConfigurer
{
    @Autowired
    private MyServlet myServlet;

    @Bean
    public ServletRegistrationBean<MyServlet> myServletBean()
    {
        ServletRegistrationBean<MyServlet> servlet = new ServletRegistrationBean<>();
        servlet.setServlet(myServlet);
        servlet.addUrlMappings("/myServlet");
        return servlet;
    }
    ...
    ...
}
```

With this approach, you can take advantage of Spring's dependency injection for servlets, filters, and listeners. Let's take a look at how you can register filters and listeners as well.

JavaMelody (`https://github.com/javamelody/javamelody/wiki`) is a library that can be used to monitor Java-based web applications. JavaMelody can provide various metrics about the running application, including:

- A summary indicating the overall number of executions, the average execution time, the CPU time, and the percentage of errors.

- The percentage of time spent on the requests when the average time exceeds a configurable threshold.

- The complete list of requests, aggregated without dynamic parameters with the number of executions, the mean execution time, the mean CPU time, the percentage of errors, and an evolution chart of execution time over time.

- Each HTTP request indicates the size of the flow response, the mean number of SQL executions, and the mean SQL time.

Integrating JavaMelody into a Java web application is very simple. You need to register `net.bull.javamelody.MonitoringFilter`, which is a filter, and `net.bull.javamelody.SessionListener`, which is a `HttpSessionListener`.

Listing 10-7 shows how to configure JavaMelody's `MonitoringFilter` and `SessionListener` as Spring beans using `FilterRegistrationBean` and `ServletListenerRegistrationBean`.

Listing 10-7. Registering JavaMelody's MonitoringFilter and SessionListener

```java
@Configuration
public class WebMvcConfig implements WebMvcConfigurer
{

    @Bean(name = "javamelodyFilter")
    public FilterRegistrationBean<MonitoringFilter> javamelodyFilterBean() {

        FilterRegistrationBean<MonitoringFilter> registration =
        new FilterRegistrationBean<>();
        registration.setFilter(new MonitoringFilter());
        registration.addUrlPatterns("/*");
        registration.setName("javamelodyFilter");
        registration.setAsyncSupported(true);
        registration.setDispatcherTypes(DispatcherType.REQUEST, DispatcherType.ASYNC);
        return registration;
    }

    @Bean(name = "javamelodySessionListener")
    public ServletListenerRegistrationBean<SessionListener> sessionListener() {
        return new ServletListenerRegistrationBean<>(new SessionListener());
    }
}
```

With this configuration, you can start the application and see JavaMelody's monitoring dashboard at `http://localhost:8080/monitoring`. See Figure 10-3.

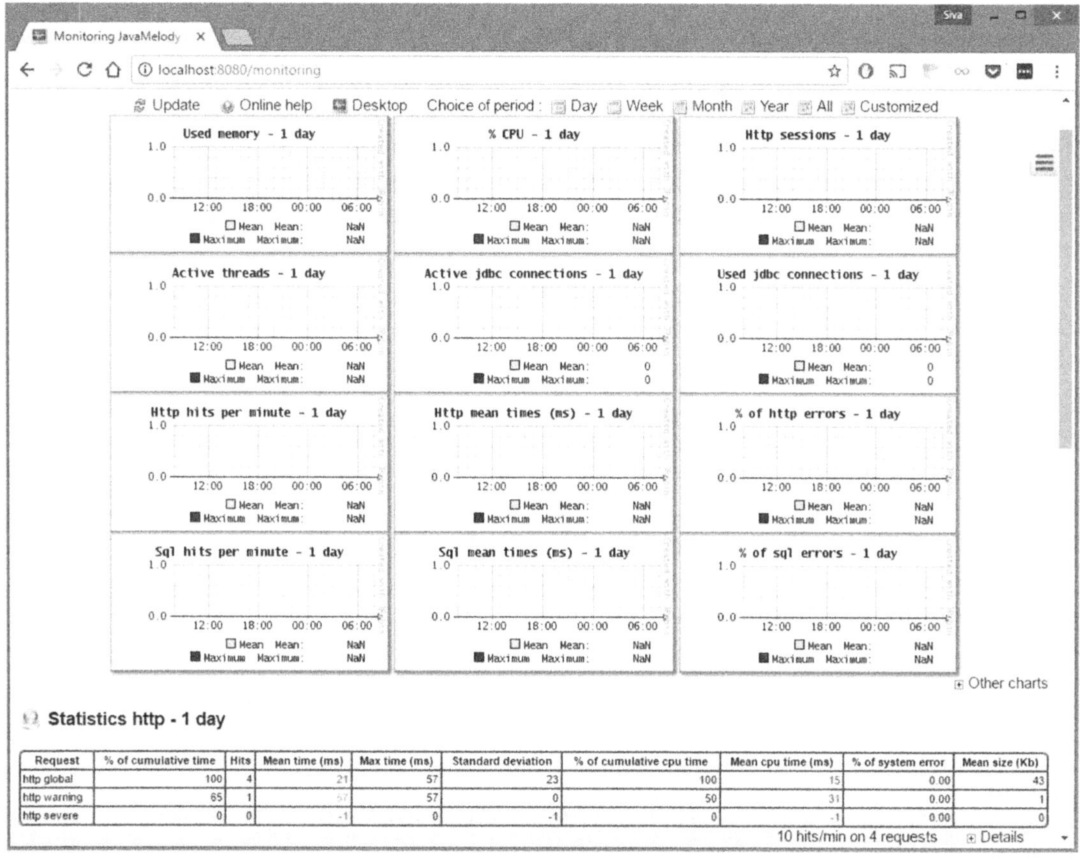

Figure 10-3. JavaMelody monitoring dashboard

Spring Boot Web Application as a Deployable WAR

The Spring Boot web application can be developed using WAR type packaging also. The first thing you do if you want to build a deployable WAR file is change the packaging type.

If you are using Maven, then in pom.xml, change the packaging type to war.

```
<packaging>war</packaging>
```

If you are using Gradle, you need to apply the WAR plugin.

```
apply plugin: 'war'
```

When you add the spring-boot-starter-web dependency. It will transitively add the spring-boot-starter-tomcat dependency as well. So you need to add spring-boot-starter-tomcat as the provided scope so that it won't get packaged inside the WAR file.

```
<dependency>
    <groupId>org.springframework.boot</groupId>
    <artifactId>spring-boot-starter-tomcat</artifactId>
    <scope>provided</scope>
</dependency>
```

If you are using Gradle, add `spring-boot-starter-tomcat` with the `providedRuntime` scope as follows:

```
dependencies {
    ...
    providedRuntime 'org.springframework.boot:spring-boot-starter-tomcat'
    ...
}
```

Finally, you need to provide a `SpringBootServletInitializer` sub-class and override its `configure()` method. You can simply make your application's entry point class extend `SpringBootServletInitializer`, as shown in Listing 10-8

Listing 10-8. Implementing SpringBootServletInitializer

```
@SpringBootApplication
public class SpringbootWebDemoApplication extends SpringBootServletInitializer {

    @Override
    protected SpringApplicationBuilder configure(SpringApplicationBuilder application) {
        return application.sources(SpringbootWebDemoApplication.class);
    }

    public static void main(String[] args) throws Exception {
        SpringApplication.run(SpringbootWebDemoApplication.class, args);
    }

}
```

Now running the Maven/Gradle build tool will produce a WAR file that can be deployed on an external server.

View Templates that Spring Boot Supports

Java Server Pages (JSP) is the most commonly used view templating technology in traditional Java-based web applications. However, there are new view templating libraries, such as Thymeleaf, Mustache, etc., that have emerged as alternatives to JSP.

Spring Boot provides autoconfiguration for the following view templating technologies.

- Thymeleaf (`http://www.thymeleaf.org/`)

- Mustache (`http://mustache.github.io/`)

- Groovy (`http://docs.groovy-lang.org/docs/next/html/documentation/template-engines.html#_the_markuptemplateengine`)

- FreeMarker (`http://freemarker.org/docs/`)

Although Spring MVC supports JSP, there are some known limitations (http://docs.spring.io/spring-boot/docs/current/reference/htmlsingle/#boot-features-jsp-limitations) to using JSP in Spring Boot applications with an embedded servlet container. But JSP works fine in Spring Boot WAR type modules.

Using the Thymeleaf View Templates

Thymeleaf is a server-side Java template engine that provides support for integrating with SpringMVC and SpringSecurity. Among the supporting view templates, Thymeleaf is the most popular one used in Spring Boot applications.

In this section, you see how you can use Thymeleaf in a Spring Boot web application.

Create a Spring Boot Maven project with the `spring-boot-starter-thymeleaf` starter.

```
<dependencies>

    <dependency>
        <groupId>org.springframework.boot</groupId>
        <artifactId>spring-boot-starter-web</artifactId>
    </dependency>
    <dependency>
        <groupId>org.springframework.boot</groupId>
        <artifactId>spring-boot-starter-thymeleaf</artifactId>
    </dependency>

</dependencies>
```

`ThymeleafAutoConfiguration` will take care of registering `TemplateResolver`, `ThymeleafViewResolver`, `SpringResourceTemplateResolver`, and `SpringTemplateEngine`. By default, Spring Boot loads the Thymeleaf view templates from the `classpath:/templates/` directory.

Now create a controller to handle the `"/home"` request.

```
@Controller
public class HomeController
{
    @GetMapping("/home")
    public String home(Model model) {
        model.addAttribute("message", "Spring Boot + Thymeleaf rocks");
        return "home";
    }
}
```

This example is adding the string `"Spring Boot + Thymeleaf rocks"` to model the key `"message"`, which you want to render in the Thymeleaf template.

Create the Thymeleaf view called `home.html` in the `src/main/resources/templates` directory.

```
<!DOCTYPE html>
<html xmlns="http://www.w3.org/1999/xhtml"
      xmlns:th="http://www.thymeleaf.org">

    <head>
        <title>Home</title>
    </head>
```

```
<body>
    <p>Welcome </p>
    <p th:text="${message}">Message</p>
</body>

</html>
```

This displays the model attribute `"message"` value in the Thymeleaf template using `th:text="${message}"`.

Now run the following entry point class.

```
@SpringBootApplication
public class SpringbootThymeleafDemoApplication
{
    public static void main(String[] args)
    {
        SpringApplication.run(SpringbootThymeleafDemoApplication.class, args);
    }
}
```

Point the browser to `http://localhost:8080/home`. You should be able to see the response `Spring Boot + Thymeleaf rocks`.

Working with Thymeleaf Forms

Thymeleaf offers very good Spring integration with support for:

- Forms with backing beans and result/error bindings

- Use of property editors and conversion services

- Displaying internationalization (i18n) messages using ResourceBundles

- Using the Spring Expression Language (Spring EL)

In this section, you see how you can create a user registration form using Thymeleaf and handle the form submission using Spring controllers.

Create a simple POJO called `User.java`, as shown in Listing 10-9.

Listing 10-9. User.java

```
public class User
{
    private Long id;
    private String name;
    private String email;
    private String password;

    //setters & getters
}
```

Create the `registration.html` file in the `src/main/resources/templates` directory, as shown in Listing 10-10.

Listing 10-10. Thymeleaf Registration View src/main/resources/templates/registration.html

```html
<!DOCTYPE html>
<html xmlns="http://www.w3.org/1999/xhtml"
    xmlns:th="http://www.thymeleaf.org">
<head>
<title>User Registration</title>
</head>
<body>

    <div>
        <h3>User Registration Form</h3>

        <form th:action="@{/registration}" th:object="${user}" method="post">

            <div>
              <label>Name</label>
              <input type="text" th:field="*{name}"/>
            </div>

            <div>
              <label>Email</label>
              <input type="text" th:field="*{email}"/>
            </div>

            <div>
              <label>Password</label>
              <input type="password" th:field="*{password}"/>
            </div>

            <div>
                <button type="submit">Submit</button>
            </div>
        </form>
    </div>

</body>
</html>
```

Create a SpringMVC controller to handle the GET and POST requests to the /registration URL, as shown in Listing 10-11.

Listing 10-11. RegistrationController.java

```java
@Controller
public class RegistrationController
{

    @GetMapping("/registration")
    public String registrationForm(Model model) {
        model.addAttribute("user", new User());
        return "registration";
    }
```

```
@PostMapping("/registration")
public String handleRegistration(User user) {
    logger.debug("Registering User : "+user);
    return "redirect:/login";
}
}
```

When you request the "/registration" URL, a GET request is triggered and will be handled by the `RegistrationController.registrationForm()` method. You are adding the User object to Model with the "user" key so that you can bind the form properties in your Thymeleaf form.

Note that this example uses two Thymeleaf attributes—`th:action` builds a context-relative URL and `th:object` specifies the model attribute name.

```
<form th:action="@{/registration}" th:object="${user}" method="post">
...
...
</form>
```

The example uses the syntax `th:field="*{propertyName}"` for form input fields so that the field will be backed by the model object property. So when you use `<input type="text" th:field="*{name}"/>`, the name input field value will be bounded to the `user.name` property. If you see the source of the rendered form, `<input type="text" th:field="*{name}"/>` is rendered as follows:

```
<input type="text" id="name" name="name" value="" />
```

Form Validation

Validating the user submitted data is crucial in web applications. Spring supports data validation using Spring's own validation framework and supports the Java Bean Validation API.

First, you need to specify the user validation rules using Java Bean validation annotations.

```
public class User
{
    private Long id;

    @NotNull
    @Size(min=3, max=50)
    private String name;

    @NotNull
    @Email(message="{invalid.email}")
    private String email;

    @NotNull
    @Size(min=6, max=50)
    private String password;

    //setters & getters
}
```

Thymeleaf provides the syntax `#fields.hasErrors('fieldName')` to check if there are any errors associated with the `fieldName` field.

```
<p th:if="${#fields.hasErrors('name')}" th:errors="*{name}" th:class="text-red">Incorrect data</p>
```

You can use `#fields.hasErrors('global')` to check whether there are any global errors (not related to any specific fields).

You can now update `registration.html` to show the validation errors, as shown in Listing 10-12.

Listing 10-12. The registration.html File with Validation Error Tags

```
<!DOCTYPE html>
<html xmlns="http://www.w3.org/1999/xhtml"
    xmlns:th="http://www.thymeleaf.org">
<head>
<title>User Registration</title>
</head>
<body>

<div>
    <h3>User Registration Form</h3>

    <form th:action="@{/registration}" th:object="${user}" method="post">

        <p th:if="${#fields.hasErrors('global')}" th:errors="*{global}"
            th:class="text-red">Incorrect data</p>

        <div th:classappend="${#fields.hasErrors('name')}? 'has-error'">
          <label>Name</label>
          <input type="text" th:field="*{name}"/>
          <p th:if="${#fields.hasErrors('name')}" th:errors="*{name}"
            th:class="text-red">Incorrect data</p>
        </div>

        <div th:classappend="${#fields.hasErrors('email')}? 'has-error'">
          <label>Email</label>
          <input type="text" th:field="*{email}"/>
          <p th:if="${#fields.hasErrors('email')}" th:errors="*{email}"
            th:class="text-red">Incorrect data</p>
        </div>

        <div th:classappend="${#fields.hasErrors('password')}? 'has-error'">
          <label>Password</label>
          <input type="password" th:field="*{password}"/>
          <p th:if="${#fields.hasErrors('password')}" th:errors="*{password}"
            th:class="text-red">Incorrect data</p>
        </div>
```

```
        <div>
            <button type="submit">Submit</button>
        </div>
    </form>
</div>

</body>
</html>
```

With this updated form if there are any form validation failures, it will show those errors next to the field and all global errors at the beginning. Observe that this example uses `th:classappend="${#fields.hasErrors('email')}? 'has-error'"` to add some CSS style dynamically if there are any errors.

You need to update the `"/registration"` POST handler method to trigger validation for the model object. You can add the `@Valid` annotation to the model parameter to perform validations on the form submit.

You also need to define the `BindingResult` parameter *immediately next to the model object*. The validation errors will be populated in `BindingResult`, which you can inspect later in your method body.

```java
@Controller
public class RegistrationController
{

    ...
    ...
    @PostMapping("/registration")
    public String handleRegistration(@Valid User user, BindingResult result) {
        logger.debug("Registering User : "+user);
        if(result.hasErrors()){
            return "registration";
        }
        return "redirect:/registrationsuccess";
    }
}
```

When the form is submitted with invalid data, those validation errors will be populated in `BindingResult`. The example checks whether there are any errors and redisplays the registration form, which will be rendered along with the errors.

Sometimes you can't express all the validation rules using annotations only. For example, you want the user e-mail to be unique. You can't implement this without checking against your database.

Next, you'll see how you can use Spring's Validation framework to implement complex validations.

You can create `UserValidator` by implementing the `org.springframework.validation.Validator` interface, as shown in Listing 10-13.

Listing 10-13. UserValidator.java

```java
@Component
public class UserValidator implements Validator
{

    @Autowired
    UserRepository userRepository;
```

```java
    @Override
    public boolean supports(Class<?> clazz)
    {
        return User.class.isAssignableFrom(clazz);
    }

    @Override
    public void validate(Object target, Errors errors)
    {
        User user = (User) target;
        String email = user.getEmail();
        User userByEmail = userRepository.findByEmail(email);
        if(userByEmail != null){
            errors.rejectValue("email",
                                "email.exists",
                                new Object[]{email},
                                "Email "+email+" already in use");
        }
    }
}
```

In the validate(Object target, Errors errors) method, you can implement any complex validation logic and register errors.

Now you can inject UserValidator into the RegistrationController and use it to validate the model object as follows:

```java
@Controller
public class RegistrationController
{
    @Autowired
    private UserValidator userValidator;

    @PostMapping("/registration")
    public String handleRegistration(@Valid User user, BindingResult result) {
        userValidator.validate(user, result);
        if(result.hasErrors()){
            return "registration";
        }
        return "redirect:/registrationsuccess";
    }
}
```

When the form is then submitted, if there are any validation failures as per the Bean Validation Constraint annotations, they will be populated in BindingResult. After that, the example checks for duplicate e-mails using userValidator.validate(user, result). This will add an error to the email property if the given e-mail already exists.

File Uploading

Spring Boot's `org.springframework.boot.autoconfigure.web.servlet.MultipartAutoConfiguration` enables multi-part uploads by default.

You can create a form with enctype="multipart/form-data" to upload a file, as shown in Listing 10-14.

Listing 10-14. File Uploading Form

```
<form action="uploadMyFile" th:action="@{/uploadMyFile}"
      method="post" enctype="multipart/form-data">
  <input type="file" name="myFile" />
  <input type="submit" />
</form>
```

You can then implement the FileUploadController to handle the request, as shown in Listing 10-15.

Listing 10-15. FileUploadController.java

```java
@PostMapping("/uploadMyFile")
public String handleFileUpload(@RequestParam("myFile") MultipartFile file)
{
    if (!file.isEmpty())
    {
        String name = file.getOriginalFilename();
        try
        {
            byte[] bytes = file.getBytes();
            Files.write(new File(name).toPath(), bytes);
        }
        catch (Exception e)
        {
            e.printStackTrace();
        }
    }
    return "redirect:/fileUpload";
}
```

Note that this example binds the file type input parameter myFile to the MultipartFile argument with @RequestParam("myFile"), from which you can extract byte[] or InputStream.

You can customize multipart configuration using the following properties:

```
spring.servlet.multipart.enabled=true
spring.servlet.multipart.max-file-size=2MB
spring.servlet.multipart.max-request-size=20MB
spring.servlet.multipart.file-size-threshold=5MB
```

Using ResourceBundles for Internationalization (i18n)

By default, Spring Boot's `org.springframework.boot.autoconfigure.context.MessageSourceAutoConfiguration` registers the MessageSource bean with the base name "messages".

You can add ResourceBundles such as `messages.properties`, `messages_en.properties`, and `messages_fr.properties` in the root classpath, which will be automatically picked up by Spring Boot. You can also customize the ResourceBundles basename using the `spring.messages.basename` property.

In addition to that, Spring Boot provides the following customization properties.

```
spring.messages.basename=messages
spring.messages.cache-seconds=-1(cache expiration in seconds. If set to -1, bundles are
cached forever)
spring.messages.encoding=UTF-8
spring.messages.fallback-to-system-locale=true
```

Create the default ResourceBundle `messages.properties` in `src/main/resources/` folder as follows:

```
app.title=SpringBoot Thymeleaf Demo
app.version=1.0
email.exists=Email {0} is already in use.
```

You can render these values in your Thymeleaf templates using `th:text="#{msgKey}"`.

```
<p th:text="#{app.title}">App Title</p>
```

You can also obtain these messages programmatically from `MessageSource`, as shown in Listing 10-16.

Listing 10-16. Reading i18n Messages Programatically

```java
@Controller
public class RegistrationController
{
    @Autowired
    private MessageSource messageSource;
    ....
    ....
    public String handleRegistration(User user)
    {
        ...
        String code="email.exists";
        Object[] args = new Object[]{email};
        String defaultMsg = "Email "+email+" already in use";
        Locale locale = Locale.getDefault();
        String errorMsg =
            messageSource.getMessage(code, args, defaultMsg, locale);
        ...
    }
}
```

ResourceBundles for Hibernate Validation Errors

Spring Boot uses Hibernate Validator as the Bean Validation API implementation. By default, Hibernate validation looks for the `ValidationMessages.properties` file in the root classpath for failure message keys. If you want to use `messages.properties` for both i18n and Hibernate Validation error messages, you can register the `Validator` bean, as shown in Listing 10-17.

Listing 10-17. Using MessageSource for Hibernate Validation Messages

```
@Configuration
public class WebConfig implements WebMvcConfigurer
{
    ...
    ...
    @Autowired
    private MessageSource messageSource;

    @Override
    public Validator getValidator() {
        LocalValidatorFactoryBean factory = new LocalValidatorFactoryBean();
        factory.setValidationMessageSource(messageSource);
        return factory;
    }
}
```

With this configuration, both the internationalization (i18n) and Hibernate Validation error message keys will be picked up from the messages*.properties files.

Error Handling

You can handle exceptions in Spring MVC applications by registering the SimpleMappingExceptionResolver bean and configuring which view to render for what type of exception, as shown in Listing 10-18.

Listing 10-18. Handling Exceptions Using SimpleMappingExceptionResolver

```
@Configuration
@EnableWebMvc
public class WebMvcConfig implements WebMvcConfigurer
{
    @Bean(name="simpleMappingExceptionResolver")
    public SimpleMappingExceptionResolver simpleMappingExceptionResolver()
    {
        SimpleMappingExceptionResolver exceptionResolver = new SimpleMappingException
        Resolver();

        Properties mappings = new Properties();
        mappings.setProperty("DataAccessException", "dbError");
        mappings.setProperty("RuntimeException", "error");

        exceptionResolver.setExceptionMappings(mappings);
        exceptionResolver.setDefaultErrorView("error");
        return exceptionResolver;
    }
}
```

You can also use the @ExceptionHandler annotation to define handler methods for specific exception types, as shown in Listing 10-19.

Listing 10-19. Handling Exceptions Using Controller Level @ExceptionHandler

```java
@Controller
public class CustomerController
{
    @GetMapping("/customers/{id}")
    public String findCustomer(@PathVariable Long id, Model model)
    {
        Customer c = customerRepository.findById(id);
        if(c == null) throw new CustomerNotFoundException();
        model.add("customer", c);
        return "view_customer";
    }

    @ExceptionHandler(CustomerNotFoundException.class)
    public ModelAndView handleCustomerNotFoundException(CustomerNotFoundException ex)
    {
        ModelAndView model = new ModelAndView("error/404");
        model.addObject("exception", ex);
        return model;
    }
}
```

The handleCustomerNotFoundException() method in CustomerController will only handle the exception CustomerNotFoundException raised from CustomerController @RequestMapping methods.

You can handle exceptions globally by creating an exception handler class annotated with @ControllerAdvice. The @ExceptionHandler methods in the @ControllerAdvice class handle errors that occur in any controller request handling method. See Listing 10-20.

Listing 10-20. Global Exception Handler Using @ControllerAdvice

```java
@ControllerAdvice
public class GlobalExceptionHandler
{
    private static final Logger logger = LoggerFactory.getLogger(GlobalExceptionHandler.class);

    @ExceptionHandler(DataAccessException.class)
    public String handleDataAccessException(HttpServletRequest request, DataAccessException ex){
        logger.info("DataAccessException Occurred:: URL="+request.getRequestURL());
        return "db_error";
    }

    @ExceptionHandler(ServletRequestBindingException.class)
    public String servletRequestBindingException(ServletRequestBindingException e) {
        logger.error("ServletRequestBindingException occurred: "+e.getMessage());
        return "validation_error"
    }
}
```

Spring Boot registers a global error handler and maps /error by default, which renders an HTML response for browser clients and a JSON response for REST clients. You can provide the custom error page by implementing ErrorController. See Listing 10-21.

Listing 10-21. Implementing a Custom ErrorController

```
@Controller
public class GenericErrorController implements ErrorController
{

    private static final String ERROR_PATH = "/error";

    @RequestMapping(ERROR_PATH)
    public String error(){
        return "errorPage.html";
    }

    @Override
    public String getErrorPath() {
        return ERROR_PATH;
    }
}
```

You can also provide custom error pages based on the HTTP error status code. Spring Boot looks for error pages in the /error folder under the static resource locations (classpath:/static, classpath:/public, etc.).

For example, you can display the src/main/resources/static/error/404.html file when a 404 error occurs. Likewise, you can also display the src/main/resources/static/error/5xx.html file for all server errors with 5xx error status codes.

Summary

This chapter discussed how to develop web applications using Spring Boot with Thymeleaf view templates. It also looked at performing form validations using the Bean Validation API and Spring's validation framework. You learned how to handle exception scenarios at the controller level and globally. In the next chapter, you will learn about developing RESTful web services using Spring Boot.

CHAPTER 11

Building REST APIs Using Spring Boot

REST (REpresentational State Transfer) is an architectural style for building distributed systems that provide interoperability between heterogeneous systems. The need for REST APIs increased a lot with the drastic increase of mobile devices. It became logical to build REST APIs and let the web and mobile clients consume the API instead of developing separate applications.

SpringMVC provides first-class support for building RESTful web services. As Spring's REST support is built on top of SpringMVC, you can leverage the knowledge of SpringMVC for building REST APIs.

Spring Data REST is a spring portfolio project that can be used to expose Spring Data repositories as REST endpoints. You can expose Spring Data JPA, Spring Data Mongo, and Spring Data Cassandra repositories as REST endpoints without much effort.

This chapter covers RESTful web services, including how you can build REST APIs using SpringMVC. Then you will learn about building REST APIs using Spring Data REST.

Introduction to RESTful Web Services

REST stands for *representational state transfer* and is an architectural style for designing distributed hypermedia systems. The term REST was coined by Roy Fielding in 2000 in his doctoral dissertation, which you can find at: `http://www.ics.uci.edu/~fielding/pubs/dissertation/rest_arch_style.htm`.

The fundamental concept of a REST-based system is the *resource*, which can be identified by a Uniform Resource Identifier (URI). For web-based systems, HTTP is the most commonly used protocol for communicating with external systems. You can identify a unique resource using a URI.

For example, a blog post can be identified by the URI `http://www.myblog.com/posts/restful-architecture`. A resource can be a *collection resource*, which represents a grouped set of resources. For example, the URI `http://www.myblog.com/posts/` represents the `posts` resource, which may contain zero or more `Post` resources, each of which can be identified by its own URI. The various operations that can be performed on a resource can be expressed using its URI along with the appropriate HTTP method (`GET`, `POST`, `PUT`, `DELETE`, etc.).

Assume for example that you're building a REST API for a blog application. The resources that can be identified in a blog domain are post, comment, and user.

Following the REST principles, you can use the following HTTP verbs:

- GET—To get a collection or a single resource
- POST—To create a new resource
- PUT—To update an existing resource
- DELETE—To delete a collection or a single resource

Now consider how you can define URIs for a blog system's resources:

- GET—http://localhost:8080/myblog/posts/: Returns a list of all posts
- GET—http://localhost:8080/myblog/posts/2: Returns a post whose ID is 2
- POST—http://localhost:8080/myblog/posts/: Creates a new Post resource
- PUT—http://localhost:8080/myblog/posts/2: Updates a POST resource whose ID is 2
- DELETE—http://localhost:8080/myblog/posts/2: Deletes a POST resource whose ID is 2
- GET—http://localhost:8080/myblog/posts/2/comments: Returns all the comments of the post whose ID is 2
- POST—http://localhost:8080/myblog/posts/2/comments: Creates a new comment for the POST whose ID is 2
- DELETE—http://localhost:8080/myblog/posts/2/comments: Deletes all the comments of the POST whose ID is 2

The most commonly used data exchange formats (ContentTypes) are JSON and XML. The typical practice of determining the input request content and output response types in web based systems are based on the ContentType and Accept header values.

REST API Using SpringMVC

SpringMVC provides support for building RESTful web services and Spring Boot makes it much easier with its autoconfiguration mechanism.

Listing 11-1 shows a SpringMVC-based REST endpoint.

Listing 11-1. SpringMVC REST Controller

```java
@Controller
public class PostController
{
    @Autowired
    PostRepository postRepository;

    @ResponseBody
    @GetMapping("/posts")
    public List<Post> listPosts()
    {
        return postRepository.findAll();
    }
}
```

It just looks like a normal SpringMVC controller, with two noticeable differences:

- Unlike the normal controller methods, which return a view name or a `ModelAndView` object, the `listPosts()` method returns a list of `Post` objects.

- The `listPosts()` request handler method is annotated with `@ResponseBody`.

The `@ResponseBody` annotation on the request handler method indicates that the return value should be bound to the response body. If you make a `GET` request to the `"/posts"` URL, you might get a JSON or XML representation of the list of `Post` objects based on the `Accept` header value.

Listing 11-2 shows another method used to create a new post.

Listing 11-2. REST Controller Method Using @RequestBody Annotation

```java
@Controller
public class PostController
{
    @Autowired
    PostRepository postRepository;
    ...
    ...
    @ResponseBody
    @PostMapping("/posts")
    public Post createPost(@RequestBody Post post)
    {
        return postRepository.save(post);
    }
}
```

In the `createPost()` handler method, the interesting part is the `@RequestBody` annotation. The `@RequestBody` annotation will take care of binding the web request body to the method parameter with the help of the registered `HttpMessageConverters`. So, when you make a `POST` request to the `"/post"` URL with a `Post` JSON body, `HttpMessageConverters` converts the JSON request body into a `Post` object and passes it to the `savePost()` method.

If all of your handler methods are REST endpoint handler methods, you can have a `@ResponseBody` at the class level instead of adding it to each method. Even better, you can use `@RestController`, which is a composed annotation of `@Controller` and `@ResponseBody`.

Now you'll take a deep look at implementing the REST API for a simple blog application using Spring Data JPA, SpringMVC, and, of course, Spring Boot.

1. Create a Spring Boot project and configure the Web and JPA starters.

Create a Spring Boot Maven project and add the following starters:

```xml
<dependency>
    <groupId>org.springframework.boot</groupId>
    <artifactId>spring-boot-starter-web</artifactId>
</dependency>

<dependency>
    <groupId>org.springframework.boot</groupId>
    <artifactId>spring-boot-starter-data-jpa</artifactId>
</dependency>
```

```xml
<dependency>
    <groupId>com.h2database</groupId>
    <artifactId>h2</artifactId>
</dependency>
```

Model the REST resources. This example assumes your blog application is a simple one where the administrator can create posts, and the blog viewers can view and add their comments to the posts. You can therefore identify that there will be User, Post, and Comment resources in the application domain.

First, you create these resources as JPA entities, as shown in Listing 11-3.

Listing 11-3. JPA Entities User.java, Post.java, and Comment.java

```java
@Entity
@Table(name = "USERS")
public class User
{
    @Id @GeneratedValue(strategy = GenerationType.IDENTITY)
    private Integer id;

    @Column(name = "name", nullable = false, length = 150)
    private String name;

    @Column(name = "email", nullable = false, length = 150)
    private String email;

    @Column(name = "password", nullable = false, length = 150)
    private String password;

    //setters & getters
}

@Entity
@Table(name = "POSTS")
public class Post
{

    @Id @GeneratedValue(strategy = GenerationType.IDENTITY)
    private Integer id;

    @Column(name = "title", nullable = false, length = 150)
    private String title;

    @Lob
    @Column(name = "content", nullable = false, columnDefinition="TEXT")
    private String content;
```

```java
    @Temporal(TemporalType.TIMESTAMP)
    @Column(name="created_on")
    private Date createdOn = new Date();

    @Temporal(TemporalType.TIMESTAMP)
    @Column(name="updated_on")
    private Date updatedOn;

    @OneToMany
    @JoinColumn(name="post_id")
    private List<Comment> comments;

    //setters & getters
}

@Entity
@Table(name = "COMMENTS")
public class Comment
{

    @Id @GeneratedValue(strategy = GenerationType.IDENTITY)
    private Integer id;

    @Column(name = "name", nullable = false, length = 150)
    private String name;

    @Column(name = "email", nullable = false, length = 150)
    private String email;

    @Lob
    @Column(name = "content", nullable = false, columnDefinition="TEXT")
    private String content;

    @Temporal(TemporalType.TIMESTAMP)
    @Column(name="created_on")
    private Date createdOn = new Date();

    @Temporal(TemporalType.TIMESTAMP)
    @Column(name="updated_on")
    private Date updatedOn;

    //setters & getters
}
```

2. Now you create the Spring Data JPA repositories for the JPA entities you just created, as shown in Listing 11-4.

Listing 11-4. JPA Repositories for the User, Post, and Comment Entities

```
public class UserRepository extends JpaRepository<User, Integer>
{
}

public class PostRepository extends JpaRepository<Post, Integer>
{
}

public class CommentRepository extends JpaRepository<Comment, Integer>
{
}
```

3. Now you create a SpringMVC controller to implement all the Post resource related REST endpoints:

```
@RestController
@RequestMapping(value="/posts")
public class PostController
{
    @Autowired
    PostRepository postRepository;

    @Autowired
    CommentRepository commentRepository;

    ...
    ...
}
```

This example uses @RestController, as all the request handler methods are REST endpoints only. Also, it annotates with @RequestMapping(value="/posts") to have the common root URL named "/posts" so that you don't have to repeat it for each method.

Before jumping on to implementing REST endpoints, first you need to create a custom exception class, called ResourceNotFoundException (Listing 11-5). It will be thrown when the client sends a request to get the details of a resource that doesn't exist.

Listing 11-5. ResourceNotFoundException.java

```java
@ResponseStatus(HttpStatus.NOT_FOUND)
public class ResourceNotFoundException extends RuntimeException
{
    public ResourceNotFoundException() {
        this("Resource not found!");
    }

    public ResourceNotFoundException(String message) {
        this(message, null);
    }

    public ResourceNotFoundException(String message, Throwable cause) {
        super(message, cause);
    }
}
```

Note that the example annotates the ResourceNotFoundException class with
@ResponseStatus(HttpStatus.NOT_FOUND) so that when the request handler
method throws ResourceNotFoundException, the proper HTTP error status code
(404 NOT_FOUND) will be returned to the client.

You'll start by implementing the endpoint for creating a new post. As per the
REST principles, you use http://localhost:8080/posts as the URI and an
HTTP POST method to create a new post. If the POST creation is successful, you
return the appropriate HTTP status code (201 CREATED) along with newly created
post as the Response body.

```java
@ResponseStatus(HttpStatus.CREATED)
@PostMapping("")
public Post createPost(@RequestBody Post post)
{
    return postRepository.save(post);
}
```

By default, if the request handling method completes successfully, the
HTTP status code 200 OK will be returned. So, you are annotating with
@ResponseStatus(HttpStatus.CREATED) explicitly to return the appropriate
HTTP status code (201 CREATED).

Next you will implement the endpoint for fetching all posts for which the
endpoint URL will be GET http://localhost:8080/posts.

```java
@GetMapping("")
public List<Post> listPosts()
{
    return postRepository.findAll();
}
```

This example is loading all the posts from the database and returning them as a response.

Next, you will implement the endpoint for fetching a post for the given ID for which the endpoint URL will be GET `http://localhost:8080/posts/{id}`.

```java
@GetMapping(value="/{id}")
public Post getPost(@PathVariable("id") Integer id)
{
    return postRepository.findById(id)
            .orElseThrow(() -> new ResourceNotFoundException
            ("No post found with id="+id));
}
```

This example is getting the `Post` object from the database for the given ID and throwing `ResourceNotFoundException` if the post is not found; otherwise, it returns the POST object.

Next, you need to implement the endpoint for updating a post for the given ID for which the endpoint URL will be PUT `http://localhost:8080/posts/{id}`.

```java
@PutMapping("/{id}")
public Post updatePost(@PathVariable("id") Integer id, @RequestBody
Post post)
{
    postRepository.findById(id)
        .orElseThrow(() -> new ResourceNotFoundException
        ("No post found with id="+id));
    return  postRepository.save(post);
}
```

The example gets the `Post` object from the database for the given ID and throws the `ResourceNotFoundException` if the post not found, otherwise updating the post.

Similarly, you can implement the endpoint by deleting a post using the HTTP DELETE method at the URI `http://localhost:8080/posts/{id}`, as follows:

```java
@DeleteMapping("/{id}")
public void deletePost(@PathVariable("id") Integer id)
{
    Post post = postRepository.findById(id)
            .orElseThrow(() -> new ResourceNotFoundException
            ("No post found with id="+id));
    postRepository.deleteById(post.getId());
}
```

Note that you are not returning any content to the client, so on successful deletion of the post, the HTTP 200 OK status code will be sent.

You can also implement the REST endpoints for creating new comments and deleting an existing comment for a given post as follows:

```
@ResponseStatus(HttpStatus.CREATED)
@PostMapping("/{id}/comments")
public void createPostComment(@PathVariable("id") Integer id,
@RequestBody Comment comment)
{
    Post post = postRepository.findById(id)
            .orElseThrow(() -> new ResourceNotFoundException
("No post found with id="+id));
    post.getComments().add(comment);
}

@DeleteMapping("/{postId}/comments/{commentId}")
public void deletePostComment(@PathVariable("postId") Integer postId,
                              @PathVariable("commentId") Integer
commentId)
{
    commentRepository.deleteById(commentId);
}
```

You can also add validation for the REST endpoint handler methods, similar to
SpringMVC controllers for traditional web applications. See Listing 11-16.

Listing 11-6. Performing Validation Using the Java Bean Validation API

```
@ResponseStatus(HttpStatus.CREATED)
@PostMapping(value="")
public Post createPost(@RequestBody @Valid Post post, BindingResult result)
{
    if(result.hasErrors()){
        //handle errors
        //throw Exception with Invalid data details
    }
    return postRepository.save(post);
}
```

This example adds the @Valid annotation to the method parameter Post so that
the post object data will be validated against the Java Bean Validation Constraints
defined on the POST properties.

4. In addition to returning a arbitrary object from request handler methods, you
    can also return ResponseEntity/HttpEntity, which provides an easy way to set
    response headers and the status code. See Listing 11-7.

Listing 11-7. Using ResponseEntity for Fine-Grained Control Over Responses

```
@PostMapping("")
public ResponseEntity<Post> createPost(@RequestBody @Valid Post post, BindingResult result)
{
    if(result.hasErrors()){
        return new ResponseEntity<>(post, HttpStatus.BAD_REQUEST);
    }
    Post savedPost = postRepository.save(post);
```

```java
HttpHeaders responseHeaders = new HttpHeaders();
responseHeaders.set("MyResponseHeader1", "MyValue1");
responseHeaders.set("MyResponseHeader2", "MyValue2");
return new ResponseEntity<>(savedPost, responseHeaders, HttpStatus.CREATED);
}
```

This code is verifying whether there are any validation errors and is returning a response with the status code `BAD_REQUEST` (400). Otherwise, it saves the post and adds custom response headers. It then returns with a status code of `CREATED` (201).

The `ResponseEntity/HttpEntity` classes can also be used along with `RestTemplate` to consume REST services, which is discussed in the next section.

5. You can test the REST endpoints using any REST client tools such as Chrome Browser's Postman (`http://www.getpostman.com/`) or the Advanced REST Client (`https://chromerestclient.appspot.com/`) extensions.

You can also use Spring's `RestTemplate` as a client to invoke RESTful services. Now you'll test the REST endpoints you have implemented using `RestTemplate`.

First, you need to populate some sample data using the SQL script, as shown in Listing 11-8.

Listing 11-8. src/test/resources/data.sql

```sql
delete from  users;

INSERT INTO users (id, email, password, name) VALUES
(1, 'admin@gmail.com', 'admin', 'Admin'),
(2, 'david@gmail.com', 'david', 'David'),
(3, 'ron@gmail.com', 'ron', 'Ron');

insert into posts(id, title, content, created_on, updated_on) values
(1, 'Introducing SpringBoot', 'SpringBoot is awesome', '2017-05-10', null),
(2, 'Securing Web applications', 'This post will show how to use SpringSecurity',
'2017-05-20', null),
(3, 'Introducing Spring Social', 'Developing social web applications using Spring Social',
'2017-05-24', null);

insert into comments(id, post_id, name, email, content, created_on, updated_on) values
(1, 1, 'John','john@gmail.com', 'This is cool', '2017-05-10', null),
(2, 1, 'Rambo','rambo@gmail.com', 'Thanks for awesome tips', '2017-05-20', null),
(3, 2, 'Paul', 'paul@gmail.com', 'Nice post buddy.', '2017-05-24', null);
```

Now you'll write a Spring Boot test that starts an embedded servlet container on a defined port (`server.port` value) and uses `RestTemplate` to invoke the REST API endpoints. See Listing 11-9.

Listing 11-9. Testing REST Endpoints Using RestTemplate

```java
@RunWith(SpringRunner.class)
@SpringBootTest(webEnvironment = SpringBootTest.WebEnvironment.DEFINED_PORT)
public class SpringbootMvcRestDemoApplicationTest
{
    private static final String ROOT_URL = "http://localhost:8080";
    RestTemplate restTemplate = new RestTemplate();
```

```java
@Test
public void testGetAllPosts()
{
    ResponseEntity<Post[]> responseEntity =
    restTemplate.getForEntity(ROOT_URL+"/posts", Post[].class);
    List<Post> posts = Arrays.asList(responseEntity.getBody());
    assertNotNull(posts);
}

@Test
public void testGetPostById()
{
    Post post = restTemplate.getForObject(ROOT_URL+"/posts/1", Post.class);
    assertNotNull(post);
}

@Test
public void testCreatePost()
{
    Post post = new Post();
    post.setTitle("Exploring SpringBoot REST");
    post.setContent("SpringBoot is awesome!!");
    post.setCreatedOn(new Date());

    ResponseEntity<Post> postResponse =
    restTemplate.postForEntity(ROOT_URL+"/posts", post, Post.class);
    assertNotNull(postResponse);
    assertNotNull(postResponse.getBody());
}

@Test
public void testUpdatePost()
{
    int id = 1;
    Post post = restTemplate.getForObject(ROOT_URL+"/posts/"+id, Post.class);
    post.setContent("This my updated post1 content");
    post.setUpdatedOn(new Date());

    restTemplate.put(ROOT_URL+"/posts/"+id, post);

    Post updatedPost = restTemplate.getForObject(ROOT_URL+"/posts/"+id, Post.class);
    assertNotNull(updatedPost);
}

@Test
public void testDeletePost()
{
    int id = 2;
    Post post = restTemplate.getForObject(ROOT_URL+"/posts/"+id, Post.class);
    assertNotNull(post);
```

```
    restTemplate.delete(ROOT_URL+"/posts/"+id);

    try {
        post = restTemplate.getForObject(ROOT_URL+"/posts/"+id, Post.class);
    }
    catch (final HttpClientErrorException e) {
        assertEquals(e.getStatusCode(), HttpStatus.NOT_FOUND);
    }
  }
}
```

You have used various methods on `RestTemplate` to invoke the REST services triggering GET, POST, PUT, and DELETE operations. You then received the responses as Java objects using the `HttpMessageConverters`.

CORS (Cross-Origin Resource Sharing) Support

For security reasons, browsers don't allow you to make AJAX requests to resources residing outside of the current origin. CORS specification (`https://www.w3.org/TR/cors/`) provides a way to specify which cross-origin requests are permitted. SpringMVC provides support for enabling CORS for REST API endpoints so that the API consumers, such as web clients and mobile devices, can make calls to REST APIs.

Class- and Method-Level CORS Configuration

You can enable CORS at the controller level or at the method level using the `@CrossOrigin` annotation. Now you'll see how you can enable CORS support on a specific request handling method.

```
@RestController
public class UserController
{

    @CrossOrigin
    @GetMapping("/users/{id}")
    public User getUser(@PathVariable Long id) {
        // ...
    }

    @DeleteMapping("/users/{id}")
    public void deleteUser(@PathVariable Long id) {
        // ...
    }
}
```

Here, the CORS support enables only the `forgetUsers()` method using the default configuration.

- All headers and origins are permitted

- Credentials are allowed

- Maximum age is set to 30 minutes

- The list of HTTP methods is set to the methods on the `@RequestMethod` annotation

You can customize these properties by providing options on the @CrossOrigin annotation.

```
@CrossOrigin(origins={"http://domain1.com", "http://domain2.com"},
                allowedHeaders="X-AUTH-TOKEN",
                allowCredentials="false",
                maxAge=15*60,
                methods={RequestMethod.GET, RequestMethod.POST }
                )
@GetMapping("/users/{id}")
public User getUser(@PathVariable Long id) {
    // ...
}
```

Similarly, you can apply the @CrossOrigin annotation at the controller class level.

```
@CrossOrigin
@RestController
public class UserController
{
    ....
    ....
}
```

When applied at the class level, the same @CrossOrigin configuration is applied to all the @RequestMapping methods. If the @CrossOrigin annotation is specified at both the class level and the method level, Spring will derive the CORS configuration by combining attributes from both annotations.

Global CORS Configuration

In addition to specifying CORS configuration at the class and method levels, you can configure it globally by implementing the WebMvcConfigurer.addCorsMappings() method. See Listing 11-10.

Listing 11-10. SpringMVC Global CORS Configuration

```
@Configuration
public class WebConfig implements WebMvcConfigurer
{
    @Override
    public void addCorsMappings(CorsRegistry registry) {
        registry.addMapping("/api/**")
        .allowedOrigins("http://localhost:3000")
        .allowedMethods("*")
        .allowedHeaders("*")
        .allowCredentials(false)
        .maxAge(3600);
    }
}
```

This configuration enables the CORS for URL pattern /api/** from the origin http://localhost:3000 only. You can specify allowedOrigins("*") to allow requests from any origin.

Exposing JPA Entities with Bi-Directional References Through RESTful Services

You need to take extra care when exposing JPA entities with bi-directional references through RESTful services. If you try to marshal a JPA parent entity (say Post) that has a collection of child entities (say List<Comment>) and the child has a reference back to the parent (Post), then the JPA marshaling will end up in infinite recursion and will throw StackOverflowError.

Assume you have the following Post and Comment entities:

```java
@Entity
@Table(name = "POSTS")
public class Post
{
    @Id @GeneratedValue(strategy = GenerationType.IDENTITY)
    private Integer id;

    @Column(name = "title", nullable = false, length = 150)
    private String title;
    ....
    ....
    @OneToMany(mappedBy="post")
    private List<Comment> comments;

    //setters & getters
}

@Entity
@Table(name = "COMMENTS")
public class Comment
{
    @Id @GeneratedValue(strategy = GenerationType.IDENTITY)
    private Integer id;

    @Column(name = "name", nullable = false, length = 150)
    private String name;
    ...
    ...
    @ManyToOne(optional=false)
    @JoinColumn(name="post_id")
    private Post post;

    //setters & getters
}
```

Here, you have a bi-directional association between the Post and Comment entities. Now assume you are exposing a REST endpoint to get a Post by its id as follows:

```
@GetMapping("/{id}")
public Post getPost(@PathVariable("id") Integer id)
{
return postRepository.findById(id)
        .orElseThrow(() -> new ResourceNotFoundException("No post found with id="+id));
}
```

If you access http://localhost:8080/posts/1, the code will enter infinite recursion and the server will throw StackOverflowError.

Spring Boot by default configures the Jackson JSON (https://github.com/FasterXML/jackson-databind) library to marshal/unmarshal Java beans into JSON and vice versa.

You can fix the infinite recursion problem by using the Jackson JSON library annotations in the following ways.

Using @JsonIgnore

You can break the infinite recursion by adding the @JsonIgnore annotation on the back reference from the child object.

```
@Entity
@Table(name = "COMMENTS")
public class Comment
{
    ...
    ...
    @JsonIgnore
    @ManyToOne(optional=false)
    @JoinColumn(name="post_id")
    private Post post;
    ...
    ...
}
```

You can add @JsonIgnore on all the properties that you want to exclude from marshaling or you can use @JsonIgnoreProperties at the class level to list all the property names to ignore.

```
@JsonIgnoreProperties({"post"})
@Entity
@Table(name = "COMMENTS")
public class Comment
{
    ....
    ....
}
```

Now you should be able to access http://localhost:8080/posts/1 and get response JSON.

Using @JsonManagedReference and @JsonBackReference

You can break the infinite recursion by using @JsonManagedReference and @JsonBackReference annotations as well.

■ **Note** The @JsonManagedReference annotation is used to indicate that the annotated property is part of a two-way linkage between fields and that its role is as a "parent" (or "forward") link. The @JsonBackReference annotation is also used to indicate that the associated property is part of a two-way linkage between fields, but its role is as a "child" (or "back") link.

You will annotate the List<Comment> collection in Post with @JsonManagedReference, as it is the parent in the context of marshaling the Post object. You will annotate the back reference property POST in the Comment class with @JsonBackReference, as it is the back link to the parent Post object.

```
@Entity
@Table(name = "POSTS")
public class Post
{
    ....
    ....
    @JsonManagedReference
    @OneToMany(mappedBy="post")
    private List<Comment> comments;

    //setters & getters
}

@Entity
@Table(name = "COMMENTS")
public class Comment
{
    ....
    ....
    @JsonBackReference
    @ManyToOne(optional=false)
    @JoinColumn(name="post_id")
    private Post post;

    //setters & getters
}
```

At times, you may need more control over the response formats and can't or don't want to directly expose database entities as REST endpoint responses. In that case, you can use Data Transfer Objects (DTOs), which you can populate from entities using Java Object Mapper libraries such as Dozer (http://dozer.sourceforge.net/), ModelMapper (http://modelmapper.org/), and MapStruct (http://mapstruct.org/).

REST API Using Spring Data REST

In the previous section, you implemented the REST API with CRUD operations for JPA entities. If your application needs are more like a REST API with CRUD operations on top of database tables, you can use Spring Data REST.

Spring Data REST builds on top of the Spring Data repositories and automatically exports them as REST resources. Spring Data REST configuration is defined in the configuration class `RepositoryRestMvcConfiguration` and you can simply import it using `@Import(RepositoryRestMvcConfiguration.class)` to activate it in our application.

Spring Boot will automatically enable Spring Data REST if you add `spring-boot-starter-data-rest` to your application.

```
<dependency>
<groupId>org.springframework.boot</groupId>
<artifactId>spring-boot-starter-data-rest</artifactId>
</dependency>
```

To expose the Spring Data repositories as REST resources with the defaults, you don't need to add any extra configuration. You can simply create the JPA entities and Spring Data JPA repositories as shown in the previous section.

Now you can run the following entry point class to start the server.

```
@SpringBootApplication
public class SpringbootDataRestDemoApplication
{
    public static void main(String[] args)
    {
        SpringApplication.run(SpringbootDataRestDemoApplication.class, args);
    }
}
```

Assuming you created the JPA entities `User`, `Post`, and `Comment` and their JPA repositories as shown in the previous section, you'll now invoke the REST services using the Postman REST client tool.

Invoke the `http://localhost:8080/posts` GET request with the Accept header set to `application/json`. This should return the response shown in Listing 11-11.

Listing 11-11. Spring Data REST Collection Resource Response

```
{
  _embedded:{
    posts:[
      {
        id:1,
        title:"Introducing SpringBoot",
        content:"SpringBoot is awesome",
        createdOn:"2017-05-09T18:30:00.000+0000",
        updatedOn:null,
        _links:{
          self:{
            href:"http://localhost:8080/api/posts/1"
          },
```

```
            post:{
               href:"http://localhost:8080/api/posts/1"
            },
            comments:{
               href:"http://localhost:8080/api/posts/1/comments"
            }
         }
      },
      {
         id:2,
         title:"Securing Web applications",
         content:"This post will show how to use SpringSecurity",
         createdOn:"2017-05-19T18:30:00.000+0000",
         updatedOn:null,
         _links:{
            self:{
               href:"http://localhost:8080/api/posts/2"
            },
            post:{
               href:"http://localhost:8080/api/posts/2"
            },
            comments:{
               href:"http://localhost:8080/api/posts/2/comments"
            }
         }
      },
      {
         id:3,
         title:"Introducing Spring Social",
         content:"Developing social web applications using Spring Social",
         createdOn:"2017-05-23T18:30:00.000+0000",
         updatedOn:null,
         _links:{
            self:{
               href:"http://localhost:8080/api/posts/3"
            },
            post:{
               href:"http://localhost:8080/api/posts/3"
            },
            comments:{
               href:"http://localhost:8080/api/posts/3/comments"
            }
         }
      }
   ]
},
_links:{
   self:{
      href:"http://localhost:8080/api/posts{?page,size,sort}",
      templated:true
   },
```

```
        profile:{
            href:"http://localhost:8080/api/profile/posts"
        },
        search:{
            href:"http://localhost:8080/api/posts/search"
        }
    },
    page:{
        size:20,
        totalElements:3,
        totalPages:1,
        number:0
    }
}
```

You can create a new Post by invoking the POST request on http://localhost:8080/posts with the Accept and Content-Type headers set to application/json. Pass the Post details to be created as JSON in request body.

```
{
  "title": "My 4th Post",
  "content": "This is my awesome 4th post",
  "createdOn": "2016-05-09T18:30:00.000+0000"
}
```

Similarly, you can update POST with id=4 by using the PUT request on http://localhost:8080/posts/4.

```
{
  "title": "My fourth Post",
  "content": "This is my awesome 4th post",
  "createdOn": "2016-05-09T18:30:00.000+0000",
  "updatedOn": "2016-05-09T18:40:00.000+0000"
}
```

You can delete POST with id=4 by using the DELETE request on http://localhost:8080/posts/4.

By default, the Spring Data REST serves up the REST resources at the root URI, "/". You can customize the path using the spring.data.rest.basePath property in application.properties.

```
spring.data.rest.basePath=/api
```

Sorting and Pagination

If the Repository extends PagingAndSortingRepository, then Spring Data REST endpoints support pagination and sorting out-of-the-box.

You can use the size query parameter to limit the number of entries returning.

```
http://localhost:8080/posts/?size=10
```

To retrieve the second page entries with five entries per page, use the page and size query parameters.

```
http://localhost:8080/posts?page=1&size=5
```

To retrieve entries sorted by some property, use the sort query parameter.

```
http://localhost:8080/posts?sort=createdOn,desc
```

Spring Data REST by default exposes all the public repository interfaces without requiring any extra configuration. But if you want to customize the defaults, you can use the @RepositoryRestResource and @RestResource annotations. You can disable a repository from being exposed as a REST resource by adding @RepositoryRestResource(exported = false).

```
@RepositoryRestResource(exported = false)
public interface CommentRepository extends JpaRepository<Comment, Integer>
{
}
```

You can disable specific methods from being exposed as REST resources by adding @RestResource (exported = false) on the methods. You can also customize the default path and rel attribute values using @RepositoryRestResource, as follows:

```
@RepositoryRestResource(path = "people", rel = "people")
public interface UserRepository extends JpaRepository<User, Integer>
{
  @Override
  @RestResource(exported = false)
  void delete(Integer id);

  @Override
  @RestResource(exported = false)
  void delete(User entity);
}
```

You can customize various properties of Spring Data REST using the spring.data.rest.* properties in the application.properties file. If you want even more control over the customization, you can register a RepositoryRestConfigurer (or extend RepositoryRestConfigurerAdapter) and implement or override the configure*() methods based on your needs.

For example, by default, the entity's primary key (id) values won't be exposed in the responses. If you want to expose the id values for certain entities, you can customize it as follows:

```
@Configuration
public class RestRepositoryConfig extends RepositoryRestConfigurerAdapter
{
    @Override
    public void configureRepositoryRestConfiguration(RepositoryRestConfiguration config)
    {
        config.exposeIdsFor(User.class);
    }
}
```

With this customization, the responses will include the id property as well.

CORS Support in Spring Data REST

Similar to SpringMVC REST endpoints, you can enable CORS support for Spring Data REST endpoints using the @CrossOrigin annotation at the repository level or globally.

```
@CrossOrigin
public interface UserRepository extends JpaRepository<User, Integer>
{
}
```

To enable CORS support globally, you can extend RepositoryRestConfigurerAdapter and provide CORS configuration, as shown in Listing 11-12.

Listing 11-12. Spring Data REST Global CORS Configuration

```
@Configuration
public class RepositoryConfig extends RepositoryRestConfigurerAdapter
{
    @Override
    public void configureRepositoryRestConfiguration(RepositoryRestConfiguration config)
    {
        config.getCorsRegistry()
                    .addMapping("/api/**")
                        .allowedOrigins("http://localhost:3000")
                        .allowedMethods("*")
                        .allowedHeaders("*")
                        .allowCredentials(false)
                        .maxAge(3600);
    }
}
```

■ **Note**   SpringMVC's CORS configuration is NOT applied to Spring Data REST endpoints.

To learn more about Spring Data REST, visit the Spring Data REST documentation at: http://docs. spring.io/spring-data/rest/docs/current/reference/html/.

Exception Handling

You can handle exceptions in REST API in the same way you handle them in the SpringMVC based web application—by using the @ExceptionHandler and @ControllerAdvice annotations. Instead of rendering a view, you can return ResponseEntity with the appropriate HTTP status code and exception details.

Instead of simply throwing an exception with the HTTP status code, it is better to provide more details about the issue, such as the error code, message, developer message, etc.

Create a class called ErrorDetails, as shown in Listing 11-13.

Listing 11-13. ErrorDetails.java

```java
public class ErrorDetails
{
    private String errorCode;
    private String errorMessage;
    private String devErrorMessage;
    private Map<String, Object> additionalData = new HashMap<>();

    //setters & getters
}
```

In the controller handler method, you can throw exception based on error conditions and handle those exceptions using the @ExceptionHandler methods, as shown in Listing 11-14.

Listing 11-14. Handling REST API Exception at Controller Level @ExceptionHandler Methods

```java
@RestController
@RequestMapping(value="/posts")
public class PostController
{
    ...
    ...

    @DeleteMapping("/{id}")
    public void deletePost(@PathVariable("id") Integer id)
    {
        Post post = postRepository.findById(id)
                .orElseThrow(() -> new ResourceNotFoundException("No post found with id="+id));
        try {
            postRepository.deleteById(post.getId());
        } catch (Exception e) {
            throw new PostDeletionException("Post with id="+id+" can't be deleted");
        }
    }

    ...
    ...

    @ExceptionHandler(PostDeletionException.class)
    public ResponseEntity<?> servletRequestBindingException(PostDeletionException e)
    {
        ErrorDetails errorDetails = new ErrorDetails();
        errorDetails.setErrorMessage(e.getMessage());
        StringWriter sw = new StringWriter();
        PrintWriter pw = new PrintWriter(sw);
        e.printStackTrace(pw);
        errorDetails.setDevErrorMessage(sw.toString());
        return new ResponseEntity<>(errorDetails, HttpStatus.INTERNAL_SERVER_ERROR);
    }
}
```

You can handle exceptions globally using the @ControllerAdvice class with the @ExceptionHandler methods, as shown in Listing 11-15.

Listing 11-15. Handling REST API Exceptions Globally Using @ExceptionHandler Methods

```
@ControllerAdvice
public class GlobalExceptionHandler
{

    @ExceptionHandler(ServletRequestBindingException.class)
    public ResponseEntity<?> servletRequestBindingException(ServletRequestBindingException e) {
        ErrorDetails errorDetails = new ErrorDetails();
        errorDetails.setErrorMessage(e.getMessage());
        errorDetails.setDevErrorMessage(getStackTraceAsString(e));
        return new ResponseEntity<>(errorDetails, HttpStatus.BAD_REQUEST);
    }

    @ExceptionHandler(Exception.class)
    public ResponseEntity<?> exception(Exception e) {
        ErrorDetails errorDetails = new ErrorDetails();
        errorDetails.setErrorMessage(e.getMessage());
        errorDetails.setDevErrorMessage(getStackTraceAsString(e));
        return new ResponseEntity<>(errorDetails, HttpStatus.INTERNAL_SERVER_ERROR);
    }

    private String getStackTraceAsString(Exception e)
    {
        StringWriter sw = new StringWriter();
        PrintWriter pw = new PrintWriter(sw);
        e.printStackTrace(pw);
        return sw.toString();
    }
}
```

The global exception handling mechanism helps you handle exceptions (like database communication errors and third-party service invocation failures) in a central place instead of handling them in each controller class.

Summary

This chapter discussed how to create REST APIs using SpringMVC and Spring Data REST. It also looked at how to handle exceptions at the controller level and globally. In the next chapter, you will learn how to build Reactive Web Applications using Spring WebFlux.

CHAPTER 12

Reactive Programming Using Spring WebFlux

Modern IT business needs have changed significantly compared to a few years ago. The amount of data that is being generated from various sources like social media sites, IoT devices, sensors, and the like is humongous. The traditional data processing models may not be suitable to process such a huge volume of data. Even though we have better hardware support these days, many of the existing APIs are synchronous and blocking APIs, which become bottlenecks to better throughput.

Reactive programming is a programming paradigm that promotes an asynchronous, non-blocking, event-driven approach to data processing. Reactive programming is gaining momentum and many of the programming languages provide reactive frameworks and libraries.

In Java, there are reactive libraries like RxJava and Reactor, which supports reactive programming. As interest in reactive programming grows in the Java community, a new initiative called *reactive streams* is starting to provide a standard for asynchronous stream processing with non-blocking back pressure. Reactive streams support will be part of the Java 9 release.

The Spring framework 5 introduced support for reactive programming with the new WebFlux module. Spring Boot 2, which uses Spring 5, also provides a starter to quickly create reactive applications using WebFlux. This chapter teaches you how to build reactive web applications using Spring WebFlux.

Introduction to Reactive Programming

Reactive programming involves modeling data and events as observable data streams and implementing data processing routines to react to the changes in those streams. A group of people put together a *Reactive Manifesto* at http://www.reactivemanifesto.org/ to describe the characteristics of a reactive system.

Reactive programming is becoming popular and there are already reactive frameworks or libraries for many of the popular programming languages.

- Project Reactor—https://projectreactor.io/

- RxJava—https://github.com/ReactiveX/RxJava

- Akka Streams—http://doc.akka.io/docs/akka/2.5.3/scala/stream/index.html

- RxJS—https://github.com/ReactiveX/rxjs

- Rx.NET—https://github.com/Reactive-Extensions/Rx.NET

- **RxScala**—http://reactivex.io/rxscala

- **RxClojure**—https://github.com/ReactiveX/RxClojure

- **RxSwift**—https://github.com/ReactiveX/RxSwift

© K. Siva Prasad Reddy 2017
K. S. Prasad Reddy, *Beginning Spring Boot 2*, DOI 10.1007/978-1-4842-2931-6_12

Reactive Streams

Reactive streams (http://www.reactive-streams.org/) is an initiative to provide a standard for asynchronous stream processing with non-blocking back pressure. The key components of reactive streams are the Publisher and Subscriber.

A Publisher is a provider of an unbounded number of sequenced elements, which are published according to the demand received from the subscriber(s).

```
public interface Publisher<T> {
    public void subscribe(Subscriber<? super T> s);
}
```

A Subscriber subscribes to the publisher for callbacks. Publishers don't automatically push data to subscribers unless subscribers request the data.

```
public interface Subscriber<T> {
    public void onSubscribe(Subscription s);
    public void onNext(T t);
    public void onError(Throwable t);
    public void onComplete();
}
```

Two popular implementations of reactive streams are RxJava (https://github.com/ReactiveX/RxJava) and Project Reactor (https://projectreactor.io/).

Project Reactor

Project Reactor is an implementation of the reactive streams specification with non-blocking and back pressure support. Reactor provides two composable reactive types—Flux and Mono—that implement the publisher but also provide a rich set of operators. A Flux represents a reactive sequence of 0..N items, whereas a Mono represents a single value or an empty result.

A Flux<T> is a standard Publisher<T> representing an asynchronous sequence of 0 to N emitted items, optionally terminated by either a success signal or an error.

A Mono<T> is a specialized Publisher<T> that emits at most one item and then optionally terminates with an onComplete signal or an onError. A Mono can be used to represent no-value asynchronous processes returning Mono<Void>.

Now you'll see how to create Mono and Flux types and how to consume data from them.

```
Mono<String> mono = Mono.just("Spring");
Mono<String> mono = Mono.empty();

Flux<String> flux = Flux.just("Spring", "SpringBoot", "Reactor");
Flux<String> flux = Flux.fromArray(new String[]{"Spring", "SpringBoot", "Reactor"});
Flux<String> flux = Flux.fromIterable(Arrays.asList("Spring", "SpringBoot", "Reactor"));
```

Until you subscribe to the publisher, no data flow will happen. You must enable logging and subscribe to the flux.

```
Flux<String> flux = Flux.just("Spring", "SpringBoot", "Reactor");
flux.log().subscribe();
```

When you run this code it will log the underlying callback method invocations as follows:

```
[main] INFO reactor.Flux.Array.1 - | onSubscribe([Synchronous Fuseable] FluxArray.
ArraySubscription)
[main] INFO reactor.Flux.Array.1 - | request(unbounded)
[main] INFO reactor.Flux.Array.1 - | onNext(Spring)
[main] INFO reactor.Flux.Array.1 - | onNext(SpringBoot)
[main] INFO reactor.Flux.Array.1 - | onNext(Reactor)
[main] INFO reactor.Flux.Array.1 - | onComplete()
```

Looking at the log statements, you can see that when you subscribe to Publisher:

- The onSubscribe() method is called when you subscribe to Publisher(Flux).

- When you call subscribe() on Publisher, a subscription is created. This subscription requests data from the publisher. In this example, it defaults to *unbounded* and hence it requests every element available.

- The onNext() callback method is called for every element.

- The onComplete() callback method is called last after receiving the last element.

- If an error occurs while consuming the next element, then onError() callback would have been called.

■ **Note** Covering Project Reactor in-depth is out of the scope of this book. Refer to the Project Reactor documentation at: http://projectreactor.io/docs/core/release/reference/ for more details.

The Spring WebFlux Reactive framework is built on top of Project Reactor, which is an implementation of the reactive streams specification.

Reactive Web Applications Using Spring WebFlux

Spring framework 5 comes with a new module called spring-webflux to support building reactive web applications. Spring WebFlux by default uses Project Reactor, which is an implementation of reactive streams for reactive support. But you can use other reactive streams implementations, like RxJava, as well. The spring-webflux module provides support for creating reactive server applications as well as reactive client applications using REST, HTML browsers, and WebSocket style communications.

Spring WebFlux can run on servlet containers with support for Servlet 3.1 non-blocking I/O APIs as well as on other async runtimes like Netty and Undertow. See Figure 12-1.

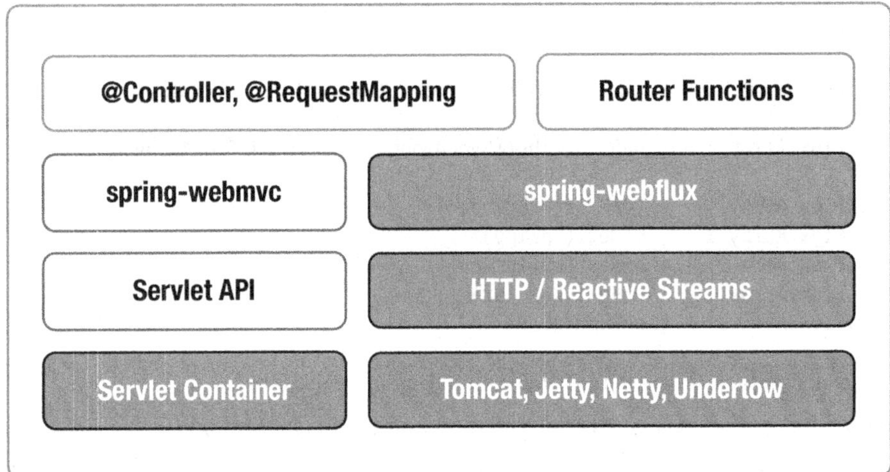

Figure 12-1. *Spring WebFlux runtime support*

Each runtime is adapted to a reactive `ServerHttpRequest` and `ServerHttpResponse`, thus exposing the body of a request and response as `Flux<DataBuffer>` instead of `InputStream` and `OutputStream` with reactive back pressure. REST-style JSON and XML serialization and deserialization and HTML view rendering is supported on top as a `Flux<Object>`.

You can develop Reactive web applications using the `spring-webflux` module in two ways:

- Using the SpringMVC style annotation based approach with `@Controller` & `@RestController`

- Using the functional style with routers and handlers

WebFlux Using the Annotation-Based Programming Model

You can build reactive web applications using the familiar Spring MVC annotations `@Controller` or `@RestController`, which also work with WebFlux. When used with WebFlux, the underlying framework components like `HandlerMapping` and `HandlerAdapter` are non-blocking and operate on the reactive `ServerHttpRequest` and `ServerHttpResponse` rather than on `HttpServletRequest` and `HttpServletResponse`.

Even though you use WebFlux reactive support at the controller layer, if you use a blocking API for data access like JDBC or JPA, your application will not be fully reactive. As of now, relational database vendors haven't provided non-blocking driver implementations. There are some NoSQL datastores such as MongoDB, Cassandra, and Redis that provide reactive drivers.

Now you'll develop a reactive web application with Spring WebFlux using the annotation based programming model. You are going to use the MongoDB Reactive Stream Driver (`https://mongodb.github.io/mongo-java-driver-reactivestreams/`) to take full advantage of MongoDB's reactive support.

Create a Spring Boot application with the Reactive web and Reactive Mongo starters.

```xml
<dependency>
    <groupId>org.springframework.boot</groupId>
    <artifactId>spring-boot-starter-webflux</artifactId>
</dependency>
<dependency>
    <groupId>org.springframework.boot</groupId>
    <artifactId>spring-boot-starter-data-mongodb-reactive</artifactId>
</dependency>
```

Use the embedded MongoDB server by adding the following dependency so that you don't need to install the MongoDB server.

```xml
<dependency>
    <groupId>de.flapdoodle.embed</groupId>
    <artifactId>de.flapdoodle.embed.mongo</artifactId>
</dependency>
```

Create a User POJO that represents a document in MongoDB, as shown in Listing 12-1.

Listing 12-1. User.java

```java
import org.springframework.data.annotation.Id;
import org.springframework.data.mongodb.core.mapping.Document;

@Document
public class User
{
    @Id
    private String id;
    private String name;
    private String email;

    //setters and getters
}
```

The Spring Data Mongo library provides `ReactiveCrudRepository`, which is similar to `CrudRepository`, but with reactive support, which will be interacting with MongoDB Reactive driver under-the-hood.

Now create a Spring Data Repository for User, as shown in Listing 12-2.

Listing 12-2. UserReactiveRepository.java

```java
import org.springframework.data.repository.reactive.ReactiveCrudRepository;

public interface UserReactiveRepository extends ReactiveCrudRepository<User, String>
{
}
```

The Spring WebFlux annotation based controllers look very similar to SpringMVC controllers except that the input and return types will use the Reactor types Mono or Flux.

Now you can implement the CRUD operations for User, as shown in Listing 12-3.

Listing 12-3. UserController.java Following the Annotation Based Reactive Programming model

```java
import org.springframework.beans.factory.annotation.Autowired;
import org.springframework.web.bind.annotation.*;
import reactor.core.publisher.Flux;
import reactor.core.publisher.Mono;

@RestController
@RequestMapping("/api/users")
public class UserController
{
    @Autowired
    private UserReactiveRepository userReactiveRepository;

    @GetMapping
    public Flux<User> allUsers() {
        return userReactiveRepository.findAll();
    }

    @GetMapping("/{id}")
    public Mono<User>  getUser(@PathVariable String id) {
        return userReactiveRepository.findById(id);
    }

    @PostMapping
    public Mono<User> saveUser(@RequestBody Mono<User> userMono) {
        return userMono.flatMap(user -> userReactiveRepository.save(user));
    }

    @DeleteMapping("/{id}")
    public Mono<Void> deleteUser(@PathVariable String id) {
        return userReactiveRepository.deleteById(id);
    }
}
```

There is nothing new in the UserController implementation except that you are using Reactor types such as Mono<User> to represent a stream of a single user object and using Flux<User> to represent a stream of one or more User objects.

One key point to remember is that, unless someone subscribes to the reactive stream pipeline, nothing happens. For example, the following method doesn't insert the user document in MongoDB.

```java
@PostMapping
public Mono<User> saveUser(@RequestBody Mono<User> userMono) {
    userMono.flatMap(user -> userReactiveRepository.save(user));
    return Mono.empty();
}
```

This just defined the stream pipeline, but nobody subscribed to it, so nothing happens. The following code will insert the user document because it is explicitly calling subscribe() on the pipeline.

```
userMono.flatMap(user -> userReactiveRepository.save(user)).subscribe();
```

The UserController.saveUser() implementation returns Mono<User> so that the web response subscribes to the pipeline. Hence, it works as expected.

WebFlux Using a Functional Programming Model

Spring framework 5 introduced a new functional style programming model built on top of the reactive foundation in addition to the annotation based programming model.

Instead of using annotations to define request handling methods, you can implement HandlerFunctions as Java 8 lambdas and map the request URL patterns to HandlerFunctions using RouterFunctions.

```
HandlerFunction<ServerResponse> echoHandlerFn =
                ( request ) -> ServerResponse.ok().body(fromObject(request.
queryParam("name")));
RequestPredicate predicate = RequestPredicates.GET("/echo");
RouterFunction<ServerResponse> routerFunction = RouterFunctions.route(predicate,
echoHandlerFn);
```

This example mapped the URL pattern GET "/echo" to echoHandlerFn, which returns the value of the request parameter "name" as the response body. You can write the same code block using Java 8 lambdas and static imports in a much more concise way, as follows:

```
route(GET("/echo"), request -> ok().body(fromObject(request.queryParam("name"))));
```

Now you can explore the key components of functional web framework.

HandlerFunction

The HandlerFunction is a functional interface that takes ServletRequest and returns ServletResponse.

```
@FunctionalInterface
public interface HandlerFunction<T extends ServerResponse>
{
    Mono<T> handle(ServerRequest request);
}
```

Here, ServerRequest and ServerResponse are immutable interfaces built on top of Reactor types. You can convert a request body into Reactor's Mono or Flux types and you can send any instance of reactive stream's Publisher as a response body.

ServerRequest

The org.springframework.web.reactive.function.server.ServerRequest interface represent a server-side HTTP request. You can retrieve information from an input HTTP request from ServerRequest using various methods, as follows:

```
HttpMethod method = request.method();
String path = request.path();
String id = request.pathVariable("id");
Map<String, String> pathVariables = request.pathVariables();
Optional<String> email = request.queryParam("email");
URI uri = request.uri();
```

You can convert a request body into a Mono or Flux using the bodyToMono() and bodyToFlux() methods.

```
Mono<User> userMono = request.bodyToMono(User.class);
Flux<User> usersFlux = request.bodyToFlux(User.class);
```

The bodyToMono() and bodyToFlux() methods are actually instances of BodyExtractor, which is used to extract the request body and deserialize it into an object.

You can use the BodyExtractors utility class to extract a request body into a Mono or Flux as follows:

```
Mono<User> userMono = request.body(BodyExtractors.toMono(User.class));
Flux<User> userFlux = request.body(BodyExtractors.toFlux(User.class));
```

You can use ParameterizedTypeReference if you want to convert a request body into a generic type.

```
ParameterizedTypeReference<Map<String, List<User>>> typeReference = new Parameterized
TypeReference<Map<String, List<User>>>() {};
Mono<Map<String, List<User>>> mapMono = request.body(BodyExtractors.toMono(typeReference));
```

ServerResponse

The org.springframework.web.reactive.function.server.ServerResponse interface represents a server-side HTTP response. The ServerResponse is an immutable interface and provides many static builder methods to construct the response with status, contentType, cookies, headers, body, etc.

The following are a few examples of how you can construct ServerResponse using builder methods.

```
ServerResponse.ok().contentType(APPLICATION_JSON).body(userMono, User.class);
ServerResponse.ok().contentType(APPLICATION_JSON).body(BodyInserters.fromObject(user));
ServerResponse.created(uri).build();
ServerResponse.notFound().build();
```

You can also render the view templates using the render() method as follows:

```
Map<String,?> modelAttributes = new HashMap<>();
modelAttributes.put("user",user);
ServerResponse.ok().render("home", modelAttributes);
```

So, essentially using these ServerResponse builder methods, you can construct the return value of the HandlerFunction.handle(ServerRequest) method.

RouterFunction

`RouterFunction` maps the incoming request to a `HandlerFunction` using `RequestPredicate`. You can use the `RouterFunctions` utility class static methods to build the `RouterFunction` as follows:

```
RouterFunctions.route(GET("/echo"), request -> ok().body(fromObject(request.
queryParam("name")))));
```

You can compose multiple route definitions into a new route definition that routes to the first handler function that matches the predicate.

```
import static org.springframework.web.reactive.function.server.RequestPredicates.*;
RouterFunctions.route(GET("/echo"), request -> ok().body(fromObject(request.queryParam("name"))))
            .and(route(GET("/home"), request -> ok().render("home")))
            .andRoute(POST("/users"), request -> ServerResponse.ok().build());
```

This example composes three route definitions into one; the incoming request will be handled by the first `HandlerFunction` that matches the `RequestPredicate`.

Suppose you need to compose multiple routes with the same prefix. Instead of repeating the URL path in every route you can use `RouterFunctions.nest()` as follows:

```
RouterFunctions.nest(path("/api/users"),
    nest(accept(APPLICATION_JSON),
        route(GET("/{id}"), request -> ServerResponse.ok().build())
        .andRoute(method(HttpMethod.GET), request -> ServerResponse.ok().build())));
```

The code maps two URLs to their handler functions. One is to `GET /api/users`, which returns all users and `GET /api/users/{id}` to return the user details for the given `id`. Instead of repeating the common path prefix `/api/users`, it uses `nest()` to compose the routes.

You can create a `RequestPredicate` using the `RequestPredicates` static methods and you can also compose request predicates using `RequestPredicate.and(RequestPredicate)` and `RequestPredicate.or(RequestPredicate)`.

```
RouterFunctions.route(path("/api/users").and(method(HttpMethod.GET)),
                    request -> ServerResponse.ok().build());
 RouterFunctions.route(GET("/api/users").or(GET("/api/users/list")),
                    request -> ServerResponse.ok().build());
```

HandlerFilterFunction

If you have to compare annotation based approaches to functional approaches, `RouterFunction` is similar to the `@RequestMapping` annotation and `HandlerFunction` is similar to the method annotated with `@RequestMapping`. The new functional web framework also provides `HandlerFilterFunction`, which is similar to the servlet `Filter` or `@ControllerAdvice` methods.

```
@FunctionalInterface
public interface HandlerFilterFunction<T extends ServerResponse, R extends ServerResponse>
{

    Mono<R> filter(ServerRequest request, HandlerFunction<T> next);

    //other methods
}
```

For example, you can filter a route based on a user role using HandlerFilterFunction as follows:

```
RouterFunction<ServerResponse> route = route(DELETE("/api/users/{id}"), request -> ok().build());

RouterFunction<ServerResponse> filteredRoute = route.filter((request, next) -> {
    if (hasAdminRole()) {
        return next.handle(request);
    }
    else {
        return ServerResponse.status(UNAUTHORIZED).build();
    }
});

private boolean hasAdminRole()
{
        //logic to check current user has ADMIN role or not
}
```

When you make a request to the /api/users/{id} URL, the filter checks whether the user has the admin role or not and decides to execute the handler function or return an UNAUTHORIZED response.

Registering HandlerFunctions as Method References

Instead of defining the HandlerFunctions using inline lambdas, it would be better to define them as methods and use method references in the route configuration, as shown in Listing 12-4.

Listing 12-4. Registering HandlerFunction with Route Using Method References

```
@Component
class EchoHandler
{
    public Mono<ServerResponse> echo(ServerRequest request)
    {
        return ServerResponse.ok().body(fromObject(request.queryParam("name")));
    }
}

@SpringBootApplication
class Applications
{
    @Autowired
    EchoHandler echoHandler;

    @Bean
    public RouterFunction<ServerResponse> echoRouterFunction() {
        return RouterFunctions.route(GET("/echo"), echoHandler::echo);
    }
}
```

Now you can build the same application that you built in an earlier section using the functional programming model. You are going to create UserHandler with methods to define HandlerFunctions for various operations and then configure RouterFunctions mapping routes to handle functions. See Listing 12-5.

Listing 12-5. UserHandler.java Using the Functional Programming Model

```java
import org.springframework.beans.factory.annotation.Autowired;
import org.springframework.http.MediaType;
import org.springframework.stereotype.Component;
import org.springframework.web.reactive.function.server.ServerRequest;
import org.springframework.web.reactive.function.server.ServerResponse;
import reactor.core.publisher.Flux;
import reactor.core.publisher.Mono;

import static org.springframework.web.reactive.function.BodyInserters.fromObject;

@Component
public class UserHandler
{
    private UserReactiveRepository userReactiveRepository;

    @Autowired
    public UserHandlerFunctions(UserReactiveRepository userReactiveRepository) {
        this.userReactiveRepository = userReactiveRepository;
    }

    public Mono<ServerResponse> getAllUsers(ServerRequest request)
    {
        Flux<User> allUsers = userReactiveRepository.findAll();
        return ServerResponse.ok().contentType(MediaType.APPLICATION_JSON_UTF8)
                .body(allUsers, User.class);
    }

    public Mono<ServerResponse> getUserById(ServerRequest request)
    {
        Mono<User> userMono = userReactiveRepository.findById(request.pathVariable("id"));
        Mono<ServerResponse> notFount = ServerResponse.notFound().build();

        return userMono.flatMap(user -> ServerResponse.ok()
                                        .contentType(MediaType.APPLICATION_JSON_UTF8)
                                        .body(fromObject(user)))
                    .switchIfEmpty(notFount);
    }

    public Mono<ServerResponse> saveUser(ServerRequest request)
    {
        Mono<User> userMono = request.bodyToMono(User.class);
        Mono<User> mono = userMono.flatMap(user -> userReactiveRepository.save(user));
        return ServerResponse.ok().body(mono, User.class);
    }
```

```java
public Mono<ServerResponse> deleteUser(ServerRequest request)
{
    String id = request.pathVariable("id");
     return ServerResponse.ok().build(userReactiveRepository.deleteById(id));
}
}
```

You have defined handler functions for CRUD operations as separate methods. Now you can configure router functions, as shown in Listing 12-6.

Listing 12-6. Application.java

```java
import org.springframework.beans.factory.annotation.Autowired;
import org.springframework.boot.SpringApplication;
import org.springframework.boot.autoconfigure.SpringBootApplication;
import org.springframework.context.annotation.Bean;
import org.springframework.http.HttpMethod;
import org.springframework.web.reactive.function.server.*;

import static org.springframework.http.MediaType.APPLICATION_JSON;
import static org.springframework.web.reactive.function.BodyInserters.fromObject;
import static org.springframework.web.reactive.function.server.RequestPredicates.*;
import static org.springframework.web.reactive.function.server.RouterFunctions.nest;
import static org.springframework.web.reactive.function.server.RouterFunctions.route;
import static org.springframework.web.reactive.function.server.ServerResponse.ok;

@SpringBootApplication
public class Application
{

    public static void main(String[] args) {
        SpringApplication.run(SpringBootWebfluxFunctionalDemoApplication.class, args);
    }

    @Autowired
    UserHandler userHandler;

    @Bean
    public RouterFunction<ServerResponse> routerFunctions() {
        return
                nest(path("/api/users"),
                        nest(accept(APPLICATION_JSON),
                                route(GET("/{id}"), userHandler::getUserById)
                                .andRoute(method(HttpMethod.GET), userHandler::getAllUsers)
                                .andRoute(DELETE("/{id}"), userHandler::deleteUser)
                                .andRoute(POST("/"), userHandler::saveUser)));
    }
}
```

You defined the router configurations and registered them as a RouterFunction bean. You can even mix the annotation-based and functional-based programming models in the same application.

By default, `spring-boot-starter-webflux` uses `reactor-netty` as the runtime engine. You can exclude `reactor-netty` and use some other server that supports reactive non-blocking I/O, such as Undertow, Jetty, or Tomcat as well.

■ **Note**   For more details on WebFlux autoconfiguration, look at the configuration classes in the `org.springframework.boot.autoconfigure.web.reactive` package.

Thymeleaf Reactive Support

Thymeleaf provides the `thymeleaf-spring5` module to support Spring framework 5 integration. The `thymeleaf-spring5` module provides reactive support so that you can use it with Spring WebFlux-based reactive applications.

Spring Boot 2 Thymeleaf starter includes the `thymeleaf-spring5` library as a dependency and autoconfigures Thymeleaf's reactive support. You can check the Thymeleaf reactive autoconfiguration in the configuration class `org.springframework.boot.autoconfigure.thymeleaf.ThymeleafAutoConfiguration`.

The new `thymeleaf-spring5` module provides `SpringWebFluxTemplateEngine`, which extends `SpringTemplateEngine` as the default template engine implementation used in the Spring WebFlux applications. The `SpringWebFluxTemplateEngine` provides three types of processing modes:

- *Full:* Thymeleaf will use FULL mode when no limit for max chunk size is specified and no data-driver context variable has been specified. All template output will be generated in memory and then sent to the server's output channels as a single `DataBuffer`.

- *Chunked:* Thymeleaf will use CHUNKED mode when a limit for max chunk size is specified but no data-driver context variable has been specified. Template output will be generated in chunks equal to or less than the specified limit in bytes and then sent to the server's output channels. After each chunk is sent to the output, the template engine will wait for the server to request more chunks by means of reactive back pressure.

- *Data-driven:* Thymeleaf will use DATA-DRIVEN mode when a data-driver variable (data stream wrapped in `IReactiveDataDriverContextVariable`) has been added to the context. In this mode, Thymeleaf will stream data from the data driver in chunks using back pressure.

Listing 12-7 shows how you can get a stream of data (`Flux<T>`) and render it using Thymeleaf reactive support.

Listing 12-7. UserListController.java Using Thymeleaf Reactive Support

```
@Controller
public class UserListController
{
    @Autowired
    private UserReactiveRepository userReactiveRepository;

    @GetMapping("/list-users")
    public String listUsers(Model model)
    {
```

```java
        Flux<User> userFlux = this.userReactiveRepository.findAll();
        List<User> userList = userFlux.collectList().block();
        model.addAttribute("users", userList);
        return "users";
    }

    @GetMapping("/list-users-chunked")
    public String listUsersChunked(Model model)
    {
        Flux<User> userFlux = this.userReactiveRepository.findAll();
        model.addAttribute("users", userFlux);
        return "users";
    }

    @GetMapping("/list-users-reactive")
    public String listUsersReactive(Model model)
    {
        Flux<User> userFlux = this.userReactiveRepository.findAll();
        model.addAttribute("users", new ReactiveDataDriverContextVariable(userFlux, 1000));
        return "users";
    }
}
```

In the listUsers() method, you are getting data from MongoDB as a reactive stream Flux<User> and fully resolving the data and then rendering the view with a complete set of data available in memory.

In the listUsersChunked() method, you are adding Flux<User> directly to the model, but you haven't specified responseMaxChunkSizeBytes, so it will be processed like FULL mode. If you configure the spring. thymeleaf.reactive.max-chunk-size=size_in_bytes property, then it will be processed in CHUNKED mode.

In the listUsersReactive() method, you are getting data from MongoDB as a reactive stream Flux<User> and wrapping it in ReactiveDataDriverContextVariable with a buffer size so that Thymeleaf will use the data-driven mode to the render view.

■ **Note** In the Thymeleaf data-driven mode, you can add only one multi-valued Publisher (flux) to the context.

Listing 12-8 shows how you can create the Thymeleaf view template to render users.

Listing 12-8. users.html Thymeleaf View

```html
<!DOCTYPE html>
<html xmlns="http://www.w3.org/1999/xhtml"
      xmlns:th="http://www.thymeleaf.org">
<head>
    <meta charset="UTF-8">
    <title>Users</title>
</head>
<body>
<table>
    <thead>
    <tr>
        <th>Name</th>
```

```
            <th>Email</th>
        </tr>
        </thead>
        <tbody>
        <tr th:each="u : ${users}">
            <td th:text="${u.name}">...</td>
            <td th:text="${u.email}">...</td>
        </tr>
        </tbody>
</table>

</body>
</html>
```

There is nothing special in this Thymeleaf view to deal with reactive streams rendering; behind the scenes Thymeleaf will handle the view resolving logic from data streams seamlessly.

You can implement the same endpoints using the web functional framework style HandlerFunctions, as shown in Listing 12-9.

Listing 12-9. UserHandler.java

```
@Component
public class UserHandler
{
    @Autowired
    private UserReactiveRepository userReactiveRepository;

    ...
    ...

    public Mono<ServerResponse> listUsers(ServerRequest request)
    {
        List<User> userList = userReactiveRepository.findAll().collectList().block();
        Map<String,Object> data = new HashMap<>();
        data.put("users", userList);
        return ServerResponse.ok().contentType(MediaType.TEXT_HTML).render("users", data);
    }

    public Mono<ServerResponse> listUsersReactive(ServerRequest request)
    {
        Flux<User> userFlux = userReactiveRepository.findAll();
        ReactiveDataDriverContextVariable users = new ReactiveDataDriverContextVariable
        (userFlux, 1000);
        Map<String,Object> data = new HashMap<>();
        data.put("users", users);
        return ServerResponse.ok().contentType(MediaType.TEXT_HTML).render("users", data);
    }

}
```

Now you can define routes to map URLs to `HandlerFunctions`, as shown in Listing 12-10.

Listing 12-10. Application.java

```java
@SpringBootApplication
public class Application
{

    @Autowired
    UserHandler userHandler;

    public static void main(String[] args) {
        SpringApplication.run(SpringBootWebfluxFunctionalDemoApplication.class, args);
    }

    ...
    ...

    @Bean
    public RouterFunction<ServerResponse> listUsersRouter() {
        return route(GET("/list-users"), userHandler::listUsers);
    }

    @Bean
    public RouterFunction<ServerResponse> listUsersReactiveRouter() {
        return route(GET("/list-users-reactive"), userHandler::listUsersReactive);
    }
}
```

If you have a large data set in MongoDB and access the endpoints /list-users and /list-users-reactive, you can clearly see that /list-users-reactive is more responsive.

Reactive WebClient

Spring provides `RestTemplate` to invoke RESTful service endpoints, which support message converters so that HTTP requests can be made using Java objects instead of preparing an input request body with JSON or XML manually.

Spring WebFlux provides WebClient as a reactive alternative to `RestTemplate` that supports non-blocking. Instead of using `InputStream` and `OutputStream` for request processing, `WebClient` uses `Flux<DataBuffer>` as the request and the response body.

Listing 12-11 shows how, as a client, you can make a request to a reactive endpoint.

Listing 12-11. Invoking Reactive REST Endpoints Using WebClient

```java
WebClient webClient = WebClient.create("http://localhost:"+port);
List<User> users = webClient.get().uri("/api/users")
                    .accept(MediaType.APPLICATION_JSON)
                    .exchange()
                    .flatMap(response -> response.bodyToFlux(User.class).collectList()).
                    block();
```

The `webClient.get().uri("/api/users").exchange()` will return a `Mono<ClientResponse>` and `ClientResponse` provides various utility methods, like the `bodyToMono()`, `bodyToFlux()` and `body(BodyExtractor)` methods to extract body content.

Testing Spring WebFlux Applications

The `spring-test` module provides `WebTestClient`, which can be used for testing reactive endpoints. Spring Boot autoconfigures the `WebTestClient` so you can autowire `WebTestClient` without having to manually configuring it.

Listing 12-12 shows how to test the reactive REST endpoint `GET /api/users` using `WebTestClient`.

Listing 12-12. Testing Reactive Endpoints Using WebTestClient

```java
import org.junit.Test;
import org.junit.runner.RunWith;
import org.springframework.beans.factory.annotation.Autowired;
import org.springframework.boot.test.context.SpringBootTest;
import static org.springframework.http.MediaType.*;
import org.springframework.test.context.junit4.SpringRunner;
import org.springframework.test.web.reactive.server.WebTestClient;

import java.util.List;

import static org.junit.Assert.assertEquals;
import static org.junit.Assert.assertNotNull;

@RunWith(SpringRunner.class)
@SpringBootTest(webEnvironment = SpringBootTest.WebEnvironment.RANDOM_PORT)
public class SpringBootWebfluxFunctionalDemoApplicationTests
{

    @Autowired
    private WebTestClient webTestClient;

    @Test
    public void getAllUsers() {
        webTestClient.get().uri("/api/users").accept(APPLICATION_JSON).exchange()
                .expectStatus().isOk()
                .expectHeader().contentType(APPLICATION_JSON)
                .expectBodyList(User.class)
                .consumeWith(result -> assertEquals(5, result.getResponseBody().size()));
    }

}
```

You can inject `WebTestClient` and use relative URLs for testing instead of providing complete URLs. Once the REST endpoint is invoked, you can assert HTTP status and `ContentType` header values and specify the class type that response body needs to be converted to.

Similarly, you can perform other operations like POST, DELETE, etc., as shown in Listing 12-13.

Listing 12-13. Performing POST Requests Using WebTestClient

```
@Test
public void createUser() {
    User user = new User(UUID.randomUUID().toString(), "Zinx", "zinx@gmail.com");
    webTestClient.post().uri("/api/users")
            .body(Mono.just(user), User.class)
            .exchange()
            .expectStatus().isOk()
            .expectHeader().contentType(MediaType.APPLICATION_JSON_UTF8)
            .expectBody(User.class)
            .consumeWith(result -> assertThat(result.getResponseBody()).isEqualToComparing
            FieldByField(user));
}
```

This example performs a POST request to /api/users to create a new User. It sends Mono<User> as the request body and gets the created User as the response body.

You can also perform JSON assertions on the response body by using JSON Path library assertions. You can invoke the GET /api/users/{id} endpoint to retrieve a particular user for the given ID and assert the response JSON, as shown in Listing 12-14.

Listing 12-14. Performing JSON Assertions on WebTestClient Response Body

```
@Test
public void getUserById() {
    String id = "uid1";
    webTestClient.get().uri("/api/users/"+id)
            .exchange()
            .expectStatus().isOk()
            .expectBody()
            .jsonPath("$.id").isEqualTo(id)
            .jsonPath("$.name").isEqualTo("Admin")
            .jsonPath("$.email").isEqualTo("admin@gmail.com");
}
```

This example asserts the response JSON using jsonPath() assertions provided by the JSON Path library. For more details on JSON Path, see https://github.com/json-path/JsonPath.

▪ **Note** You will learn more about testing Spring Boot applications in Chapter 15.

Summary

This chapter showed you how to build reactive web applications using the Spring WebFlux framework, which is a new module introduced in Spring 5. You built a reactive application using the MongoDB reactive stream driver and WebFlux with the annotation-based model and the functional style programming model. In the next chapter, you learn how to secure traditional web applications and REST APIs using Spring Security.

CHAPTER 13

Securing Web Applications

Security is an important aspect of software application design. It ensures that only those who have authority to access the secured resources can do so. When it comes to securing an application, two primary things you'll need to take care of are authentication and authorization. Authentication refers to the process of verifying the user, which is typically done by asking for credentials. Authorization refers to the process of verifying whether or not the user is allowed to do a certain activity.

Spring Security is a powerful and flexible security framework for securing Java-based web applications. Even though Spring Security is commonly used with Spring-based applications, you can use it to secure non-Spring-based web applications too.

This chapter explains how to use the Spring Boot Security starter to secure SpringMVC-based web applications and how to secure service layer components using method-level security. The chapter also explores how to configure Spring Security to secure the REST API.

Spring Security in Spring Boot Web Application

Spring Security is a framework for securing Java-based applications at various layers with great flexibility and customizability. Spring Security provides authentication and authorization support against database authentication, LDAP, form authentication, JA-SIG central authentication service, Java Authentication and Authorization Service (JAAS), and many more. Spring Security provides support for dealing with common attacks like CSRF, XSS, and session fixation protection, with minimal configuration.

Spring Security can be used to secure the application at various layers, such as web URLs, service layer methods, etc. Spring Security from version 3.2 onward provides Java configuration support for security. Using Spring Security in Spring Boot application became easier with its autoconfiguration features.

Adding the Spring Security Starter (`spring-boot-starter-security`) to an Spring Boot application will:

* Enable HTTP basic security

* Register the `AuthenticationManager` bean with an in-memory store and a single user

* Ignore paths for commonly used static resource locations (such as `/css/**`, `/js/**`, `/images/**`, etc.)

* Enable common low-level features such as XSS, CSRF, caching, etc.

You'll get started by looking at how to secure a Spring Boot application using Spring Security. First, create a Spring Boot project with the Web, Thymeleaf, and Spring Security starters.

© K. Siva Prasad Reddy 2017
K. S. Prasad Reddy, *Beginning Spring Boot 2*, DOI 10.1007/978-1-4842-2931-6_13

```
<dependency>
    <groupId>org.springframework.boot</groupId>
    <artifactId>spring-boot-starter-web</artifactId>
</dependency>
<dependency>
    <groupId>org.springframework.boot</groupId>
    <artifactId>spring-boot-starter-thymeleaf</artifactId>
</dependency>
<dependency>
    <groupId>org.springframework.boot</groupId>
    <artifactId>spring-boot-starter-security</artifactId>
</dependency>
```

Now if you run the application and access `http://localhost:8080`, you will be prompted to enter the user credentials. The default user is user and the password is auto-generated. You can find it in the console log.

```
Using default security password: 78fa095d-3f4c-48b1-ad50-e24c31d5cf35
```

You can change the default user credentials in `application.properties` as follows:

```
security.user.name=admin
security.user.password=secret
security.user.role=USER,ADMIN
```

Okay, that's nice for a quick demo. But in your actual projects, you may want to implement role-based access control using a persistence datastore such as a database. Also, you might want to fine-tune the access to resources (URLs, service layer methods, etc.) based on roles. Now you'll see how to customize the default Spring Security autoconfiguration to meet your needs.

First, you'll create the database tables shown in Figure 13-1 to store users and roles.

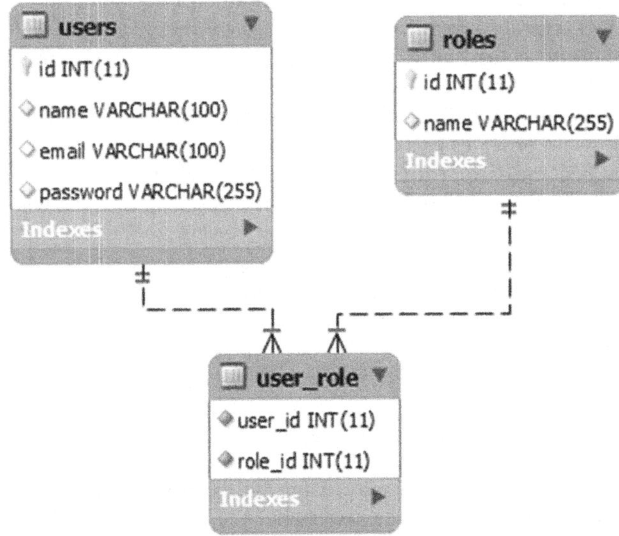

Figure 13-1. *Users and roles database tables*

You are going to use the Spring Data JPA starter to talk to your database.

```xml
<dependency>
    <groupId>org.springframework.boot</groupId>
    <artifactId>spring-boot-starter-data-jpa</artifactId>
</dependency>
<dependency>
    <groupId>com.h2database</groupId>
    <artifactId>h2</artifactId>
</dependency>
```

Create the JPA entities called users and roles, as shown in Listings 13-1 and 13-2.

Listing 13-1. User JPA Entity

```java
@Entity
@Table(name="users")
public class User
{
    @Id @GeneratedValue(strategy=GenerationType.AUTO)
    private Integer id;

    @Column(nullable=false, unique=true)
    private String email;

    @Column(nullable=false)
    private String password;

    @ManyToMany(cascade=CascadeType.MERGE)
    @JoinTable(
            name="user_role",
            joinColumns={@JoinColumn(name="USER_ID",
                            referencedColumnName="ID")},
            inverseJoinColumns={@JoinColumn(name="ROLE_ID",
                            referencedColumnName="ID")})
    private List<Role> roles;

    //setters and getters
}
```

Listing 13-2. Role JPA Entity

```java
@Entity
@Table(name="roles")
public class Role
{
    @Id @GeneratedValue(strategy=GenerationType.AUTO)
    private Integer id;
```

```java
@Column(nullable=false, unique=true)
private String name;

@ManyToMany(mappedBy="roles")
private List<User> users;

//setters and getters
}
```

Next, create the Spring Data JPA repository for the user entity, as shown in Listing 13-3.

Listing 13-3. Spring Data JPA Repository Interface UserRepository.java

```java
public interface UserRepository extends JpaRepository<User, Integer>
{
    Optional<User> findByEmail(String email);
}
```

Spring Security uses the UserDetailsService interface, which contains the loadUserByUsername(String username) method to look up UserDetails for a given username. The UserDetails interface represents an authenticated user object and Spring Security provides an out-of-the-box implementation of org.springframework.security.core.userdetails.User.

Now you implement a UserDetailsService to get UserDetails from database, as shown in Listing 13-4.

Listing 13-4. UserDetailsService Implementation

```java
@Service
@Transactional
public class CustomUserDetailsService implements UserDetailsService
{

    @Autowired
    private UserRepository userRepository;

    @Override
    public UserDetails loadUserByUsername(String userName)
            throws UsernameNotFoundException {
        User user = userRepository.findByEmail(userName)
                    .orElseThrow(() -> new UsernameNotFoundException("Email "+userName+"
                    not found"));
        return new org.springframework.security.core.userdetails.User(
                user.getEmail(),
                user.getPassword(),
                getAuthorities(user)
                );
    }
```

```java
    private static Collection<? extends GrantedAuthority> getAuthorities(User user)
    {
        String[] userRoles = user.getRoles()
                                      .stream()
                                      .map((role) -> role.getName())
                                      .toArray(String[]::new);
        Collection<GrantedAuthority> authorities = AuthorityUtils.createAuthorityList(userRoles);
        return authorities;
    }
}
```

Spring Boot implemented the default Spring Security autoconfiguration in
SecurityAutoConfiguration. To switch the default web application security configuration and
provide your own customized security configuration, you can create a configuration class that extends
WebSecurityConfigurerAdapter and is annotated with @EnableWebSecurity.

Now you'll create a configuration class that extends WebSecurityConfigurerAdapter to customize the
default Spring Security configuration, as shown in Listing 13-5.

Listing 13-5. Customized Spring Security Configuration Extending WebSecurityConfigurerAdapter

```java
@Configuration
@EnableWebSecurity
public class WebSecurityConfig extends WebSecurityConfigurerAdapter {

    @Autowired
    private UserDetailsService customUserDetailsService;

    @Bean
    public PasswordEncoder passwordEncoder() {
        return new BCryptPasswordEncoder();
    }

    @Autowired
    public void configureGlobal(AuthenticationManagerBuilder auth)
        throws Exception
    {
        auth
            .userDetailsService(customUserDetailsService)
            .passwordEncoder(passwordEncoder());
    }

    @Override
    protected void configure(HttpSecurity http) throws Exception {
        http
            .authorizeRequests()
                .antMatchers("/resources/", "/webjars/","/assets/")
                    .permitAll()
                .antMatchers("/").permitAll()
                .antMatchers("/admin/").hasRole("ADMIN")
                .anyRequest().authenticated()
                .and()
```

```
        .formLogin()
            .loginPage("/login")
            .defaultSuccessUrl("/home")
            .failureUrl("/login?error")
            .permitAll()
            .and()
        .logout()
            .logoutRequestMatcher(new AntPathRequestMatcher("/logout"))
            .logoutSuccessUrl("/login?logout")
            .permitAll()
            .and()
        .exceptionHandling()
            .accessDeniedPage("/accessDenied");
    }
}
```

This example configures `CustomUserDetailsService` and `BCryptPasswordEncoder` to be used by `AuthenticationManager` instead of the default in-memory database with a single-user with a plaintext password.

The `configure(HttpSecurity http)` method is configured to:

- Ignore the static resource paths `"/resources/**"`, `"/webjars/**"`, and `"/assets/**"`

- Allow everyone to have access to the root URL `"/"`

- Restrict access to URLs that start with `/admin/` to only users with the `ADMIN` role

- All other URLs should be accessible to authenticated users only

You are also configuring custom form-based login parameters and making them accessible to everyone. By default, the logout request works only with the HTTP `POST` method, so this example configures it to be used with any HTTP method, which makes it accessible to everyone.

The example also configures the URL to redirect the users to the `/accessDenied` URL if they try to access a resource they don't have access to.

You are going to use Thymeleaf view templates for rendering views. The `thymeleaf-extras-springsecurity4` module provides Thymeleaf Spring Security dialect attributes (`sec:authentication`, `sec:authorize`, etc.) to conditionally render parts of the view based on authentication status, logged-in user roles, etc.

Add the following dependency to use the Thymeleaf Spring Security dialect.

```
<dependency>
    <groupId>org.thymeleaf.extras</groupId>
    <artifactId>thymeleaf-extras-springsecurity4</artifactId>
</dependency>
```

Now you need to create a configuration class for providing MVC configuration, as shown in Listing 13-6.

Listing 13-6. Spring WebMVC Configuration

```
@Configuration
public class WebConfig implements WebMvcConfigurer
{
    @Override
    public void addViewControllers(ViewControllerRegistry registry)
    {
        registry.addViewController("/login").setViewName("login");
        registry.addViewController("/home").setViewName("home");
        registry.addViewController("/admin/home").setViewName("adminhome");
        registry.addViewController("/accessDenied").setViewName("403");
    }

    @Bean
    public SpringSecurityDialect securityDialect() {
        return new SpringSecurityDialect();
    }
}
```

This example configures view controllers to specify which view to render for which URL. Also, it registers SpringSecurityDialect to enable using the Thymeleaf Spring Security dialect.

Now that you have all the configuration ready, it's time to create views using Thymeleaf.

Create src/main/resources/templates/login.html, as shown in Listing 13-7.

Listing 13-7. Thymeleaf Login View

```
<!DOCTYPE html>
<html xmlns="http://www.w3.org/1999/xhtml"
      xmlns:th="http://www.thymeleaf.org"
      xmlns:sec="http://www.thymeleaf.org/thymeleaf-extras-springsecurity3">
  <head>
    <title>SpringBoot Security</title>
  </head>

  <body>

    <form action="login" th:action="@{/login}" method="post">

        <div th:if="${param.error}">
            <span>Invalid Email and Password.</span>
        </div>

        <input type="email" name="username" placeholder="Email" />
        <input type="password" name="password" placeholder="Password" />
        <button type="submit">LogIn</button>

    </form>

  </body>
</html>
```

This code creates the login form with the `username` and `password` fields and renders a login error if there is an error request parameter. The code configures the login form `failureUrl` to `"/login?error"`, so if the users provide incorrect credentials, they will be redirected to the `/login?error` URL.

Next, create `src/main/resources/templates/home.html`, as shown in Listing 13-8.

Listing 13-8. Thymeleaf Home View

```
<!DOCTYPE html>
<html xmlns="http://www.w3.org/1999/xhtml"
      xmlns:th="http://www.thymeleaf.org"
      xmlns:sec="http://www.thymeleaf.org/thymeleaf-extras-springsecurity3">
  <head>
    <title>SpringBoot Security</title>
  </head>

  <body>

    <p>Welcome <span sec:authentication="principal.username">User</span></p>
    <p><a th:href="@{/logout}">Logout</a></p>

    <div sec:authorize="hasRole('ROLE_ADMIN')">
        <h3>You will see this only if you are ADMIN</h3>
        <p><a th:href="@{/admin/home}">Admin Home</a></p>
    </div>

  </body>
</html>
```

The code configures `"/home"` as `defaultSuccessUrl`, so after successful authentication, users will be redirected to the `/home` URL, which will render the `home.html` view.

In the `home.html` view, you are using `sec:authentication="principal.username"` to display the authenticated username. This example also conditionally renders the link to the admin's home page only if the authenticated user has the role `ROLE_ADMIN`. This is done by using `sec:authorize="hasRole ('ROLE_ADMIN')"`.

Create `src/main/resources/templates/adminhome.html`, as shown in Listing 13-9.

Listing 13-9. Thymeleaf Adminhome View

```
<!DOCTYPE html>
<html xmlns="http://www.w3.org/1999/xhtml"
      xmlns:th="http://www.thymeleaf.org"
      xmlns:sec="http://www.thymeleaf.org/thymeleaf-extras-springsecurity3">
  <head>
    <title>SpringBoot Security</title>
  </head>
  <body>
    <p>Welcome Administrator(<span sec:authentication="principal.username">User</span>)</p>
    <p><a th:href="@{/logout}">Logout</a></p>
  </body>
</html>
```

Next, create `src/main/resources/templates/403.html`, as shown in Listing 13-10.

Listing 13-10. AccessDenied View 403.html

```
<!DOCTYPE html>
<html>
  <head>
    <title>Access Denied</title>
  </head>
  <body>
      <p>You are not authorized to view this page!!</p>
  </body>
</html>
```

If the logged-in user doesn't have the ROLE_ADMIN role and tries to access the /admin/home URL, then Spring Security will throw AccessDeniedException. The code then redirects the user to the /accessDenied URL when AccessDeniedException occurs. That's because the example maps the /accessDenied URL to view the 403.html file.

Instead of configuring exceptionHandling().accessDeniedPage("/accessDenied"), you can simply configure exceptionHandling(); which will throw AccessDeniedException with the HTTP status code 403. You can then place the 403.html file in the src/main/resources/public/error/ folder, which will automatically be picked up by the Spring Boot error-handling mechanism.

Before running this application, you need to initialize the database with some sample data for users and roles, as shown in Listing 13-11.

Listing 13-11. src/main/resources/data.sql

```
delete from  user_role;
delete from  roles;
delete from  users;

INSERT INTO roles (id, name) VALUES
(1, 'ROLE_ADMIN'),
(2, 'ROLE_USER');

INSERT INTO users (id, email, password, name) VALUES
(1, 'admin@gmail.com', '$2a$10$hKDVYxLefVHV/vtuPhWD3OigtRyOykRLDdUAp8OZ1crSoS1lFqaFS',
'Admin'),
(2, 'siva@gmail.com', '$2a$10$UFEPYW7Rx1qZqdHajzOnB.VBR3rvm7OI7uSix4RadfQiNhkZOi2fi',
'Siva'),
(3, 'user@gmail.com', '$2a$10$ByIUiNaRfBKSV6urZoBBxe4UbJ/sS6u1ZaPORHF9AtNWAuVPVz1by',
'DemoUser');

insert into user_role(user_id, role_id) values
(1,1),
(1,2),
(3,2);
```

The passwords are encrypted using the BCryptPasswordEncoder.encode(plan_tx_password) method.

Run the application and go to `http://localhost:8080/home`. You will be redirected to the login page, as you are not yet authenticated. After submitting the valid credentials (such as `admin@gmail.com/admin`), you will be redirected to the home page. If you have logged in as a user with the ADMIN role, you should be able to see the text **You will see this only if you are ADMIN** and a link to *Admin Home*. If you click on the Admin Home link, you should be able to see the Admin Home page.

If you have logged in as a normal user (`user@gmail.com/user`), you will not be able to see **You will see this only if you are ADMIN** and a link to Admin Home. If you try to access the Admin Home URL by directly entering `http://localhost:8080/admin/home`, you will be redirected to the Access Denied page (the `403.html` view).

Implementing the Remember-Me Feature

Spring Security provides the Remember-Me feature so that applications can remember the identity of a user between sessions. To use the Remember-Me functionality, you just need to send the HTTP parameter `remember-me`.

```
<form th:action="@{/login}" method="post">
    <input type="email" name="username"/>
    <input type="password" name="password" />
    <input type="checkbox" name="remember-me"> Remember Me
    <button type="submit">LogIn</button>
</form>
```

Spring Security provides the following two implementations of the Remember-Me feature out-of-the-box:

- Simple hash-based token as **a** cookie—This approach creates a token by hashing the user identity information and setting it as a cookie on the client browser.

- **Persistent token**—This approach uses a persistent store like a relational database to store the tokens.

Simple Hash-Based Token as Cookie

You can enable the Remember-Me feature in the Security configuration which by default use hash-based token approach, as shown in Listing 13-12.

Listing 13-12. Spring Security Configuration Enabling Remember-Me

```
@Configuration
@EnableWebSecurity
public class WebSecurityConfig extends WebSecurityConfigurerAdapter
{
    ...
    ...

    @Override
    protected void configure(HttpSecurity http) throws Exception {
        http
            .authorizeRequests()
                .antMatchers("/resources/**", "/webjars/**","/assets/**").permitAll()
```

```
                .antMatchers("/").permitAll()
                .antMatchers("/admin/**").hasRole("ADMIN")
                .anyRequest().authenticated()
                .and()
            .formLogin()
                .loginPage("/login")
                .defaultSuccessUrl("/home")
                .failureUrl("/login?error")
                .permitAll()
                .and()
            .logout()
                .logoutRequestMatcher(new AntPathRequestMatcher("/logout"))
                .logoutSuccessUrl("/login?logout")
                .deleteCookies("remember-me")
                .permitAll()
                .and()
            .rememberMe()
                .and()
            .exceptionHandling()
                ;
    }
}
```

With this configuration, when you log in by selecting the Remember Me checkbox, a cookie will be set with remember-me and will contain the hash-based token as a value. Now if you close and reopen the browser and go to the application, you will be automatically authenticated. Also note that the remember-me cookie is deleted when the user logs out.

This hash-based token as a cookie approach is implemented by Spring Security using org.springframework.security.web.authentication.rememberme.TokenBasedRememberMeServices. The remember-me cookie token value is generated as follows:

```
base64(username + ":" + expirationTime + ":" + md5Hex(username + ":" + expirationTime + ":"
password + ":" + key))
```

The default expirationTime is two weeks (1209600 seconds) and key is a random generated string (UUID.randomUUID().toString()).

You can customize the cookie name, expiration time, and key as follows:

```
.rememberMe()
    .key("my-secure-key")
    .rememberMeCookieName("my-remember-me-cookie")
    .tokenValiditySeconds(24 * 60 * 60)
    .and()
```

With this customization, after successful authentication, it will create the remember-me cookie with the name my-remember-me-cookie. It will be valid for one day (24 * 60 * 60 seconds).

■ **Caution**   In this approach, the generated token contains the MD5 hashed password and is a potential security vulnerability if the cookie is captured.

Persistent Tokens

Spring Security provides another implementation of the Remember-Me feature, which can be used to store the generated tokens in a persistent storage such as a database. The persistent tokens approach is implemented using `org.springframework.security.web.authentication.rememberme.PersistentTokenBasedRememberMeServices`, which internally uses the `PersistentTokenRepository` interface to store the tokens.

Spring provides the following two implementations of `PersistentTokenRepository` out-of-the-box.

- `InMemoryTokenRepositoryImpl` can be used to store tokens in-memory (not recommended for production use).

- `JdbcTokenRepositoryImpl` can be used to store tokens in a database.

The `JdbcTokenRepositoryImpl` stores the tokens in the `persistent_logins` table. See Listing 13-13.

Listing 13-13. persistent_logins table

```
create table persistent_logins
(
    username varchar(64) not null,
    series varchar(64) primary key,
    token varchar(64) not null,
    last_used timestamp not null
);
```

Now you'll see how to configure Remember-Me functionality to use a relational database to store the tokens. See Listing 13-14.

Listing 13-14. Configuring Remember-Me Using Persistent Tokens

```
@Configuration
@EnableWebSecurity
public class WebSecurityConfig extends WebSecurityConfigurerAdapter
{
    @Autowired
    private UserDetailsService customUserDetailsService;

    @Autowired
    private DataSource dataSource;

    ...
    ...

    @Override
    protected void configure(HttpSecurity http) throws Exception {
        http

            ...
            ...

            .rememberMe()
                .tokenRepository(persistentTokenRepository())
                .tokenValiditySeconds(24 * 60 * 60)
```

```
            .and()
        .exceptionHandling()
            ;
    }

    PersistentTokenRepository persistentTokenRepository(){
        JdbcTokenRepositoryImpl tokenRepositoryImpl = new JdbcTokenRepositoryImpl();
        tokenRepositoryImpl.setDataSource(dataSource);
        return tokenRepositoryImpl;
    }
}
```

Now when you successfully log in with the Remember-Me checkbox selected, the generated token will be stored in the persistent_logins table.

This approach generates a unique series value for the user, together with random token data to create a token and set it as a cookie. Every time the user then logs in with the cookie, a new random token data will be generated, but the series value will be intact for that user.

Cross-Site Request Forgery

Cross-Site Request Forgery (CSRF) is an attack that lets users execute unwanted actions on an authenticated web application. Suppose you go to the genuinesite.com web site and authenticate yourself. This may set cookies on your browser, including an authentication token. Now, if you open the malicioussite.com web site on the same browser but in a different tab, you can send a request from malicioussite.com to genuinesite.com with unwanted data. This data will send the request along with the cookies set by genuinesite.com.

Spring Security provides CSRF protection and is enabled by default. Spring Security provides CSRF protection by using org.springframework.security.web.csrf.CsrfFilter. The CsrfFilter will intercept all the requests, ignore the GET, HEAD, TRACE, and OPTIONS requests, and check whether a valid CSRF token is present for all the other requests (such as POST, PUT, DELETE, etc.). If the CSRF token is missing or contains an invalid token, then it will throw AccessDeniedException.

You should send the state-changing requests (such as POST, PUT, DELETE, etc.) with the CSRF token as a hidden parameter in the request. You can manually insert the token as follows:

```
<form method="post" action="/users">
    ...
    ...
    <input
      type="hidden"
      th:name="${_csrf.parameterName}"
      th:value="${_csrf.token}" />
</form>
```

If you are using Spring Security and Thymeleaf, the CSRF token will be automatically included if the <form> has the th:action attribute and method is anything other than GET, HEAD, TRACE, or OPTIONS.

Suppose you have the following Thymeleaf form.

```
<form th:action="@{/messages}" method="post">
    <textarea name="content" cols="50" rows="5"></textarea>
    <input type="submit" value="Submit"/>
</form>
```

When it is rendered, if you see the page source, you can see the CSRF token inserted automatically as a hidden parameter.

```
<form action="/messages" method="post">
    <input type="hidden" name="_csrf" value="57f12f98-d62c-4d01-88c0-a11cf9ed980a"/>
    <textarea name="content" cols="50" rows="5"></textarea>
    <input type="submit" value="Submit"/>
</form>
```

■ **Note**   If you use the `action` attribute instead of setting the `th:action` or `method` value to any of GET, HEAD, TRACE, or OPTIONS, the CSRF token won't be inserted automatically.

If you submit the form without a CSRF token or with an invalid CSRF token, then `AccessDeniedException` will be thrown with the 403 HTTP status code.

Method-Level Security

You have learned how to secure web applications by protecting access to web URLs. But the service-layer methods that are supposed to be invoked only by authenticated users are still accessible without restriction if users have the Spring bean. You can use Spring not only for developing web applications but also for batch-processing applications, integration servers, etc., which doesn't provide a web interface. So, you may need to secure the methods access based on roles and permissions.

Spring Security provides method-level security using the @Secured annotation. It also supports the JSR-250 security annotation @RolesAllowed. From version 3.0, Spring Security has provided an expression-based security configuration using the @PreAuthorize and @PostAuthorize annotations, which provides more fine-grained control.

You can enable method-level security using the @EnableGlobalMethodSecurity annotation on any configuration class, as follows:

```
@Configuration
@EnableWebSecurity
@EnableGlobalMethodSecurity(securedEnabled = true,
                           prePostEnabled=true,
                           jsr250Enabled=true)
public class WebSecurityConfig extends WebSecurityConfigurerAdapter
{
    ...
    ...
}
```

- `secureEnabled`: Defines whether @Secured is enabled.

- `prePostEnabled`: Defines whether the pre/post annotations @PreAuthorize and @PostAuthorize are enabled.

- `jsr250Enabled`: Defines whether the JSR-250 annotation @RolesAllowed is enabled.

Once you enable method-level security, you can annotate the SpringMVC controller request-handling methods, service-layer methods, or any Spring components with @Secured, @PreAuthorize, or @RolesAllowed in order to define your security restrictions. See Listing 13-15.

Listing 13-15. SpringMVC REST Controller Using Method-Level Security Annotations

```
@RestController
public class AdminRestController
{
    @Autowired
    private UserService userService;

    @PreAuthorize("hasRole('ADMIN') OR hasRole('USER')")
    @PutMapping("/admin/users/{id}")
    public User updateUser(@RequestBody User user)
    {
        userService.updateUser(user);
        return user;
    }

    @Secured("ROLE_ADMIN")
    @DeleteMapping("/admin/users/{id}")
    public void deleteUser(@PathVariable("id") Integer userId)
    {
        userService.deleteUser(userId);
    }
}
```

Similarly, you can secure service-layer methods using the @Secured, @PreAuthorize, or @RolesAllowed annotations.

```
@Service
@Transactional
public class UserService
{
    @PreAuthorize("hasRole('ADMIN')")
    public void deleteUser(Integer userId)
    {
        ....
    }
}
```

You can use the @Secured, @PreAuthorize, or @RolesAllowed annotations at the class level as well, which applies security configuration to all the methods in that class.

You can use the Spring Expression Language (SpEL) to define the security expressions as follows:

- `hasRole(role)`: Returns true if the current user has the specified role.

- `hasAnyRole(role1,role2)`: Returns true if the current user has any of the supplied roles.

- `isAnonymous()`: Returns true if the current user is an anonymous user.

- `isAuthenticated()`: Returns true if the user is not anonymous.

- `isFullyAuthenticated()`: Returns true if the user is not an anonymous or *Remember-Me* user.

You can combine these expressions using the logical operators AND, OR, and NOT(!).

```
@PreAuthorize("hasRole('ADMIN') OR hasRole('USER')")
```

```
@PreAuthorize("isFullyAuthenticated() AND hasRole('ADMIN')")
```

```
@PreAuthorize("!isAnonymous()")
```

Although defining security restrictions using `@Secured` and `@PreAuthorize` looks similar, there are some minor differences to be noted.

The `@Secured("ROLE_ADMIN")` annotation is the same as `@PreAuthorize("hasRole('ROLE_ADMIN')")`. The `@Secured({"ROLE_USER", "ROLE_ADMIN")` is considered as `ROLE_USER OR ROLE_ADMIN`, so you cannot express the AND condition using `@Secured`. You can define the same with `@PreAuthorize("hasRole('ADMIN') OR hasRole('USER')")`, which is easier to understand. You can express AND, OR, or NOT(!) as well.

```
@PreAuthorize("!isAnonymous() AND hasRole('ADMIN')")
```

■ **Note** The `@PreAuthorize` annotation is more powerful compared to `@Secured`/`@RolesAllowed`, so it's better to use `@PreAuthorize`.

Securing the REST API Using Spring Security

In the previous section, you learned how to secure a traditional web application using Spring Security. The default behavior of some of the Spring Security components is suitable to web applications. To secure a REST API, however, you need to customize the components behavior to better suit the REST semantics. Follow these steps to do so:

1. Set up `AuthenticationEntryPoint`.

   By default, when a user tries to access a secured resource without logging in, Spring Security's `AuthenticationEntryPoint` redirects the user to the login URL. However, for the REST API, it would make more sense to return the HTTP status code 401 (`SC_UNAUTHORIZED`) when an unauthorized user tries to access secured resource.

   Spring Security provides several implementations of `AuthenticationEntryPoint` out-of-the-box. Among them, `org.springframework.boot.autoconfigure. security.Http401AuthenticationEntryPoint` provides the exact behavior you want—return the HTTP status code 401 `SC_UNAUTHORIZED`. See Listing 13-16.

Listing 13-16. AuthenticationEntryPoint for the REST API

```
public class Http401AuthenticationEntryPoint
            implements AuthenticationEntryPoint
{
    private final String headerValue;

    public Http401AuthenticationEntryPoint(String headerValue) {
        this.headerValue = headerValue;
    }

    @Override
    public void commence(HttpServletRequest request,
                         HttpServletResponse response,
                         AuthenticationException authException)
                    throws IOException, ServletException
    {
        response.setHeader("WWW-Authenticate", this.headerValue);
        response.sendError(HttpServletResponse.SC_UNAUTHORIZED,
                authException.getMessage());
    }
}
```

2. Set up AuthenticationSuccessHandler.

    By default, Spring Security uses
    SavedRequestAwareAuthenticationSuccessHandler, which implements
    AuthenticationSuccessHandler to redirect the user to redirectUrl with the 301
    MOVED PERMANENTLY HTTP status code. But for REST APIs, it would make sense
    to return the status code 200 OK, along with the authenticated user details as the
    response body for a successful authentication.

    Listing 13-17 shows how to implement a custom
    AuthenticationSuccessHandler as a Spring bean so that you can take advantage
    of HttpMessageConverters to send User details as the response body.

Listing 13-17. AuthenticationSuccessHandler for the REST API

```
@Component
public class RestAuthenticationSuccessHandler
            extends SavedRequestAwareAuthenticationSuccessHandler
{
    private final ObjectMapper mapper;

    @Autowired
    public RestAuthenticationSuccessHandler
                (MappingJackson2HttpMessageConverter messageConverter) {
        this.mapper = messageConverter.getObjectMapper();
    }
```

```
@Override
public void onAuthenticationSuccess(HttpServletRequest request,
                                    HttpServletResponse response,
                                    Authentication authentication)
                        throws IOException, ServletException
{
    response.setStatus(HttpServletResponse.SC_OK);

    UserDetails userDetails = (UserDetails) authentication.getPrincipal();
    PrintWriter writer = response.getWriter();
    mapper.writeValue(writer, userDetails);
    writer.flush();
    writer.close();
}
}
```

3. Set up `AuthenticationFailureHandler`.

    Spring Security provides `SimpleUrlAuthenticationFailureHandler`, which
    implements `AuthenticationFailureHandler` to redirect to `defaultFailureUrl`
    if `defaultFailureUrl` is not null. If `defaultFailureUrl` is null, then it will simply
    return the HTTP status code 401 `SC_UNAUTHORIZED`. See Listing 13-18.

Listing 13-18. AuthenticationFailureHandler for the REST API

```
public class SimpleUrlAuthenticationFailureHandler implements
        AuthenticationFailureHandler {
    protected final Log logger = LogFactory.getLog(getClass());

    private String defaultFailureUrl;
    ....
    ....

    public SimpleUrlAuthenticationFailureHandler() {
    }

    public SimpleUrlAuthenticationFailureHandler(String defaultFailureUrl) {
        setDefaultFailureUrl(defaultFailureUrl);
    }

    public void onAuthenticationFailure(HttpServletRequest request,
            HttpServletResponse response, AuthenticationException exception)
            throws IOException, ServletException {

        if (defaultFailureUrl == null) {
            logger.debug("No failure URL set, sending 401 Unauthorized error");

            response.sendError(HttpServletResponse.SC_UNAUTHORIZED,
                    "Authentication Failed: " + exception.getMessage());
```

```
        }
        else {
            ....
            ....
        }
    }
    ...
    ...
}
```

So, you can use `SimpleUrlAuthenticationFailureHandler` without setting the `defaultFailureUrl` value, which will be suitable for the REST API.

4. Set up `LogoutSuccessHandler`.

When a user logs out of Spring Security, it uses `SimpleUrlLogoutSuccessHandler`, which implements `LogoutSuccessHandler` to redirect the user to a default target URL. For the REST API, you should return the HTTP status code 200 OK, similar to `AuthenticationSuccessHandler`.

Spring Security provides `HttpStatusReturningLogoutSuccessHandler`, which you can use to simply return the HTTP status code 200, as shown in Listing 13-19.

Listing 13-19. LogoutSuccessHandler for the REST API

```
public class HttpStatusReturningLogoutSuccessHandler
                    implements LogoutSuccessHandler
{
    private final HttpStatus httpStatusToReturn;
    ....
    ....

    public HttpStatusReturningLogoutSuccessHandler() {
        this.httpStatusToReturn = HttpStatus.OK;
    }

    public void onLogoutSuccess(HttpServletRequest request,
                               HttpServletResponse response,
                               Authentication authentication)
                    throws IOException, ServletException
    {
        response.setStatus(httpStatusToReturn.value());
        response.getWriter().flush();
    }
}
```

You now have all the Spring Security customizations in place for securing the REST API. It's time to hook them up with the Spring Security configuration. See Listing 13-20.

Listing 13-20. Spring Security Customized Configuration for the REST API

```
@Configuration
@EnableWebSecurity
@EnableGlobalMethodSecurity(securedEnabled = true)
public class WebSecurityConfig extends WebSecurityConfigurerAdapter {

    @Autowired
    private UserDetailsService customUserDetailsService;

    @Autowired
    private RestAuthenticationSuccessHandler authenticationSuccessHandler;

    @Bean
    public PasswordEncoder passwordEncoder() {
        return new BCryptPasswordEncoder();
    }

    @Autowired
    public void configureGlobal(AuthenticationManagerBuilder auth)
        throws Exception
    {
        auth.userDetailsService(customUserDetailsService)
            .passwordEncoder(passwordEncoder());
    }

    @Override
    protected void configure(HttpSecurity http) throws Exception {
        http
            .csrf().disable()
            .authorizeRequests()
                .antMatchers("/","/register","/forgotPassword").permitAll()
                .antMatchers("/admin/").hasRole("ADMIN")
                .and()

            .exceptionHandling()
                .authenticationEntryPoint(
                    new Http401AuthenticationEntryPoint("Basic realm=\"MyApp\""))
                .and()

            .formLogin()
                .permitAll()
                .loginProcessingUrl("/login")
                .successHandler(authenticationSuccessHandler)
                .failureHandler(new SimpleUrlAuthenticationFailureHandler())
                .and()
            .logout()
                .permitAll()
```

```
        .logoutRequestMatcher(new AntPathRequestMatcher("/logout"))
        .logoutSuccessHandler(
                new HttpStatusReturningLogoutSuccessHandler())
    ;


    }
}
```

You have the complete configuration in place to secure the REST API. Now, before making a request to a secured resource, the client needs to be authenticated. Otherwise, the 401 UNAUTHORIZED response code will be returned. In this example, you'll use Postman REST client (https://www.getpostman.com/) to verify that the REST API is secured.

If you open the Postman client and send a GET request to http://localhost:8080/api/posts, you will see the following response, as you are not yet authenticated.

```
{
  "timestamp": 1496547074713,
  "status": 401,
  "error": "Unauthorized",
  "message": "Full authentication is required to access this resource",
  "path": "/api/posts"
}
```

Now send a POST request to http://localhost:8080/login with form-data set to the username and password values. This will produce the following response:

```
{
    "password":null,
    "username":"admin@gmail.com",
    "authorities":[
        {"authority":"ROLE_ADMIN"},
        {"authority":"ROLE_USER"}
    ],
    "accountNonExpired":true,
    "accountNonLocked":true,
    "credentialsNonExpired":true,
    "enabled":true,
    "name":"admin@gmail.com"
}
```

Now that you have been authenticated, send a GET request to http://localhost:8080/api/posts again. You should be successful.

Summary

This chapter explored how to secure traditional web applications built with SpringMVC and Thymeleaf by using the Spring Security starter. You also learned how to secure the REST API built with Spring Boot by customizing Spring Security. The next chapter looks at the Spring Boot Actuator.

CHAPTER 14

Spring Boot Actuator

Spring Boot is an opinionated framework that autoconfigures various application components based on several criteria, like the starters you used, the properties configuration, and the active environment profile(s).

- Is there a way to know which components (which Spring beans) are automatically registered by Spring Boot?

- Is it possible to check all the configuration parameters applied for the current running application?

- Can you determine which request URL will be handled by which controller?

- Can you get metrics on the application, such as memory usage, thread allocation, etc.?

The answer to all these questions is yes. You can perform all these activities with the Spring Boot Actuator.

This chapter introduces the Spring Boot Actuator and explores the various actuator endpoints that provide lots of useful information about running Spring Boot applications. You will also learn how to secure actuator endpoints, enable CORS for actuator endpoints, and implement custom health checks and metrics. Finally, the chapter looks into using JMX to monitor your application using JConsole.

Introducing the Spring Boot Actuator

The Spring Boot Actuator module provides production-ready features such as monitoring, metrics, health checks, etc. The Spring Boot Actuator enables you to monitor the application using HTTP endpoints and JMX.

Spring Boot provides `spring-boot-starter-actuator` to autoconfigure Actuator. You can take advantage of Actuator's features in order to monitor a Spring Boot application, as you'll see in this section.

First, create a Spring Boot application with the Web, Data-JPA, and Actuator starters.

```
<dependencies>
    <dependency>
        <groupId>org.springframework.boot</groupId>
        <artifactId>spring-boot-starter-web</artifactId>
    </dependency>
    <dependency>
        <groupId>org.springframework.boot</groupId>
        <artifactId>spring-boot-starter-data-jpa</artifactId>
    </dependency>
</dependencies>
```

© K. Siva Prasad Reddy 2017
K. S. Prasad Reddy, *Beginning Spring Boot 2*, DOI 10.1007/978-1-4842-2931-6_14

```xml
<dependency>
    <groupId>org.springframework.boot</groupId>
    <artifactId>spring-boot-starter-actuator</artifactId>
</dependency>
<dependency>
    <groupId>com.h2database</groupId>
    <artifactId>h2</artifactId>
</dependency>
</dependencies>
```

Run the entry point class `SpringbootActuatorDemoApplication`.

```java
@SpringBootApplication
public class SpringbootActuatorDemoApplication
{
    public static void main(String[] args)
    {
        SpringApplication.run(SpringbootActuatorDemoApplication.class, args);
    }
}
```

You can see the console output displaying the request mapping provided by the Spring Boot Actuator.

```
... EndpointHandlerMapping      : Mapped "{[/application/health || /application/health.json],
                                  methods=[GET],....
... EndpointHandlerMapping      : Mapped "{[/application/loggers/{name:.*}],methods=[GET],...
... EndpointHandlerMapping      : Mapped "{[/application/loggers/{name:.*}],methods=[POST],...
... EndpointHandlerMapping      : Mapped "{[/application/loggers || /application/loggers.json],
                                  methods=[GET],...
... EndpointHandlerMapping      : Mapped "{[/application/auditevents || /application/
                                  auditevents.json],methods=[GET],...
... EndpointHandlerMapping      : Mapped "{[/application/dump || /application/dump.json],
                                  methods=[GET],...
... EndpointHandlerMapping      : Mapped "{[/application/env/{name:.*}],methods=[GET],...
... EndpointHandlerMapping      : Mapped "{[/application/env || /application/env.json],
                                  methods=[GET],...
... EndpointHandlerMapping      : Mapped "{[/application/beans || /application/beans.json],
                                  methods=[GET],...
... EndpointHandlerMapping      : Mapped "{[/application || /application.json],methods=[GET],...
... EndpointHandlerMapping      : Mapped "{[/application/trace || /application/trace.json],
                                  methods=[GET],...
... EndpointHandlerMapping      : Mapped "{[/application/metrics/{name:.*}],methods=[GET],...
... EndpointHandlerMapping      : Mapped "{[/application/metrics || /application/metrics.json],
                                  methods=[GET],...
... EndpointHandlerMapping      : Mapped "{[/application/info || /application/info.json],
                                  methods=[GET],...
... EndpointHandlerMapping      : Mapped "{[/application/logfile || /application/logfile.json],
                                  methods=[GET || HEAD]}" ...
... EndpointHandlerMapping      : Mapped "{[/application/autoconfig || /application/
                                  autoconfig.json],methods=[GET],...
```

```
... EndpointHandlerMapping       : Mapped "{[/application/docs],produces=[text/html]}" ...
... EndpointHandlerMapping       : Mapped "{[/application/docs/],produces=[text/html]}" ...
... EndpointHandlerMapping       : Mapped "{[/application/heapdump || /application/heapdump.json],
                                    methods=[GET],...
... EndpointHandlerMapping       : Mapped "{[/application/mappings || /application/mappings.json],
                                    methods=[GET],...
... EndpointHandlerMapping       : Mapped "{[/application/configprops || /application/
                                    configprops.json],methods=[GET],...
```

There are lots of endpoints that are automatically added by the Spring Boot Actuator. The next section explores various Actuator endpoints in detail.

Exploring Actuator's Endpoints

The Actuator endpoints listed in Table 14-1 are autoconfigured by the Actuator starter with the default settings.

Table 14-1. *Spring Boot Actuator Endpoints*

ID	Description	Sensitive Default
info	Displays arbitrary application info.	false
health	Shows application basic health info for unauthenticated users and full details for authenticated users.	false
beans	Shows a list of all Spring beans configured in the application.	true
autoconfig	Displays an autoconfiguration report showing all autoconfiguration candidates and the reason they were/were not applied.	true
mappings	Displays a collated list of all @RequestMapping paths.	true
configprops	Displays a collated list of all @ConfigurationProperties.	true
metrics	Shows metrics information for the current application.	true
env	Exposes properties from Spring's ConfigurableEnvironment.	true
trace	Displays trace information (by default, the last 100 HTTP requests).	true
dump	Performs a thread dump.	true
loggers	Shows and modifies the configuration of loggers in the application.	true
auditevents	Exposes audit events information for the current application.	true
flyway	Shows any Flyway database migrations that have been applied.	true
liquibase	Shows any Liquibase database migrations that have been applied.	true
actuator	Provides a hypermedia-based "discovery page" for the other endpoints. Requires Spring HATEOAS to be on the classpath.	true
shutdown	Allows the application to be gracefully shut down (not enabled by default).	true

Table 14-2 lists the additional Actuator endpoints that are available based on certain conditions.

Table 14-2. *Additional Spring Boot Actuator Endpoints for SpringMVC Applications*

ID	Description	Sensitive Default
docs	Displays documentation, including example requests and responses, for the Actuator's endpoints. Requires `spring-boot-actuator-docs` to be on the classpath.	false
heapdump	Returns a GZip-compressed hprof heap dump file.	true
jolokia	Exposes JMX beans over HTTP (when `Jolokia` is on the classpath).	true
logfile	Returns the contents of the logfile (if the `logging.file` or `logging.path` properties have been set).	true

The sensitive actuator endpoints can be accessed by authenticated users only. You will learn how to configure security for endpoints in later sections, so for now you can disable security for actuator endpoints by setting the following property.

```
management.security.enabled=false
```

By default actuator endpoints run on the same HTTP port (`server.port`) with `/application` as the base path prefix.

In this section, you will explore several commonly used Actuator endpoints.

The /info Endpoint

If you added any information about the application in the `application.properties` file using the `info.app.*` properties, as shown in Figure 14-1, then you can view it at the `http://localhost:8080/application/info` endpoint.

```
info.app.name=Beginning Spring Boot 2
info.app.description=This is a SpringBoot Demo app
info.app.version=1.0.0
```

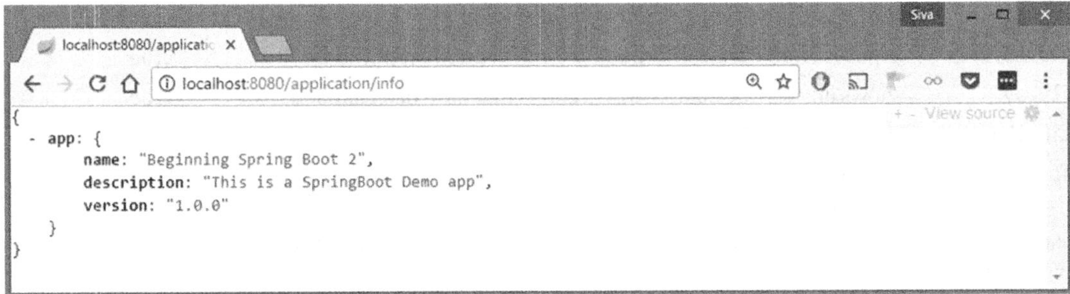

Figure 14-1. *Spring Boot Actuator /info endpoint*

The /health Endpoint

The /health endpoint shows the health of the application, including the disk space, databases, etc. Go to http://localhost:8080/application/health to check the health of the application, as shown in Figure 14-2.

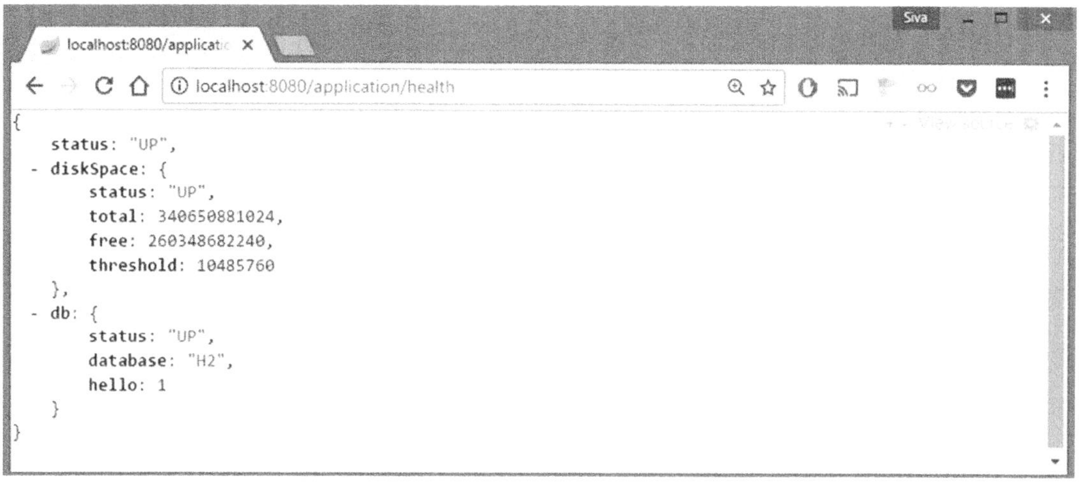

Figure 14-2. Spring Boot Actuator /health endpoint

By default, the /health endpoint shows only whether the application is UP or DOWN for unauthorized users. If the user is authorized or management security is disabled, the /health endpoint shows additional information, such as disk space, databases, health, etc.

The /beans Endpoint

The /beans endpoint shows all the beans registered in your application, including the beans you explicitly configured and the beans autoconfigured by Spring Boot.

Point your browser to http://localhost:8080/application/beans. You should be able to see output similar to what's shown in Figure 14-3.

Figure 14-3. *Spring Boot Actuator /beans endpoint*

The /autoconfig Endpoint

The /autoconfig endpoint shows the autoconfiguration report, which is categorized into positiveMatches and negativeMatches.

If you go to http://localhost:8080/application/autoconfig, you should see an autoconfiguration report similar to the one in Figure 14-4.

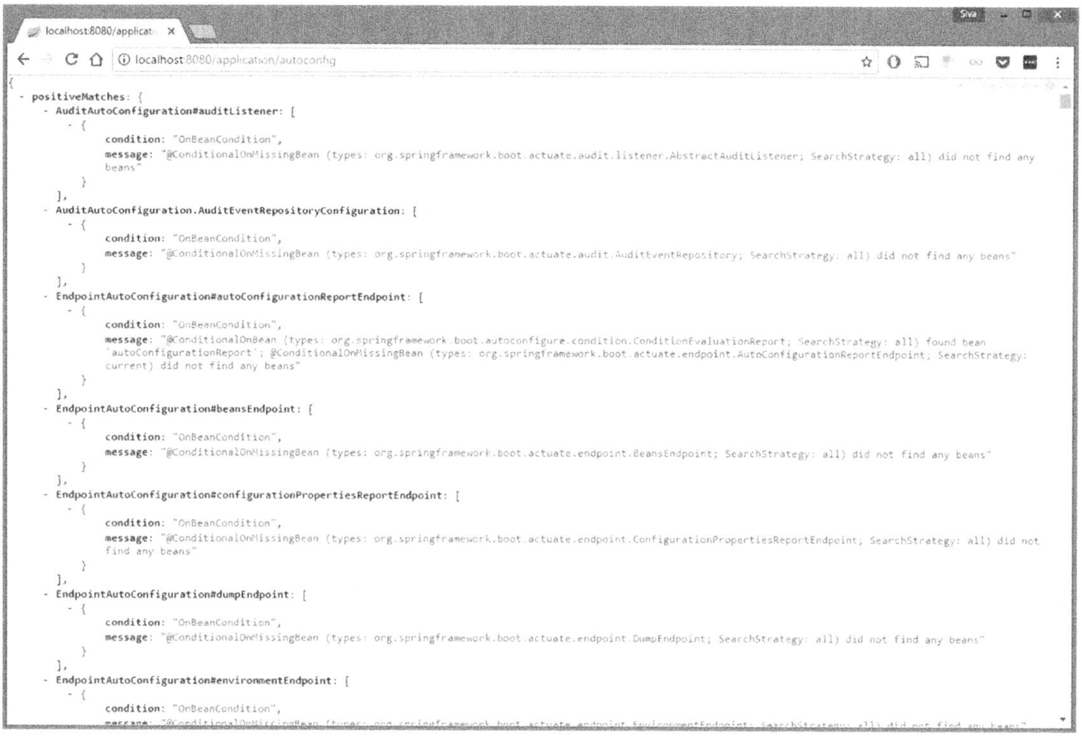

Figure 14-4. *Spring Boot Actuator /autoconfig endpoint*

The elements in positiveMatches are the conditions matched by various @Conditional components. For example:

```
DataSourceAutoConfiguration: [
    {
        condition: "OnClassCondition",
        message: "@ConditionalOnClass classes found: javax.sql.DataSource,org.
        springframework.jdbc.datasource.embedded.EmbeddedDatabaseType"
    }
]
```

Since this example added the data-jpa starter and H2 driver, the classes javax.sql.DataSource and org.springframework.jdbc.datasource.embedded.EmbeddedDatabaseType are found in the classpath and hence DataSourceAutoConfiguration becomes a positive match.

The elements in negativeMatches are the conditions not matched by various @Conditional components. For example:

```
JooqAutoConfiguration: [
    {
        condition: "OnClassCondition",
        message: "required @ConditionalOnClass classes not found: org.jooq.DSLContext"
    }
]
```

As there aren't JOOQ libraries on the application classpath, @ConditionalOnClass could not find the org.jooq.DSLContext class and hence JooqAutoConfiguration became a negative match.

The /mappings Endpoint

The /mappings endpoint shows all the @RequestMapping paths declared in the application. This is very helpful for checking which request path will be handled by which controller method.

If you go to http://localhost:8080/application/mappings, you should see all the mappings shown in Figure 14-5.

```
{
  - /webjars/**: {
        bean: "resourceHandlerMapping"
    },
  - /**: {
        bean: "resourceHandlerMapping"
    },
  - /application/docs/**: {
        bean: "resourceHandlerMapping"
    },
  - /**/favicon.ico: {
        bean: "faviconHandlerMapping"
    },
  - {[/error]}: {
        bean: "requestMappingHandlerMapping",
        method: "public org.springframework.http.ResponseEntity<java.util.Map<java.lang.String, java.lang.Object>>
        org.springframework.boot.autoconfigure.web.servlet.error.BasicErrorController.error(javax.servlet.http.HttpServletRequest)"
    },
  - {[/error],produces=[text/html]}: {
        bean: "requestMappingHandlerMapping",
        method: "public org.springframework.web.servlet.ModelAndView
        org.springframework.boot.autoconfigure.web.servlet.error.BasicErrorController.errorHtml(javax.servlet.http.HttpServletRequest,jav.
    },
  - {[/application/docs/],produces=[text/html]}: {
        bean: "endpointHandlerMapping",
        method: "public java.lang.String org.springframework.boot.actuate.endpoint.mvc.DocsMvcEndpoint.browse()"
    },
  - {[/application/docs],produces=[text/html]}: {
        bean: "endpointHandlerMapping",
        method: "public java.lang.String org.springframework.boot.actuate.endpoint.mvc.DocsMvcEndpoint.redirect()"
    },
  - {[/application/trace || /application/trace.json],methods=[GET],produces=[application/vnd.spring-boot.actuator.v2+json ||
    application/json]}: {
        bean: "endpointHandlerMapping",
```

Figure 14-5. *Spring Boot Actuator /mappings endpoint*

The /configprops Endpoint

The /configprops shows all the configuration properties defined by the @ConfigurationProperties beans, including your own configuration properties defined in the application.properties or YAML files.

If you go to http://localhost:8080/application/configprops, you should see all the configuration properties, as shown in Figure 14-6.

```
{
 - spring.jpa-org.springframework.boot.autoconfigure.orm.jpa.JpaProperties: {
       prefix: "spring.jpa",
     - properties: {
           showSql: true,
         - hibernate: {
               ddlAuto: "update",
               naming: { }
           },
           generateDdl: false,
           properties: { }
       }
   },
 - endpoints-org.springframework.boot.actuate.endpoint.EndpointProperties: {
       prefix: "endpoints",
     - properties: {
           enabled: true
       }
   },
 - docsMvcEndpoint: {
       prefix: "endpoints.docs",
     - properties: {
           path: "/docs",
         - curies: {
               enabled: false
           },
           sensitive: false,
           enabled: true
       }
   },
 - spring.transaction-org.springframework.boot.autoconfigure.transaction.TransactionProperties: {
       prefix: "spring.transaction",
       properties: { }
   },
 - management.info-org.springframework.boot.actuate.autoconfigure.InfoContributorProperties: {
       prefix: "management.info",
     - properties: {
         - git: {
               mode: "SIMPLE"
           }
```

Figure 14-6. *Spring Boot Actuator /configprops endpoint*

The /metrics Endpoint

The /metrics endpoint shows various metrics about the current application, such as how much memory it is using, how much memory is free, the size of the heap being used, the number of threads used, and so on.

If you go to http://localhost:8080/application/metrics, you should see all the configuration properties shown in Figure 14-7.

```
localhost:8080/applicati ×

←  →  C  ⌂   ⓘ localhost:8080/application/metrics                    ⊕ ☆  ...

{
    mem: 492168,
    mem.free: 249150,
    processors: 4,
    instance.uptime: 964621,
    uptime: 974961,
    systemload.average: -1,
    heap.committed: 417280,
    heap.init: 131072,
    heap.used: 168129,
    heap: 1842688,
    nonheap.committed: 77016,
    nonheap.init: 2496,
    nonheap.used: 74890,
    nonheap: 0,
    threads.peak: 29,
    threads.daemon: 23,
    threads.totalStarted: 33,
    threads: 25,
    classes: 10164,
    classes.loaded: 10164,
    classes.unloaded: 0,
    gc.ps_scavenge.count: 10,
    gc.ps_scavenge.time: 152,
    gc.ps_marksweep.count: 2,
    gc.ps_marksweep.time: 163,
    httpsessions.max: -1,
    httpsessions.active: 0,
    datasource.primary.active: 0,
    datasource.primary.usage: 0,
    gauge.response.application.autoconfig: 1399,
    gauge.response.application.configprops: 362,
    gauge.response.application.beans: 229,
    gauge.response.application.mappings: 8,
    counter.status.200.application.beans: 1,
    counter.status.200.application.autoconfig: 1,
    counter.status.200.application.configprops: 1,
    counter.status.200.application.mappings: 1
}
```

Figure 14-7. *Spring Boot Actuator /metrics endpoint*

The /env Endpoint

The /env endpoint will expose all the properties from the Spring's ConfigurableEnvironment interface, such as a list of active profiles, application properties, system environment variables, and so on.

If you go to http://localhost:8080/application/env, you should be able to see all the environment details shown in Figure 14-8.

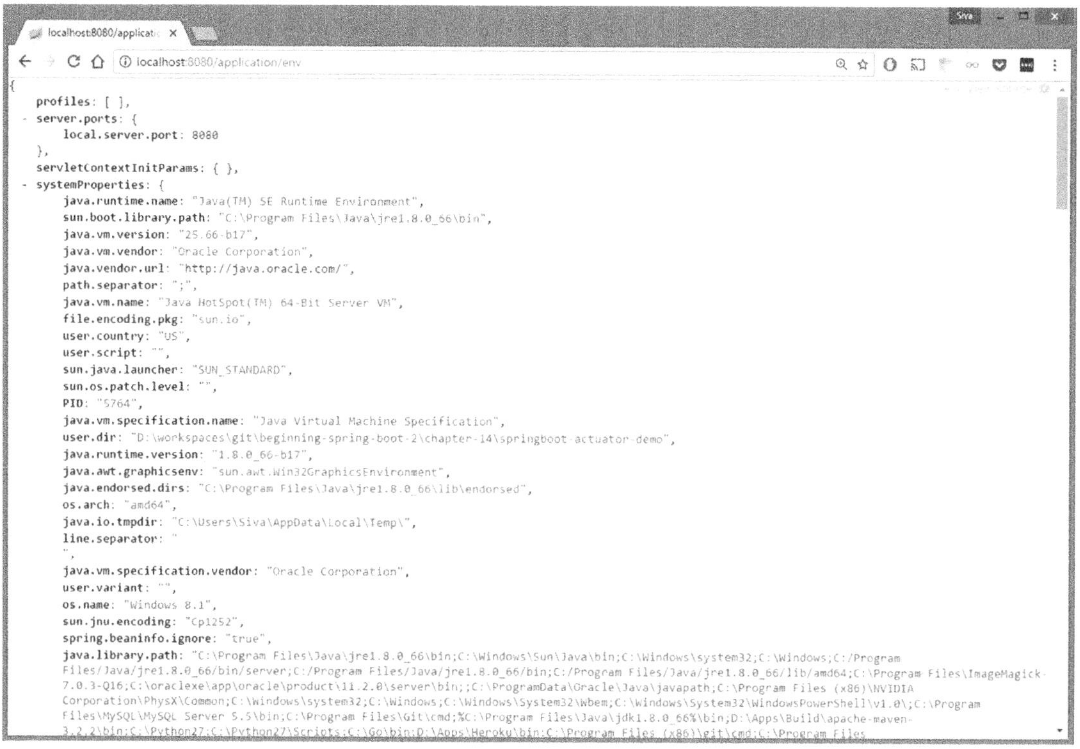

Figure 14-8. *Spring Boot Actuator /env endpoint*

The /trace Endpoint

The /trace endpoint shows the tracing information of the last few HTTP requests, which is very helpful for debugging the request/response details, like headers, cookies, etc. Go to http://localhost:8080/application/trace to view the HTTP request tracing details, as shown in Figure 14-9.

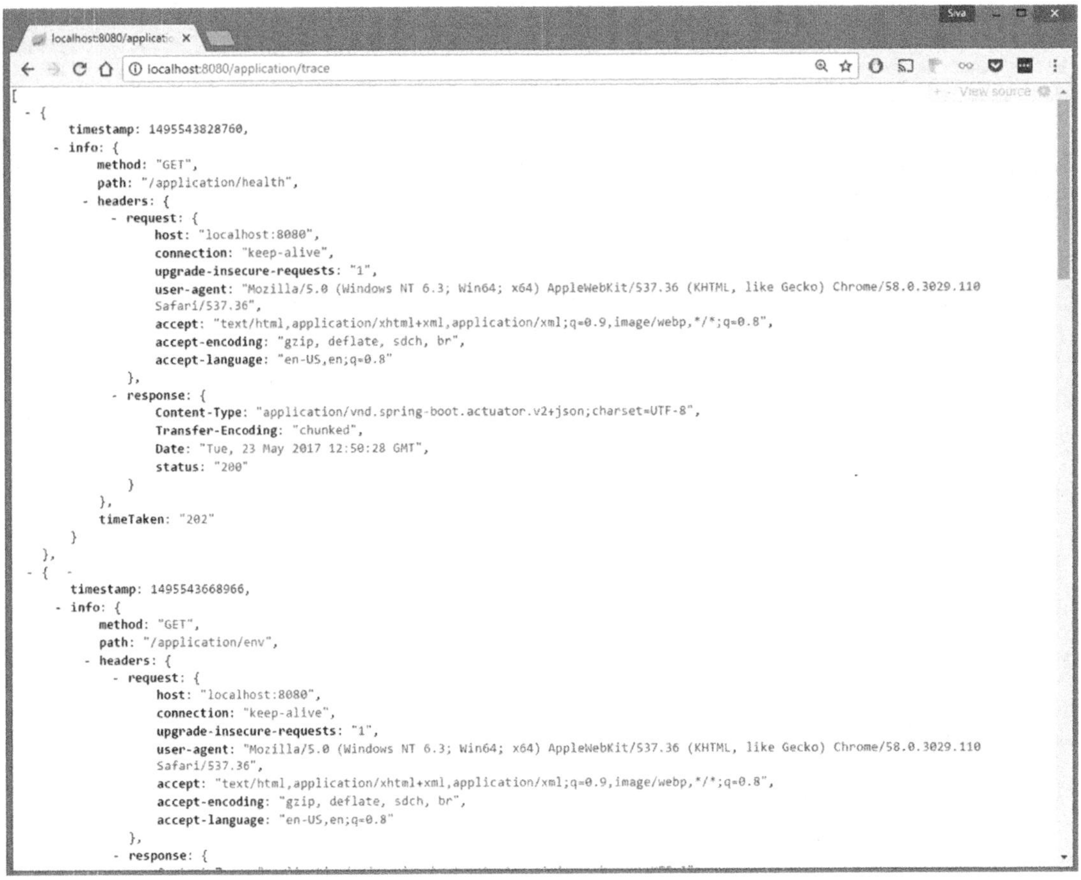
localhost:8080/applicati
localhost:8080/application/trace
View source
[
- {
timestamp: 1495543828760,
- info: {
method: "GET",
path: "/application/health",
- headers: {
- request: {
host: "localhost:8080",
connection: "keep-alive",
upgrade-insecure-requests: "1",
user-agent: "Mozilla/5.0 (Windows NT 6.3; Win64; x64) AppleWebKit/537.36 (KHTML, like Gecko) Chrome/58.0.3029.110 Safari/537.36",
accept: "text/html,application/xhtml+xml,application/xml;q=0.9,image/webp,*/*;q=0.8",
accept-encoding: "gzip, deflate, sdch, br",
accept-language: "en-US,en;q=0.8"
},
- response: {
Content-Type: "application/vnd.spring-boot.actuator.v2+json;charset=UTF-8",
Transfer-Encoding: "chunked",
Date: "Tue, 23 May 2017 12:50:28 GMT",
status: "200"
}
},
timeTaken: "202"
}
},
- {
timestamp: 1495543668966,
- info: {
method: "GET",
path: "/application/env",
- headers: {
- request: {
host: "localhost:8080",
connection: "keep-alive",
upgrade-insecure-requests: "1",
user-agent: "Mozilla/5.0 (Windows NT 6.3; Win64; x64) AppleWebKit/537.36 (KHTML, like Gecko) Chrome/58.0.3029.110 Safari/537.36",
accept: "text/html,application/xhtml+xml,application/xml;q=0.9,image/webp,*/*;q=0.8",
accept-encoding: "gzip, deflate, sdch, br",
accept-language: "en-US,en;q=0.8"
},
- response: {

Figure 14-9. *Spring Boot Actuator /trace endpoint*

The /dump Endpoint

You can view the thread dump of your application with the details of the running threads and the stack trace of the JVM at `http://localhost:8080/application/dump endpoint`. See Figure 14-10.

```
[
  - {
        threadName: "DestroyJavaVM",
        threadId: 40,
        blockedTime: -1,
        blockedCount: 0,
        waitedTime: -1,
        waitedCount: 0,
        lockName: null,
        lockOwnerId: -1,
        lockOwnerName: null,
        inNative: false,
        suspended: false,
        threadState: "RUNNABLE",
        stackTrace: [ ],
        lockedMonitors: [ ],
        lockedSynchronizers: [ ],
        lockInfo: null
  },
  - {
        threadName: "http-nio-8080-AsyncTimeout",
        threadId: 38,
        blockedTime: -1,
        blockedCount: 0,
        waitedTime: -1,
        waitedCount: 1691,
        lockName: null,
        lockOwnerId: -1,
        lockOwnerName: null,
        inNative: false,
        suspended: false,
        threadState: "TIMED_WAITING",
      - stackTrace: [
          - {
                methodName: "sleep",
                fileName: null,
                lineNumber: -2,
                className: "java.lang.Thread",
                nativeMethod: true
            },
          - {
```

Figure 14-10. *Spring Boot Actuator /dump endpoint*

The /loggers Endpoint

The /loggers endpoint allows you to view and configure the log levels of your application at runtime. You can view the logging levels of all loggers at http://localhost:8080/application/loggers, as shown in Figure 14-11.

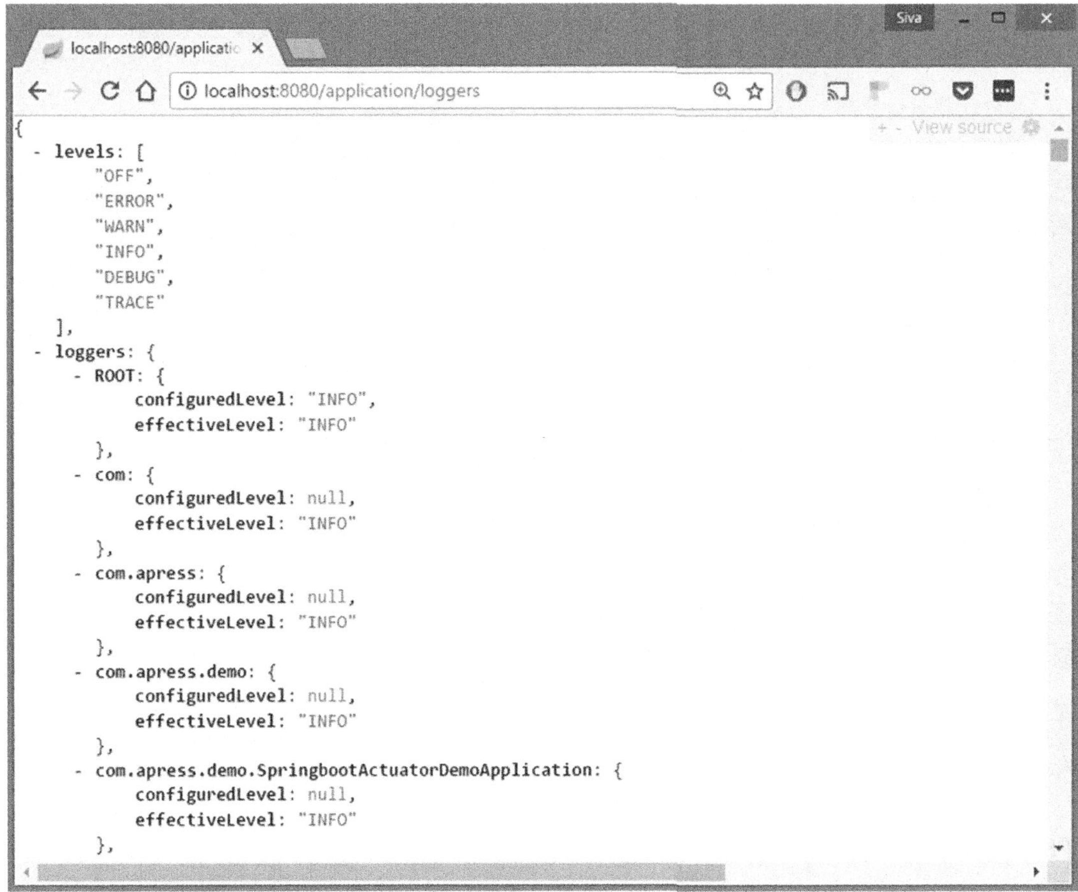

Figure 14-11. *Spring Boot Actuator /loggers endpoint*

You can view the logging level of a specific logger at `http://localhost:8080/application/{loggerName}`. For example, if you want to view the logging level of the `com.apress.demo` logger, go to `http://localhost:8080/application/loggers/com.apress.demo`.

```
{
configuredLevel: null,
effectiveLevel: "INFO"
}
```

You can update the logging level of a logger at runtime by issuing a POST request to `http://localhost:8080/application/{loggerName}`. Suppose you want to change the logging level of `com.apress.demo` to DEBUG. You can send a POST request to the `http://localhost:8080/application/loggers/com.apress.demo` URL with the following request body JSON.

```
{
    configuredLevel: "DEBUG"
}
```

```
> curl -i -X POST -H 'Content-Type: application/json' -d '{"configuredLevel": "DEBUG"}'
http://localhost:8080/application/loggers/com.apress.demo
```

Now, if you again check the logging level of the com.apress.demo logger by issuing a GET request to
http://localhost:8080/application/loggers/com.apress.demo, you will see the updated logging
configuration.

```
{
    configuredLevel: "DEBUG",
    effectiveLevel: "DEBUG"
}
```

The /logfile Endpoint

If you enabled file-based logging by setting logging.file or logging.path or using the native file
configuration files (logback.xml, log4j.properties, etc.), you can use the /logfile endpoint to view the
log file content. Go to http://localhost:8080/application/logfile, as shown in Figure 14-12.

Figure 14-12. *Spring Boot Actuator /logfile endpoint*

The /shutdown Endpoint

The /shutdown endpoint can be used to gracefully shut down the application, which is not enabled by
default. You can enable this endpoint by adding the following property to application.properties.

```
endpoints.shutdown.enabled=true
```

After adding this property, you can send the HTTP POST method to `http://localhost:8080/application/shutdown` to invoke the `/shutdown` endpoint.

Once the `/shutdown` endpoint is invoked successfully, you should see the following message:

```
{
    "message": "Shutting down, bye..."
}
```

■ **Note**   Be careful about enabling /shutting down an endpoint. Enable or shut down an endpoint only when it is absolutely required and be sure to protect the endpoint with the appropriate security configuration.

The /actuator Endpoint

The `/actuator` endpoint provides a hypermedia-based "discovery page" for the other endpoints. To activate this endpoint, you need to have the following Spring HATEOAS dependency.

```
<dependency>
    <groupId>org.springframework.hateoas</groupId>
    <artifactId>spring-hateoas</artifactId>
</dependency>
```

Go to `http://localhost:8080/application/` to see the list of actuator endpoints, as shown in Figure 14-13.

```
{
 - links: [
    - {
        rel: "self",
        href: "http://localhost:8080/application"
      },
    - {
        rel: "docs",
        href: "http://localhost:8080/application/docs"
      },
    - {
        rel: "trace",
        href: "http://localhost:8080/application/trace"
      },
    - {
        rel: "loggers",
        href: "http://localhost:8080/application/loggers"
      },
    - {
        rel: "mappings",
        href: "http://localhost:8080/application/mappings"
      },
    - {
        rel: "beans",
        href: "http://localhost:8080/application/beans"
      },
    - {
        rel: "info",
        href: "http://localhost:8080/application/info"
      },
    - {
        rel: "env",
        href: "http://localhost:8080/application/env"
      },
    - {
        rel: "health",
        href: "http://localhost:8080/application/health"
      },
    - {
        rel: "auditevents",
        href: "http://localhost:8080/application/auditevents"
      },
```

Figure 14-13. *Spring Boot Actuator /actuator endpoint*

You can customize the actuator endpoint URL by setting the `endpoints.actuator.path` property.

```
endpoints.actuator.path=/actuator
```

Now you can access the Actuator endpoint at `http://localhost:8080/application/actuator`.

Customizing Actuator Endpoints

By default, the Spring Boot Actuator endpoints run on the same port and the default management context-path is "`/application`". You can customize these properties using the following properties.

```
management.context-path=/management
management.port=9090
```

With this customization, you can access Actuator endpoints at `http://localhost:9090/management/` as the base path. The `/health` endpoint would become `http://localhost:8080/management/health`.

You can change endpoint IDs, sensitivity, and enabled values using the `endpoints.{endpointName}.*` properties.

```
endpoints.beans.id=springbeans
endpoints.beans.sensitive=false
endpoints.beans.enabled=true
```

With these customizations, you can access the `/beans` endpoint at `http://localhost:8080/application/springbeans`.

You can also selectively enable/disable an endpoint using the `endpoints.{endpoint}.enabled` property.

```
endpoints.trace.enabled=false
endpoints.shutdown.enabled=true
```

You can enable/disable all endpoints using `endpoints.enabled` property and selectively override for specific endpoints. For example, if you want to disable all endpoints except /info then configure as follows:

```
endpoints.enabled=false
endpoints.info.enabled=true
```

You can set sensitivity for all endpoints using the `endpoints.sensitive` property and selectively override for specific endpoints. For example, if you want to make all endpoints non-sensitive except for /trace, you can configure it as follows:

```
endpoints.sensitive=false
endpoints.trace.sensitive=true
```

If you don't want to expose the endpoints over HTTP, you can disable this option by adding the following property.

```
management.port=-1
```

Securing Actuator Endpoints

By default all sensitive endpoints are secured and only authenticated users who have the ACTUATOR role can access those endpoints. You can change the ACTUATOR role name to something else, say SUPERADMIN, by setting the following property.

```
management.security.roles=SUPERADMIN
```

If you have the Spring Boot Security starter on the classpath, the Actuator endpoints will be secured by Spring Security.

Add the Security starter dependency to `pom.xml`.

```
<dependency>
    <groupId>org.springframework.boot</groupId>
    <artifactId>spring-boot-starter-security</artifactId>
</dependency>
```

Instead of using the default user credentials, you can configure the security user credential in `application.properties` as follows.

```
security.user.name=admin
security.user.password=secret
security.user.role=USER,ADMIN,ACTUATOR
```

Now if you try to access any endpoint, say `http://localhost:8080/application/beans`, you will be prompted to enter credentials.

But most likely you will be using a custom Spring Security configuration backed by a datastore for user credentials, so you can configure Actuator endpoints for security as needed.

If, for any reason, you want to disable security for your Actuator endpoints, you can set the following property:

```
management.security.enabled=false
```

This will disable security for all Actuator endpoints. *You are strongly advised to secure the Actuator endpoints, especially if your application is publicly accessible.*

Implementing Custom Health Indicators

Spring Boot provides the following `HealthIndicator` implementations out-of-the-box. They are autoconfigured by default.

- `CassandraHealthIndicator`
- `DiskSpaceHealthIndicator`
- `DataSourceHealthIndicator`
- `ElasticsearchHealthIndicator`
- `JmsHealthIndicator`
- `MailHealthIndicator`
- `MongoHealthIndicator`
- `RabbitHealthIndicator`
- `RedisHealthIndicator`
- `SolrHealthIndicator`

In addition to these, you can also implement your own `HealthIndicators` based on your application health check needs.

Suppose you need to download some feed data from a remote server on a regular interval basis and there is an endpoint to invoke for checking the server reachability.

To implement a custom `HealthIndicator`, you need to register a Spring bean that implements the `HealthIndicator` interface. You can implement a `HealthIndicator` to ping the feed server, as shown in Listing 14-1.

Listing 14-1. Implementing a Custom HealthIndicator

```java
import java.util.Date;
import org.springframework.boot.actuate.health.Health;
import org.springframework.boot.actuate.health.HealthIndicator;
import org.springframework.stereotype.Component;
import org.springframework.web.client.RestClientException;
import org.springframework.web.client.RestTemplate;

@Component
public class FeedServerHealthIndicator implements HealthIndicator
{
    @Override
    public Health health() {
        RestTemplate restTemplate = new RestTemplate();
        String url = "http://feedserver.com/ping";
        try {
            String resp = restTemplate.getForObject(url, String.class);
            if("OK".equalsIgnoreCase(resp)){
                return Health.up().
                        build();
            } else {
                return Health.down()
                        .withDetail("ping_url", url)
                        .withDetail("ping_time", new Date())
                        .build();
            }
        } catch (RestClientException e) {
            return Health.down(e)
                    .withDetail("ping_url", url)
                    .withDetail("ping_time", new Date())
                    .build();
        }
    }
}
```

Now, when you go to the `http://localhost:8080/application/health` URL and the feed server is not reachable, you will see the following response:

```
{
    status: "DOWN",
    feedServer: {
        status: "DOWN",
        error: "org.springframework.web.client.HttpClientErrorException: 410 Gone",
        ping_url: "http://feedserver.com/ping",
        ping_time: 1495777475435
    },
    diskSpace: {
        status: "UP",
        total: 340650881024,
```

```
        free: 260343615488,
        threshold: 10485760
    },
    db: {
        status: "UP",
        database: "H2",
        hello: 1
    }
}
```

Having health checks for various application components and integration points will help you monitor the overall application health.

Capturing Custom Application Metrics

You have already seen how you can use Actuator's /metrics endpoint to view various application metrics, such as memory, heap, thread pool, and datasource information. In addition to that, you can also record your own metrics by using CounterService and GaugeService.

CounterService can be used to increment, decrement, and reset a named counter value. GaugeService can be used to submit a named metric value for further analysis.

Suppose you want to capture the count of successful and failed login attempts. You can use CounterService to record those metrics, as shown in Listing 14-2.

Listing 14-2. Using CounterService to Record Login Metrics

```java
import org.springframework.beans.factory.annotation.Autowired;
import org.springframework.boot.actuate.metrics.CounterService;
import org.springframework.stereotype.Service;

@Service
public class LoginService
{
    @Autowired
    private CounterService counterService;

    public boolean login(String email, String password)
    {
        if("admin@gmail.com".equalsIgnoreCase(email) && "admin".equals(password)){
            counterService.increment("counter.login.success");
            return true;
        } else {
            counterService.increment("counter.login.failure");
            return false;
        }
    }
}
```

Now if you invoke the `LoginService.login()` method with correct and incorrect credentials, you can see those metrics at `http://localhost:8080/application/metrics` endpoint.

```
{
    mem: 491423,
    mem.free: 155266,
    ....
    ....
    datasource.primary.active: 0,
    datasource.primary.usage: 0,
    gauge.response.application.health: 1679,
    gauge.response.application.metrics: 12,
    ...
    ...
    counter.login.failure: 2,
    counter.login.success: 3,
    ....
    ...
}
```

Suppose you want to capture the time needed to invoke a third-party web service. You can use GaugeService to record the time taken for this web service call. The default GaugeService implementation will store the data in-memory, but you can create an implementation to feed the data into your analytical tools. See Listing 14-3.

Listing 14-3. Using GaugeService to Record Response Times

```
import org.springframework.beans.factory.annotation.Autowired;
import org.springframework.boot.actuate.metrics.GaugeService;
import org.springframework.stereotype.Service;
import org.springframework.web.client.RestClientException;
import org.springframework.web.client.RestTemplate;
import com.apress.demo.models.GitHubUser;

@Service
public class GitHubService {

    @Autowired
    GaugeService gaugeService;

    public GitHubUser getUserInfo(String username)
    {
        RestTemplate restTemplate = new RestTemplate();
        String url = "https://api.github.com/users/"+username;
        GitHubUser gitHubUser = null;
        try {
            long start = System.currentTimeMillis();
            gitHubUser = restTemplate.getForObject(url, GitHubUser.class);
            long end = System.currentTimeMillis();
            gaugeService.submit("gauge.guthub.response-time", (end-start));
        } catch (RestClientException e) {
```

```
        e.printStackTrace();
    }
    return gitHubUser;
}
}
```

Now if you invoke the GitHubService.getUserInfo() method, the time taken for the call will be recorded using GaugeService. You can look at those metrics at the http://localhost:8080/application/metrics endpoint.

```
{
    mem: 491423,
    mem.free: 155266,
    ....
    ....
    datasource.primary.active: 0,
    datasource.primary.usage: 0,
    ...
    gauge.guthub.response-time: 126,
    ...
    ...
}
```

CORS Support for Actuator Endpoints

In order to access the Actuator endpoints from other origins, you need to enable CORS support for them. CORS support is disabled by default and you need to set the endpoints.cors.allowed-origins property to enable it.

```
endpoints.cors.allowed-origins=http://remoteserver.com
endpoints.cors.allowed-methods=GET,POST
```

You can also add other CORS properties using the endpoints.cors.* properties.

Monitoring and Management Over JMX

By default Spring Boot exposes Actuator endpoints as JMX MBeans under the org.springframework.boot domain. You can use JConsole, which comes with JDK, to view JMX MBeans.

Run JConsole from C:\\Program Files\\Java\\jdk1.8.0_45\\bin\\jconsole.exe. Select the Spring Boot application main class and click Connect. If you see a dialog box that says "Secure Connection Failed. Retry Insecurely?", click on Insecure Connection.

By default, you will be on the Overview tab. Click on the MBeans tab.

Now expand the org.springframework.boot domain, where you'll find Actuator endpoints exported as MBeans. See Figure 14-14.

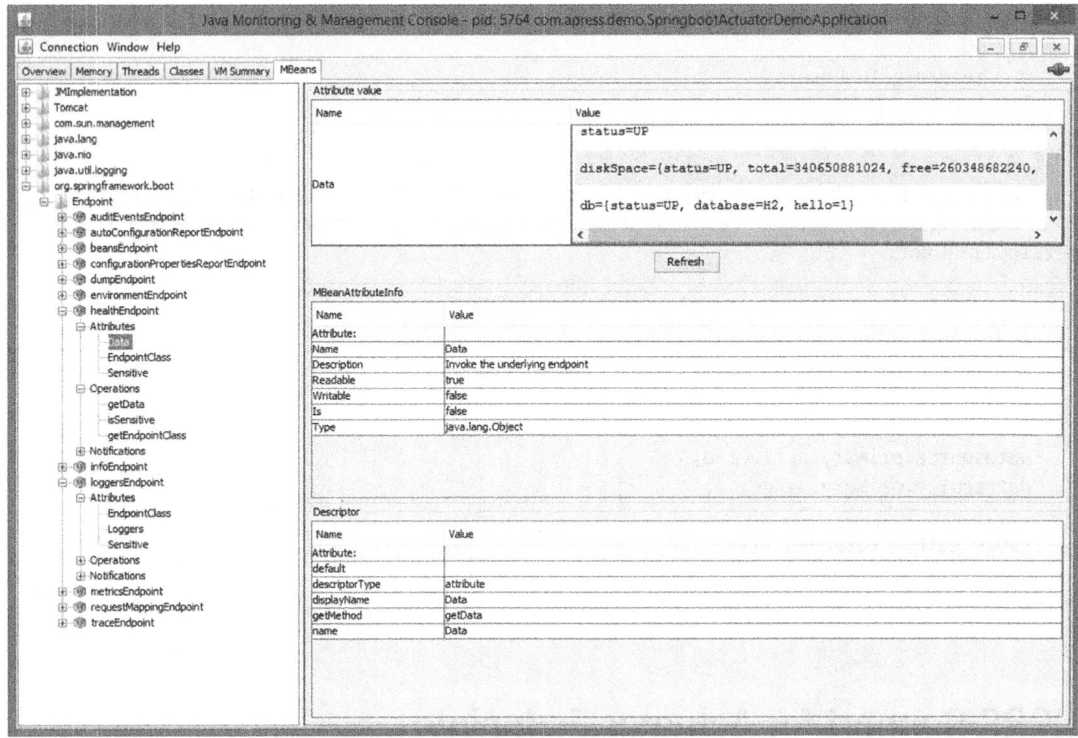

Figure 14-14. *Spring Boot Actuator JMX monitoring*

You can customize the domain name by using the `endpoints.jmx.domain` property.

```
endpoints.jmx.domain=mydomain
```

You can disable exposing endpoints over JMX by setting `endpoints.jmx.enabled=false`.

Summary

In this chapter, you explored the Spring Boot Actuator, which includes very helpful production support features. You learned about the various endpoints, including how to customize them and how to invoke them over HTTP and JMX. In the next chapter, you will learn how to test Spring Boot applications.

CHAPTER 15

Testing Spring Boot Applications

Testing is an important part of software development. It helps developers verify the correctness of the functionality. JUnit and TestNG are two of the most popular testing libraries used in Java projects.

Test Driven Development (TDD) is a popular development practice where you write tests first and write just enough production code to pass the tests. You write various types of tests, such as unit tests, integration tests, performance tests, etc. Unit tests focus on testing one component in isolation, whereas integration tests verify the behavior of a feature, which could possibly involve multiple components. While doing integration testing, you may have to mock the behavior of dependent components such as third-party web service classes, database method invocations, etc. There are mocking libraries like Mockito, PowerMock, and jMock, for mocking the object's behavior.

The dependency injection (DI) design pattern encourages programming to practice and write testable code. With dependency injection, you can inject mock implementations for testing and real implementations for production. At its core, Spring is a dependency injection container and it provides great support for testing various parts of an application.

In this chapter, you will learn how to test Spring components in Spring Boot applications. You will take a detailed look at how to test slices of applications, such as web components (regular MVC Controllers, REST API endpoints), Spring data repositories, and secured controller/service methods using the @WebMvcTest, @DataJpaTest, and the @JdbcTest annotations.

Testing Spring Boot Applications

One of the key reasons for the popularity of the Spring framework is its great support for testing. Spring provides SpringRunner, which is a custom JUnit runner helping to load the Spring ApplicationContext by using @ContextConfiguration(classes=AppConfig.class).

A typical Spring unit/integration test is shown in Listing 15-1.

Listing 15-1. Typical Spring JUnit Test

```
@RunWith(SpringRunner.class)
@ContextConfiguration(classes=AppConfig.class)
public class UserServiceTests
{
    @Autowired
    UserService userService;
```

```java
@Test
public void should_load_all_users()
{
    List<User> users = userService.getAllUsers();
    assertNotNull(users);
    assertEquals(10, users.size());
}
}
```

The Spring Boot application is also nothing but a Spring application, so you can use all of Spring's testing features in your Spring Boot applications as well.

However, some of the Spring Boot features, like loading external properties and logging, are available only if you create `ApplicationContext` using the `SpringApplication` class, which you'll typically use in your entry point class. These additional Spring Boot features won't be available if you use `@ContextConfiguration`.

```java
@SpringBootApplication
public class SpringbootTestingDemoApplication
{
    public static void main(String[] args)
    {
        SpringApplication.run(SpringbootTestingDemoApplication.class, args);
    }
}
```

Spring Boot provides the `@SpringBootTest` annotation, which uses `SpringApplication` behind the scenes to load `ApplicationContext` so that all the Spring Boot features will be available. See Listing 15-2.

Listing 15-2. Typical Spring Boot JUnit Test

```java
@RunWith(SpringRunner.class)
@SpringBootTest
public class SpringbootTestingDemoApplicationTests
{
    @Autowired
    UserService userService;

    @Test
    public void should_load_all_users()
    {
        ...
        ...
    }
}
```

For `@SpringBootTest`, you can pass Spring configuration classes, Spring bean definition XML files, and more, but in Spring Boot applications, you'll typically use the entry point class.

The Spring Boot Test starter `spring-boot-starter-test` pulls in the JUnit, Spring Test, and Spring Boot Test modules, along with the following most commonly used mocking and asserting libraries:

- Mockito—A Java mocking framework found at `http://site.mockito.org/`.

- Hamcrest—A matcher/predicates library for data assertion found at `http://hamcrest.org/JavaHamcrest/`.

- AssertJ—A fluent assertion library found at `https://joel-costigliola.github.io/assertj/`.

- JSONassert—An assertion library for JSON found at `https://github.com/skyscreamer/JSONassert`.

- JsonPath—XPath for JSON found at `https://github.com/json-path/JsonPath`.

Now you'll see how to create a simple Spring Boot web application with a simple REST endpoint.

```
<dependencies>
    <dependency>
        <groupId>org.springframework.boot</groupId>
        <artifactId>spring-boot-starter-web</artifactId>
    </dependency>
    <dependency>
        <groupId>org.springframework.boot</groupId>
        <artifactId>spring-boot-starter-test</artifactId>
        <scope>test</scope>
    </dependency>
</dependencies>
```

First create an entry point class called `Application.java`, as follows:

```
@SpringBootApplication
public class Application
{
    public static void main(String[] args)
    {
        SpringApplication.run(Application.class, args);
    }
}
```

Listing 15-3 shows how to create a simple REST endpoint called /ping.

Listing 15-3. Spring REST Controller

```
@RestController
public class PingController
{
    @GetMapping("/ping")
    public String ping()
    {
        return "OK";
    }
}
```

Now if you run the application, you can invoke the REST endpoint `http://localhost:8080/ping`, which gives the response "OK". Now you can write a test for the /ping endpoint. See Listing 15-4.

Listing 15-4. Testing Spring REST Endpoint Using TestRestTemplate

```java
import static org.assertj.core.api.Assertions.assertThat;

import org.junit.Test;
import org.junit.runner.RunWith;
import org.springframework.beans.factory.annotation.Autowired;
import org.springframework.boot.test.context.SpringBootTest;
import org.springframework.boot.test.context.SpringBootTest.WebEnvironment;
import org.springframework.boot.test.web.client.TestRestTemplate;
import org.springframework.http.HttpStatus;
import org.springframework.http.ResponseEntity;
import org.springframework.test.context.junit4.SpringRunner;

@RunWith(SpringRunner.class)
@SpringBootTest(webEnvironment=WebEnvironment.RANDOM_PORT)
public class PingControllerTests
{
    @Autowired
    TestRestTemplate restTemplate;

    @Test
    public void testPing()
    {
        ResponseEntity<String> respEntity = restTemplate.getForEntity("/ping", String.class);
        assertThat(respEntity.getStatusCode()).isEqualTo(HttpStatus.OK);
        assertThat(respEntity.getBody()).isEqualTo("OK");
    }
}
```

As you need to test the REST endpoint, you start the embedded servlet container by specifying the webEnvironment attribute of @SpringBootTest.

The default webEnvironment value is WebEnvironment.MOCK, which doesn't start an embedded servlet container.

You can use various webEnvironment values based on how you want to run the tests.

- MOCK (default)—Loads a WebApplicationContext and provides a mock servlet environment. It will not start an embedded servlet container. If servlet APIs are not on your classpath, this mode will fall back to creating a regular non-web ApplicationContext.

- RANDOM_PORT— Loads a ServletWebServerApplicationContext and starts an embedded servlet container listening on a random available port.

- DEFINED_PORT—Loads a ServletWebServerApplicationContext and starts an embedded servlet container listening on a defined port (server.port).

- NONE—Loads an ApplicationContext using SpringApplication but does not provide a servlet environment.

The TestRestTemplate bean will be registered automatically only when @SpringBootTest is started with an embedded servlet container.

While running the integration tests that start the embedded servlet containers, it is better to use WebEnvironment.RANDOM_PORT so that it won't conflict with other running applications, especially in Continuous Integration (CI) environments where multiple builds run in parallel.

You can specify which configuration classes to use to build ApplicationContext by using the classes attribute of the @SpringBootTest annotation. If you don't specify any classes explicitly, it will automatically search for nested @Configuration classes and will fall back to searching for @SpringBootConfiguration classes. The @SpringBootApplication is annotated with @SpringBootConfiguration so @SpringBootTest would pick up the application's entry point class.

Testing with Mock Implementations

While performing unit testing, you may want to mock calls to external services like database interactions and web service invocations. You can create mock implementations to be used in tests and real implementations used in production.

Say you have an EmployeeRepository file that talks to the database and gets employee data, as shown in Listing 15-5.

Listing 15-5. EmployeeRepository.java

```java
public interface EmployeeRepository
{
    List<Employee> findAllEmployees();
}
```

Suppose you have EmployeeService, which depends on EmployeeRepository, with getMaxSalariedEmployee() and a few other employee-related methods. See Listing 15-6.

Listing 15-6. EmployeeService.java

```java
@Service
public class EmployeeService
{
    private EmployeeRepository employeeRepository;

    @Autowired
    public EmployeeService(EmployeeRepository employeeRepository)
    {
      this.employeeRepository = employeeRepository;
    }

    public Employee getMaxSalariedEmployee()
    {
        Employee emp = null;
        List<Employee> emps = employeeRepository.findAllEmployees();
        //loop through emps and find max salaried emp
        return emp;
    }
}
```

Now you can create a mock `EmployeeRepository` file for testing, as shown in Listing 15-7.

Listing 15-7. MockEmployeeRepository.java

```java
@Repository
@Profile("test")
public class MockEmployeeRepository implements EmployeeRepository
{
    public List<Employee> findAllEmployees()
    {
        return Arrays.asList(
            new Employee(1, "A", 50000),
            new Employee(2, "B", 75000),
            new Employee(3, "C", 43000)
        );
    }
}
```

Now you'll create a real implementation of `EmployeeRepository` for production, as shown in Listing 15-8.

Listing 15-8. JdbcEmployeeRepository.java

```java
@Service
@Profile("production")
public class JdbcEmployeeRepository implements EmployeeRepository
{
    @Autowired
    private JdbcTemplate jdbcTemplate;

    public List<Employee> findAllEmployees()
    {
        return jdbcTemplate.query(...);
    }
}
```

You can use the `@ActiveProfiles` annotation to specify which profiles to use so that only the beans associated with those profiles will be activated. See Listing 15-9.

Listing 15-9. Testing with Mock implementation Using Profiles

```java
@ActiveProfiles("test")
@RunWith(SpringRunner.class)
@SpringBootTest
public class ApplicationTests
{
    @Autowired
    EmployeeService employeeService;

    @Test
    public void test_getMaxSalariedEmployee()
    {
        Employee emp = employeeService.getMaxSalariedEmployee();
        assertNotNull(emp);
```

```
        assertEquals(2, emp.getId());
        assertEquals("B", emp.getName());
        assertEquals(75000, emp.getSalary());
    }
}
```

As you have enabled the `test` profile, `MockEmployeeRepository` will be injected into `EmployeeService`. You can activate the `production` profile while running the application in production as follows:

```
java -jar myapp.jar -Dspring.profiles.active=production
```

While running the main application, the `production` profile will be used and `JdbcEmployeeRepository` will be injected into `EmployeeService`.

In addition to providing mock data, you may also need to simulate other behaviors, like throwing exceptions when certain methods are called. But creating mock implementations for every use case can be tedious. You can use mocking libraries to create mock objects without actually creating classes with mock behavior. The next section looks into how to unit test using the popular mocking library, Mockito.

Testing with Mockito

Mockito is a popular Java mocking framework that can be used along with JUnit. Mockito lets you write tests by mocking the external dependencies with the desired behavior.

For example, assume you are invoking some external web service. When it fails due to some communication failures, you want to retry three times before giving up. To test the retry behavior, that external web service should throw an exception that may not be in your control. You can use Mockito to simulate this behavior so that you can test the retry functionality.

Suppose you are importing user data from a third-party using a web service, as shown in Listing 15-10.

Listing 15-10. UsersImporter.java

```
@Service
public class UsersImporter
{
    public List<User> importUsers() throws UserImportServiceCommunicationFailure
    {
        List<User> users = new ArrayList<>();
        //get users by invoking some web service
        //if any exception occurs throw UserImportServiceCommunicationFailure

        //dummy data
        users.add(new User());
        users.add(new User());
        users.add(new User());

        return users;
    }
}
```

UserService uses UsersImporter to get user data and retries three times in case a UserImportService CommunicationFailure occurs. See Listing 15-11.

Listing 15-11. UsersImportService.java

```java
@Service
@Transactional
public class UsersImportService
{
    private Logger logger = LoggerFactory.getLogger(UserService.class);

    private UsersImporter usersImporter;

    @Autowired
    public UsersImportService(UsersImporter usersImporter)
    {
        this.usersImporter = usersImporter;
    }

    public UsersImportResponse importUsers()
    {
        int retryCount = 0;
        int maxRetryCount = 3;
        for (int i = 0; i < maxRetryCount; i++)
        {
            try
            {
                List<User> importUsers = usersImporter.importUsers();
                logger.info("Import Users: "+importUsers);
                break;
            } catch (UserImportServiceCommunicationFailure e)
            {
                retryCount++;
                logger.error("Error: "+e.getMessage());
            }
        }
        if(retryCount >= maxRetryCount)
            return new UsersImportResponse(retryCount, "FAILURE");
        else
            return new UsersImportResponse(0, "SUCCESS");
    }
}

public class UsersImportResponse
{
    private int retryCount;
    private String status;
    //setters & getters
}
```

This code invokes the usersImporter.importUsers() method and, if it throws UserImportService CommunicationFailure, it retries three times.

If you want to test if usersImporter.importUsers() returns the result without getting an exception, then UsersImportResponse(0, "SUCCESS") should be returned; otherwise, UsersImportResponse(3, "FAILURE") should be returned.

You can use @Mock to create a mock object and @InjectMocks to inject the dependencies with mocks. You can use @RunWith(MockitoJUnitRunner.class) to initialize the mock objects or trigger the mock object initialization using MockitoAnnotations.initMocks(this) in the JUnit @Before method. See Listing 15-12.

Listing 15-12. Testing Using Mockito Mock Objects

```
import static org.assertj.core.api.Assertions.assertThat;
import static org.mockito.BDDMockito.*;

import org.junit.Test;
import org.junit.runner.RunWith;
import org.mockito.InjectMocks;
import org.mockito.Mock;
import org.mockito.junit.MockitoJUnitRunner;

import com.apress.demo.exceptions.UserImportServiceCommunicationFailure;
import com.apress.demo.model.UsersImportResponse;

@RunWith(MockitoJUnitRunner.class)
public class UsersImportServiceMockitoTest
{
    @Mock
    private UsersImporter usersImporter;

    @InjectMocks
    private UsersImportService usersImportService;

    @Test
    public void should_retry_3times_when_UserImportServiceCommunicationFailure_occured()
    {
        given(usersImporter.importUsers()).willThrow(new UserImportServiceCommunication
        Failure());

        UsersImportResponse response = usersImportService.importUsers();

        assertThat(response.getRetryCount()).isEqualTo(3);
        assertThat(response.getStatus()).isEqualTo("FAILURE");
    }

}
```

Here you are simulating the failure condition while importing users using the web service as follows:

```
given(usersImporter.importUsers()).willThrow(new UserImportServiceCommunicationFailure());
```

So, when you call userService.importUsers() and the mock usersImporter object throws UserImportServiceCommunicationFailure, it will retry three times. Similarly, you can use Mockito to simulate any kind of behavior to meet these test cases.

Spring Boot provides the @MockBean annotation that can be used to define a new Mockito mock bean or replace a Spring bean with a mock bean and inject that into their dependent beans. Mock beans will be automatically reset after each test method. See Listing 15-13.

Listing 15-13. Testing Using Spring Boot's @MockBean Mocks

```
import static org.assertj.core.api.Assertions.assertThat;
import static org.mockito.BDDMockito.*;

import org.junit.Test;
import org.junit.runner.RunWith;
import org.springframework.beans.factory.annotation.Autowired;
import org.springframework.boot.test.context.SpringBootTest;
import org.springframework.boot.test.mock.mockito.MockBean;
import org.springframework.test.context.junit4.SpringRunner;

import com.apress.demo.exceptions.UserImportServiceCommunicationFailure;
import com.apress.demo.model.UsersImportResponse;

@RunWith(SpringRunner.class)
@SpringBootTest
public class UsersImportServiceMockitoTest
{
    @MockBean
    private UsersImporter usersImporter;

    @Autowired
    private UsersImportService usersImportService;

    @Test
    public void should_retry_3times_when_UserImportServiceCommunicationFailure_occured()
    {
        given(usersImporter.importUsers()).willThrow(new UserImportServiceCommunication
        Failure());

        UsersImportResponse response = usersImportService.importUsers();

        assertThat(response.getRetryCount()).isEqualTo(3);
        assertThat(response.getStatus()).isEqualTo("FAILURE");
    }
}
```

Here, Spring Boot will create a Mockito mock object for UsersImporter and inject it into the UsersImportService bean.

Testing Slices of Application Using @*Test Annotations

While testing various components of the application, you may want to load a subset of the Spring ApplicationContext beans, which are related to the subject under test (SUT). For example, when testing a SpringMVC controller, you may want to load only the MVC layer components and provide mock service-layer beans as dependencies.

Spring Boot provides annotations like @WebMvcTest, @DataJpaTest, @DataMongoTest, @JdbcTest, and @JsonTest to test slices of the application.

Testing SpringMVC Controllers Using @WebMvcTest

Spring Boot provides the @WebMvcTest annotation, which will autoconfigure SpringMVC infrastructure components and load only @Controller, @ControllerAdvice, @JsonComponent, Filter, WebMvcConfigurer, and HandlerMethodArgumentResolver components. Other Spring beans (annotated with @Component, @Service, @Repository, etc.) will not be scanned when using this annotation.

Now you'll see how to create a controller that adds data to the model and renders a Thymeleaf view. See Listing 15-14.

Listing 15-14. TodoController.java

```java
import org.springframework.beans.factory.annotation.Autowired;
import org.springframework.stereotype.Controller;
import org.springframework.ui.Model;
import org.springframework.web.bind.annotation.GetMapping;

import com.apress.demo.repositories.TodoRepository;

@Controller
public class TodoController
{
    @Autowired
    TodoRepository todoRepository;

    @GetMapping("/todolist")
    public String showTodos(Model model)
    {
        model.addAttribute("todos", todoRepository.findAll());
        return "todos";
    }
}
```

Listing 15-15 shows how to write a test for TodoController using @WebMvcTest.

Listing 15-15. Testing SpringMVC Controller Using MockMvc

```java
import static org.mockito.BDDMockito.*;
import static org.springframework.test.web.servlet.request.MockMvcRequestBuilders.get;
import static org.springframework.test.web.servlet.result.MockMvcResultMatchers.*;

import static org.hamcrest.Matchers.*;

import java.util.Arrays;

import org.junit.Test;
import org.junit.runner.RunWith;
import org.springframework.beans.factory.annotation.Autowired;
import org.springframework.boot.test.autoconfigure.web.servlet.WebMvcTest;
```

```java
import org.springframework.boot.test.mock.mockito.MockBean;
import org.springframework.http.MediaType;
import org.springframework.test.context.junit4.SpringRunner;
import org.springframework.test.web.servlet.MockMvc;

import com.apress.demo.entities.Todo;
import com.apress.demo.repositories.TodoRepository;

@RunWith(SpringRunner.class)
@WebMvcTest(controllers= TodoController.class)
public class TodoControllerTests
{
    @Autowired
    private MockMvc mvc;

    @MockBean
    private TodoRepository todoRepository;

    @Test
    public void testShowAllTodos() throws Exception
    {
        Todo todo1 = new Todo(1, "Todo1",false);
        Todo todo2 = new Todo(2, "Todo2",true);

        given(this.todoRepository.findAll()).willReturn(Arrays.asList(todo1, todo2));

        this.mvc.perform(get("/todolist")
            .accept(MediaType.TEXT_HTML))
                .andExpect(status().isOk())
                .andExpect(view().name("todos"))
                .andExpect(model().attribute("todos", hasSize(2)))
                ;

        verify(todoRepository, times(1)).findAll();
    }
}
```

You have annotated the test with @WebMvcTest(controllers = TodoController.class) by explicitly specifying which controller you are testing. As @WebMvcTest doesn't load other regular Spring beans and TodoController depends on TodoRepository, you provided a mock bean using the @MockBean annotation. The @WebMvcTest autoconfigures MockMvc, which can be used to test controllers without starting an actual servlet container.

In this test method, you set the expected behavior on todoRepository.findAll() to return a list of two Todo objects. Then you issue a GET request to "/todolist" and assert various things on response.

Testing SpringMVC REST Controllers Using @WebMvcTest

Similar to how you can test SpringMVC controllers, you can test REST controllers as well. You can write assertions on response data using JsonPath or JSONassert libraries.

Create a `TodoRestController`, as shown in Listing 15-16.

Listing 15-16. TodoRestController.java.

```java
import java.util.Optional;
import org.springframework.beans.factory.annotation.Autowired;
import org.springframework.web.bind.annotation.GetMapping;
import org.springframework.web.bind.annotation.PathVariable;
import org.springframework.web.bind.annotation.RestController;

import com.apress.demo.entities.Todo;
import com.apress.demo.repositories.TodoRepository;

@RestController
public class TodoRestController
{
    @Autowired
    private TodoRepository todoRepository;

    @GetMapping("/api/todos/{id}")
    public Optional<Todo> findById(@PathVariable Integer id)
    {
        return todoRepository.findById(id);
    }
}
```

You can write a test for `TodoRestController`, as shown in Listing 15-17.

Listing 15-17. Testing SpringMVC REST Controller Using MockMvc

```java
import static org.hamcrest.CoreMatchers.*;
import static org.mockito.BDDMockito.*;
import static org.springframework.test.web.servlet.request.MockMvcRequestBuilders.get;
import static org.springframework.test.web.servlet.result.MockMvcResultMatchers.jsonPath;
import static org.springframework.test.web.servlet.result.MockMvcResultMatchers.status;

import java.util.Optional;

import org.junit.Test;
import org.junit.runner.RunWith;
import org.springframework.beans.factory.annotation.Autowired;
import org.springframework.boot.test.autoconfigure.web.servlet.WebMvcTest;
import org.springframework.boot.test.mock.mockito.MockBean;
import org.springframework.http.MediaType;
import org.springframework.test.context.junit4.SpringRunner;
import org.springframework.test.web.servlet.MockMvc;

import com.apress.demo.entities.Todo;
import com.apress.demo.repositories.TodoRepository;
```

```java
@RunWith(SpringRunner.class)
@WebMvcTest(controllers= TodoRestController.class)
public class TodoRestControllerTests
{
    @Autowired
    private MockMvc mvc;

    @MockBean
    private TodoRepository todoRepository;

    @Test
    public void testFindTodoById() throws Exception
    {
        Todo todo = new Todo(1, "Todo1", false);
        given(this.todoRepository.findById(1)).willReturn(Optional.of(todo));

        this.mvc.perform(get("/api/todos/1")
                .accept(MediaType.APPLICATION_JSON))
                .andExpect(status().isOk())
                .andExpect(jsonPath("$.id", is(1)))
                .andExpect(jsonPath("$.text", is("Todo1")))
                .andExpect(jsonPath("$.done", is(false)));

        verify(todoRepository, times(1)).findById(1);
    }
}
```

You are testing the TodoRestController endpoint "/api/todos/{id}" in the same way you tested TodoController, but you are using the JSON Path assertions to verify the returned JSON response data.

Testing Secured Controller/Service Methods

In Chapter 13, you learned how to secure web applications and REST APIs and apply method-level security. Spring provides several ways to test these secured resources as well.

You'll now see how you can test secured resources.

Add the following dependencies to enable Spring Security and security testing capabilities.

```xml
<dependency>
    <groupId>org.springframework.boot</groupId>
    <artifactId>spring-boot-starter-security</artifactId>
</dependency>

<dependency>
    <groupId>org.springframework.security</groupId>
    <artifactId>spring-security-test</artifactId>
    <scope>test</scope>
</dependency>
```

When you add the Security starter without custom security configurations, MVC endpoints will be secured using HTTP basic authentication with a default user and generated password. Instead of using the default credentials, you can configure credentials in `application.properties` as follows:

```
security.user.name=admin
security.user.password=admin123
security.user.role=USER,ADMIN
```

You can use the autoconfigured `TestRestTemplate` to test REST endpoints, passing the HTTP basic auth parameters, as shown in Listing 15-18.

Listing 15-18. Testing REST Endpoint with TestRestTemplate Using HTTP Basic Authentication

```
@RunWith(SpringRunner.class)
@SpringBootTest(webEnvironment=WebEnvironment.RANDOM_PORT)
public class PingControllerTests
{
    @Autowired
    TestRestTemplate restTemplate;

    @Test
    public void testPing() throws Exception
    {
        ResponseEntity<String> respEntity =
                restTemplate.withBasicAuth("admin", "admin123")
                .getForEntity("/ping", String.class);
        assertThat(respEntity.getStatusCode()).isEqualTo(HttpStatus.OK);
        assertThat(respEntity.getBody()).isEqualTo("OK");
    }
}
```

Note that you have passed the credentials using `restTemplate.withBasicAuth("admin", "admin123")`. Also note that by using `TestRestTemplate`, you can invoke REST endpoints using relative paths like `"/ping"` instead of specifying the complete URL `http://localhost:<port>/ping`. This is very convenient when using `RANDOM_PORT`. But if you want to construct a URL yourself, you can get the `RANDOM_PORT` value using the `@LocalServerPort` as follows:

```
import org.springframework.boot.web.server.LocalServerPort;

@LocalServerPort
int port;
```

You might want to customize the default Spring Security configuration and use form-based authentication instead of HTTP basic authentication.

Now you'll see how to customize Spring Security to configure a few in-memory user details and enable method-level security, as shown in Listing 15-19.

Listing 15-19. Custom Spring Security Configuration

```
@Configuration
@EnableWebSecurity
@EnableGlobalMethodSecurity(securedEnabled = true, prePostEnabled=true)
public class WebSecurityConfig extends WebSecurityConfigurerAdapter
{
    @Autowired
    protected void configureGlobal(AuthenticationManagerBuilder auth) throws Exception
    {
        auth
        .inMemoryAuthentication()
                .withUser("user").password("password").roles("USER").and()
                .withUser("admin").password("admin123").roles("USER", "ADMIN");
    }

    @Override
    protected void configure(HttpSecurity http) throws Exception {
        http.authorizeRequests()
            .antMatchers("/api/todos/**").hasRole("USER")
            .antMatchers("/admin/**").hasRole("ADMIN")
            .antMatchers("/ping").hasAnyRole("USER","ADMIN")
            .anyRequest().authenticated()
        ;
    }
}
```

You have customized the Security configuration and the httpBasic authentication is not enabled.
So you can't use TestRestTemplate with basic auth parameters to test the secured REST endpoints. You
can use @WebMvcTest and invoke the REST endpoint using MockMvc, which allows you to pass security user
credentials.

When using @WebMvcTest, the Spring Security HTTP basic authentication will be used by default
instead of the custom Security configuration that you manually configured. You can turn off basic
authentication using the secure=false attribute of @WebMvcTest and load the security configuration using
@ContextConfiguration, as shown in Listing 15-20.

Listing 15-20. Testing REST Controllers Using a Custom Spring Security Configuration

```
@RunWith(SpringRunner.class)
@WebMvcTest(controllers= TodoRestController.class, secure=false)
@ContextConfiguration(classes={SpringbootTestingDemoApplication.class,
WebSecurityConfig.class})
public class TodoRestControllerTests
{
    @Autowired
    private MockMvc mvc;

    @MockBean
    private TodoRepository todoRepository;

    //@Test methods
}
```

Listing 15-21 shows you how to test the GET /api/todos/{id} endpoint using MockMvc.

Listing 15-21. Testing a Secured REST Endpoint Using MockMvc

```
@Test
public void testFindTodoById() throws Exception
{
    Todo todo = new Todo(1, "Todo1", false);

    given(this.todoRepository.findById(1)).willReturn(Optional.of(todo));

    this.mvc.perform(get("/api/todos/1")
            .with(user("admin").password("admin123").roles("USER","ADMIN"))
            .accept(MediaType.APPLICATION_JSON))
            .andExpect(status().isOk())
            .andExpect(jsonPath("$.id", is(1)))
            .andExpect(jsonPath("$.text", is("Todo1")))
            .andExpect(jsonPath("$.done", is(false)));

    verify(todoRepository, times(1)).findById(1);
}
```

Here you are mocking todoRepository.findById(1) method and trigger GET request using MockMvc.perform() and you are passing the security user credentials using .with(user("admin"). password("admin123").roles("USER","ADMIN")).

Listing 15-22 shows you how to test the POST /api/todos endpoint to create a new Todo.

Listing 15-22. Testing a Secured REST Endpoint with a CSRF Token Using MockMvc

```
@Autowired
private ObjectMapper objectMapper;

@Test
public void testCreateTodo() throws Exception
{
    Todo todo = new Todo(null, "New Todo1", false);
    String content = objectMapper.writeValueAsString(todo);

    given(this.todoRepository.save(any(Todo.class))).willReturn(todo);

    this.mvc.perform(post("/api/todos")
            .contentType(MediaType.APPLICATION_JSON_VALUE)
            .content(content)
            .with(csrf())
            .with(user("admin").password("admin123").roles("USER","ADMIN"))
            .accept(MediaType.APPLICATION_JSON_VALUE))
            .andExpect(status().isOk())
            .andExpect(MockMvcResultMatchers.content().json(content))
            .andReturn()
            ;
    verify(todoRepository, times(1)).save(any(Todo.class));
}
```

It is similar to the previous test method, but you are performing a POST request using `MockMvc.perform()` and you are setting the CSRF token using `with(csrf())`. As it is a POST request and CSRF is enabled, you should send the CSRF token; otherwise, it will throw `AccessDeniedException` with the HTTP status code 403.

In addition to using the `configure(HttpSecurity http)` method to configure security constraints, you can also use the `@Secured` or `@PreAuthorize` annotations to secure REST endpoints. See Listing 15-23.

Listing 15-23. AdminRestController with Secured Methods Using Annotations

```java
@RestController
public class AdminRestController
{
    @Autowired
    private UserService userService;

    @Secured("ROLE_ADMIN")
    @DeleteMapping("/admin/users/{id}")
    public void deleteUser(@PathVariable("id") Integer userId)
    {
        userService.deleteUser(userId);
    }
}
```

The REST endpoint `DELETE /admin/users/{id}` can be accessed by the users with the `ADMIN` role. You can test the REST endpoints secured by the `@Secured` or `@PreAuthorize` annotations in the same way using `MockMvc`, as shown in Listing 15-24.

Listing 15-24. Testing REST Endpoints Secured with the @Secured Annotation Using MockMvc

```java
@RunWith(SpringRunner.class)
@WebMvcTest(controllers= AdminRestController.class, secure=false)
@ContextConfiguration(classes={SpringbootTestingDemoApplication.class,
WebSecurityConfig.class})
public class AdminRestControllerTests
{
    @Autowired
    private MockMvc mvc;

    @MockBean
    private UserService userService;

    @Test
    public void testAdminDeleteUser() throws Exception
    {
        Mockito.doNothing()
            .when(userService)
            .deleteUser(Mockito.any(Integer.class));

        this.mvc.perform(delete("/admin/users/2")
                .with(csrf())
                .with(user("admin").password("admin123").roles("ADMIN"))
```

```
                .accept(MediaType.APPLICATION_JSON))
                .andExpect(status().isOk());

        verify(userService, times(1)).deleteUser(2);
    }
}
```

In addition to securing the web layer, you can also secure any Spring components by using method-level security and annotating the methods with @Secured or @PreAuthorize. You can also annotate these annotations at the class level, which applies the security configuration for all the methods in that class.

Listing 15-25 shows you how to secure the UserService methods using @Secured and @PreAuthorize.

Listing 15-25. UserService.java with Method-Level Security

```
@Service
@Transactional
public class UserService
{
    private UserRepository userRepository;

    @Autowired
    public UserService(UserRepository repo)
    {
        this.userRepository = repo;
    }

    public Optional<User> findUserById(Integer userId)
    {
        return userRepository.findById(userId);
    }

    @Secured("ROLE_USER")
    public void createUser(User user)
    {
        userRepository.save(user);
    }

    @PreAuthorize("isAuthenticated()")
    public void updateUser(User user)
    {
        userRepository.save(user);
    }

    @Secured("ROLE_ADMIN")
    public void deleteUser(Integer userId)
    {
        userRepository.delete(userId);
    }
}
```

In UserService, you have configured the deleteUser() method to be accessible for ADMIN users only, the createUser() method to be accessible for users with the USER only, and the updateUser() method to be accessed by any authenticated user.

Approach One

You can use the JUnit @Before method to initialize Spring Security user authentication and the @After method to clear SecurityContextHolder. See Listing 15-26.

Listing 15-26. Testing Secured Methods Using AuthenticationManager

```
@RunWith(SpringRunner.class)
@SpringBootTest(webEnvironment=WebEnvironment.RANDOM_PORT)
public class SpringbootTestingDemoApplicationTests
{
    @Autowired
    private UserService userService;

    @Autowired
    private ApplicationContext context;

    private Authentication authentication;

    @Before
    public void init() {
        AuthenticationManager authenticationManager =
                this.context.getBean(AuthenticationManager.class);
        this.authentication = authenticationManager.authenticate(
            new UsernamePasswordAuthenticationToken("admin", "admin123"));
    }

    @After
    public void close() {
        SecurityContextHolder.clearContext();
    }

    @Test(expected = AuthenticationCredentialsNotFoundException.class)
    public void deleteUserUnauthenticated() {
        userService.deleteUser(3);
    }

    @Test
    public void deleteUserAuthenticated() {
        SecurityContextHolder.getContext().setAuthentication(this.authentication);
        userService.deleteUser(3);
    }
}
```

Here, you are invoking the deleteUserUnauthenticated() test method without authentication. That means that userService.deleteUser() will throw AuthenticationCredentialsNotFoundException. But in the deleteUserAuthenticated() test case, you are setting user authentication with valid user credentials to the ADMIN role, so it will allow you to invoke the userService.deleteUser() method.

Approach Two

Spring Security 4.0 introduced the @WithMockUser annotation, which allows you to test secured resources even more easily. The @WithMockUser will by default initialize user authentication with the username set to user, the password set to password, and the role set to ROLE_USER.

```
@Test
@WithMockUser
public void createUserWithMockUser() {
    User user = new User();
    user.setName("Yosin");
    user.setEmail("yosin@gmail.com");
    user.setPassword("yosin123");

    userService.createUser(user);
}
```

As userService.createUser() is allowed to be called by users with the ROLE_USER role, you can simply add @WithMockUser to run the createUserWithMockUser() test case.

You can also explicitly provide username, password, and roles to @WithMockUser, as follows.

```
@Test
@WithMockUser(username="admin", password="admin123", roles={"USER","ADMIN"})
public void deleteUserAuthenticatedWithMockUser() {
    userService.deleteUser(2);
}
```

Approach Three

In real applications, you may have used custom UserDetailsService and a custom implementation of UserDetails. In these cases, you can use @WithUserDetails to initialize user authentication loaded by using a custom UserDetailsService.

```
@Test
@WithUserDetails
public void createUserWithUserDetails()
{
    ...
}
```

You can also pass a specific username as @WithUserDetails("admin"), which initializes the user authentication with the admin user details loaded by using custom UserDetailsService.

For more details on Spring Security testing, visit the reference documentation at http://docs.spring.io/spring-security/site/docs/current/reference/htmlsingle/#test.

Testing Persistence Layer Components Using @DataJpaTest and @JdbcTest

You might want to test the persistence layer components of your application, which doesn't require loading of many components like controllers, security configuration, and so on. Spring Boot provides the @DataJpaTest and @JdbcTest annotations to test the Spring beans, which talk to relational databases.

Spring Boot provides the @DataJpaTest annotation to test the persistence layer components that will autoconfigure in-memory embedded databases and scan for @Entity classes and Spring Data JPA repositories. The @DataJpaTest annotation doesn't load other Spring beans (@Components, @Controller, @Service, and annotated beans) into ApplicationContext.

Now you'll see how to test the Spring Data JPA repositories in a Spring Boot application. Create a Spring Boot Maven project with the Data-JPA and Test starters.

```xml
<dependencies>
    <dependency>
        <groupId>org.springframework.boot</groupId>
        <artifactId>spring-boot-starter-data-jpa</artifactId>
    </dependency>
    <dependency>
        <groupId>com.h2database</groupId>
        <artifactId>h2</artifactId>
    </dependency>
    <dependency>
        <groupId>org.springframework.boot</groupId>
        <artifactId>spring-boot-starter-test</artifactId>
        <scope>test</scope>
    </dependency>
</dependencies>
```

Create a JPA entity called User and a Spring Data JPA repository called UserRepository, as shown in Listing 15-27.

Listing 15-27. JPA Entity User.java and Data JPA Repository UserRepository.java

```java
@Entity
@Table(name="users")
public class User
{
    @Id @GeneratedValue(strategy=GenerationType.AUTO)
    private Integer id;

    @Column(nullable=false)
    private String name;

    @Column(nullable=false, unique=true)
    private String email;

    @Column(nullable=false)
    private String password;

    //setters & getters
}

public interface UserRepository extends JpaRepository<User, Integer>
{
    User findByEmail(String email);
}
```

You can initialize the USERS table with some static data using src/main/resources/data.sql. See Listing 15-28.

Listing 15-28. src/main/resources/data.sql

```
insert into users(id, email, password, name) values
(1, 'admin@gmail.com','admin','Admin'),
(2, 'siva@gmail.com','siva','Siva'),
(3, 'test@gmail.com','test','Test');
```

Now you can test UserRepository using the @DataJpaTest annotation, as shown in Listing 15-29.

Listing 15-29. Testing Spring Data JPA Repositories Using @DataJpaTest

```
@RunWith(SpringRunner.class)
@DataJpaTest
public class UserRepositoryTests
{
    @Autowired
    private UserRepository userRepository;

    @Test
    public void testFindByEmail() {
        User user = userRepository.findByEmail("admin@gmail.com");
        assertNotNull(user);
        assertEquals(1, user.getId());
        assertEquals("admin", user.getName());
    }
}
```

When you run UserRepositoryTests, Spring Boot will autoconfigure the H2 in-memory embedded database (as you have the H2 database driver in the classpath) and run the tests.

If you want to run the tests against the actual registered database, you can annotate the test with @AutoConfigureTestDatabase(replace=Replace.NONE), which will use the registered DataSource instead of an in-memory datasource. You can use Replace.AUTO_CONFIGURED to replace autoconfigured DataSource and use Replace.ANY (the default) to replace any datasource bean that's autoconfigured or explicitly defined.

The @DataJpaTest tests are transactional and rolled back at the end of each test by default. You can disable this default rollback behavior for a single test or for an entire test class by annotating with @Transactional(propagation = Propagation.NOT_SUPPORTED). See Listing 15-30.

Listing 15-30. @DataJpaTest with Custom Transactional Behavior

```
@RunWith(SpringRunner.class)
@DataJpaTest
public class UserRepositoryTests
{
    @Autowired
    private UserRepository userRepository;

    @Test
    @Transactional(propagation = Propagation.NOT_SUPPORTED)
```

```
    public void testCreateUser() {
        User user = new User(null, "john@gmail.com", "john", "John");
        userRepository.save(user);
        //assertions
    }

    @Test
    public void testUpdateUser() {
        User user = userRepository.findByEmail("admin@gmail.com");
        user.setName("Administrator")
        userRepository.save(user);
        //assertions
    }
}
```

When the testCreateUser() test method runs, the changes will not be rolled back, whereas the database changes made in testUpdateUser() will be automatically rolled back.

The @DataJpaTest annotation also autoconfigures TestEntityManager, which is an alternative to the JPA EntityManager to be used in JPA tests. See Listing 15-31.

Listing 15-31. @DataJpaTest Using TestEntityManager

```
@RunWith(SpringRunner.class)
@DataJpaTest
public class UserRepositoryTests
{

    @Autowired
    private UserRepository userRepository;

    @Autowired
    private TestEntityManager entityManager;

    @Test
    public void testFindByEmail() {
        User user = new User(null, "john@gmail.com", "john", "John");
        Integer id = entityManager.persistAndGetId(user, Integer.class);

        User john = userRepository.findByEmail("john@gmail.com");
        assertNotNull(john);
        assertEquals(id, john.getId());
        assertEquals("john", user.getName());
    }
}
```

The TestEntityManager provides some convenient methods—like persistAndGetId(), persistAndFlush(), and persistFlushFind()—which are useful in tests.

Similar to the @DataJpaTest annotation, you can use @JdbcTest to test plain JDBC-related methods using JdbcTemplate. The @JdbcTest annotation also autoconfigures in-memory embedded databases and runs the tests in a transactional manner.

Now you'll create a JdbcUserRepository to perform database operations using JdbcTemplate. See Listing 15-32.

Listing 15-32. JdbcUserRepository.java

```
public class JdbcUserRepository
{
   private JdbcTemplate jdbcTemplate;

   public JdbcUserRepository(JdbcTemplate jdbcTemplate) {
    this.jdbcTemplate = jdbcTemplate;
   }

   public List<User> findAll() {
      ....
      ....
   }
}
```

Listing 15-33 shows you how to test JdbcUserRepository methods using @JdbcTest.

Listing 15-33. Testing JDBC Operations Using @JdbcTest

```
@RunWith(SpringRunner.class)
@JdbcTest
public class JdbcUserRepositoryTests
{
    @Autowired
    private JdbcTemplate jdbcTemplate;

    private JdbcUserRepository userRepository;

    @Before
    public void init()
    {
        userRepository = new JdbcUserRepository(jdbcTemplate);

        jdbcTemplate.execute("create table people(id int, name varchar(100))");
        jdbcTemplate.execute("insert into people(id, name) values(1, 'John')");
        jdbcTemplate.execute("insert into people(id, name) values(2, 'Remo')");
        jdbcTemplate.execute("insert into people(id, name) values(3, 'Dale')");
    }

  @Test
  public void testFindAllUsers() throws Exception
  {
     List<User> users = userRepository.findAll();
     assertThat(users.size()).isEqualTo(3);
  }
}
```

As @jdbcTest will not load any regular @Component Spring beans, this example manually creates the JdbcUserRepository instance by using the autoconfigured JdbcTemplate bean.

Similar to @DataJpaTest and @jdbcTest, Spring Boot provides other annotations like @DataMongoTest, @DataNeo4jTest, @JooqTest, @JsonTest, and @DataLdapTest to test slices of application.

Summary

In this chapter, you learned about various techniques that test Spring Boot applications. You looked at testing controllers, REST API endpoints, and service-layer methods. You also learned how to test secured methods and REST endpoints using the Spring Security test module. In the next chapter, you will look at how to create your own Spring Boot Starter.

CHAPTER 16

Creating a Custom Spring Boot Starter

The main purpose of Spring Boot is to increase developer productivity by taking an opinionated view of the application and autoconfiguring the Spring `ApplicationContext`. Spring Boot provides starters for a wide range of commonly used frameworks and libraries. Spring Boot's autoconfiguration mechanism takes care of configuring Spring Beans on your behalf based on various criteria.

In addition to the Spring Boot Starters that come out-of-the-box, you can also create your own starter modules. You may have some reusable modules developed in your organization that are used in many applications. You can create your own custom Spring Boot Starter to utilize those reusable modules in a much simpler way in Spring Boot applications.

This chapter looks into how to create a custom Spring Boot Starter. To demonstrate it, you are going to create `twitter4j-spring-boot-starter`, which will autoconfigure Twitter4j, which is a Java library that interacts with the Twitter API.

Introducing Twitter4j

Twitter4j provides Java bindings for the Twitter REST API. In order to use Twitter4j, you need to add the following Maven dependency.

```
<dependency>
        <groupId>org.twitter4j</groupId>
        <artifactId>twitter4j-core</artifactId>
        <version>4.0.4</version>
</dependency>
```

© K. Siva Prasad Reddy 2017

K. S. Prasad Reddy, *Beginning Spring Boot 2*, DOI 10.1007/978-1-4842-2931-6_16

The Twitter4j API main entry point is the `Twitter` class and you can create an instance of Twitter, as shown in Listing 16-1.

Listing 16-1. Using the Twitter4j API

```
ConfigurationBuilder cb = new ConfigurationBuilder();
cb.setDebugEnabled(true)
  .setOAuthConsumerKey("your-consumer-key-here")
  .setOAuthConsumerSecret("your-consumer-secret-here")
  .setOAuthAccessToken("your-access-token-here")
  .setOAuthAccessTokenSecret("your-access-token-secret-here");

TwitterFactory tf = new TwitterFactory(cb.build());
Twitter twitter = tf.getInstance();
```

Now you can use `Twitter` instance to get the latest tweets, as follows:

```
List<Status> statuses = twitter.getHomeTimeline();
for (Status status : statuses)
{
    System.out.println(status.getUser().getName() + ":" + status.getText());
}
```

You are going to create a Spring Boot Starter for Twitter4j so that you can autowire `Twitter` instances without having to explicitly register them.

Custom Spring Boot Starter

In Chapter 3, you learned how Spring Boot autoconfiguration works by using the `@Conditional` feature.

Spring Boot Starter is typically aimed at autoconfiguring some library or framework based on the presence of a class or a configuration property or depends on whether a bean of a particular type is already registered or not.

Creating a custom Spring Boot Starter generally involves:

- Creating an autoconfigure module that autoconfigures Spring Beans based on some criteria

- Creating a starter module that provides a dependency to the autoconfigure module along with the dependent libraries

So, you are going to create:

- The `twitter4j-spring-boot-autoconfigure` module, which contains Twitter4j autoconfiguration bean definitions.

- The `twitter4j-spring-boot-starter` module, which pulls in the `twitter4j-spring-boot-autoconfigure` and `twitter4j-core` dependencies.

After creating the custom Twitter4j starter, you will build a Spring Boot application using `twitter4j-spring-boot-starter`.

Create the twitter4j-spring-boot-autoconfigure Module

Now you will create a module called `twitter4j-spring-boot-autoconfigure` and add the Maven dependencies such as `spring-boot-autoconfigure`, `twitter4j-core`, and `spring-boot-starter-test`. See Listing 16-2.

Listing 16-2. twitter4j-spring-boot-autoconfigure/pom.xml

```xml
<?xml version="1.0" encoding="UTF-8"?>
<project xmlns="http://maven.apache.org/POM/4.0.0"
    xmlns:xsi="http://www.w3.org/2001/XMLSchema-instance"
    xsi:schemaLocation="http://maven.apache.org/POM/4.0.0
                        http://maven.apache.org/maven-v4_0_0.xsd">
    <modelVersion>4.0.0</modelVersion>

    <groupId>com.apress</groupId>
    <artifactId>twitter4j-spring-boot-autoconfigure</artifactId>
    <packaging>jar</packaging>
    <version>1.0-SNAPSHOT</version>

    <properties>
        <project.build.sourceEncoding>UTF-8</project.build.sourceEncoding>
        <maven.compiler.source>1.8</maven.compiler.source>
        <maven.compiler.target>1.8</maven.compiler.target>
        <twitter4j.version>4.0.4</twitter4j.version>
        <spring-boot.version>2.0.0.BUILD-SNAPSHOT</spring-boot.version>
    </properties>

    <dependencyManagement>
        <dependencies>
            <dependency>
                <groupId>org.springframework.boot</groupId>
                <artifactId>spring-boot-dependencies</artifactId>
                <version>${spring-boot.version}</version>
                <type>pom</type>
                <scope>import</scope>
            </dependency>
        </dependencies>
    </dependencyManagement>

    <dependencies>
        <dependency>
            <groupId>org.springframework.boot</groupId>
            <artifactId>spring-boot-autoconfigure</artifactId>
        </dependency>
        <dependency>
            <groupId>org.springframework.boot</groupId>
            <artifactId>spring-boot-configuration-processor</artifactId>
            <optional>true</optional>
        </dependency>
```

```xml
        <dependency>
        <groupId>org.springframework.boot</groupId>
        <artifactId>spring-boot-starter-test</artifactId>
        <scope>test</scope>
        </dependency>
        <dependency>
            <groupId>org.twitter4j</groupId>
            <artifactId>twitter4j-core</artifactId>
            <version>${twitter4j.version}</version>
            <optional>true</optional>
        </dependency>
    </dependencies>

</project>
```

Note that this example specifies twitter4j-core as an optional dependency because twitter4j-core should be added to the project only when twitter4j-spring-boot-starter is added to the project.

Twitter4j Properties to Hold the Twitter4j Config Parameters

Now you'll create Twitter4jProperties.java to bind the Twitter4j OAuth config parameters that start with twitter4j.* using @ConfigurationProperties. See Listing 16-3.

Listing 16-3. Twitter4jProperties.java

```java
package com.apress.spring.boot.autoconfigure;

import org.springframework.boot.context.properties.ConfigurationProperties;

@ConfigurationProperties(prefix= Twitter4jProperties.TWITTER4J_PREFIX)
public class Twitter4jProperties
{

    public static final String TWITTER4J_PREFIX = "twitter4j";

    private Boolean debug = false;

    private OAuth oauth = new OAuth();

    public Boolean getDebug() {
        return debug;
    }

    public void setDebug(Boolean debug) {
        this.debug = debug;
    }

    public OAuth getOauth() {
        return oauth;
    }
```

```java
    public static class OAuth {

        private String consumerKey;
        private String consumerSecret;
        private String accessToken;
        private String accessTokenSecret;

        public String getConsumerKey() {
            return consumerKey;
        }
        public void setConsumerKey(String consumerKey) {
            this.consumerKey = consumerKey;
        }
        public String getConsumerSecret() {
            return consumerSecret;
        }
        public void setConsumerSecret(String consumerSecret) {
            this.consumerSecret = consumerSecret;
        }
        public String getAccessToken() {
            return accessToken;
        }
        public void setAccessToken(String accessToken) {
            this.accessToken = accessToken;
        }
        public String getAccessTokenSecret() {
            return accessTokenSecret;
        }
        public void setAccessTokenSecret(String accessTokenSecret) {
            this.accessTokenSecret = accessTokenSecret;
        }

    }
}
```

The @ConfigurationProperties annotation allows you to bind a set of properties with a common prefix to Java bean properties. With this configuration object, you can configure the Twitter4j properties in application.properties, as shown in Listing 16-4.

Listing 16-4. application.properties

```
twitter4j.debug=true
twitter4j.oauth.consumer-key=your-consumer-key-here
twitter4j.oauth.consumer-secret=your-consumer-secret-here
twitter4j.oauth.access-token=your-access-token-here
twitter4j.oauth.access-token-secret=your-access-token-secret-here
```

Twitter4j Autoconfiguration to Autoconfigure Twitter4j

Now you create an autoconfiguration class called `Twitter4jAutoConfiguration`, which contains the bean definitions that will be automatically configured based on some criteria.

What is that criteria?

- If `twitter4j.TwitterFactory.class` is on the classpath

- If the `TwitterFactory` bean is not already defined explicitly

So, you are going to autoconfigure `TwitterFactory` and the Twitter beans if there is a `TwitterFactory` class in the classpath and if the `TwitterFactory` bean is not already registered.

Create the `Twitter4jAutoConfiguration` class, as shown in Listing 16-5.

Listing 16-5. Twitter4jAutoConfiguration.java

```java
package com.apress.spring.boot.autoconfigure;

import org.apache.commons.logging.Log;
import org.apache.commons.logging.LogFactory;
import org.springframework.beans.factory.annotation.Autowired;
import org.springframework.boot.autoconfigure.condition.ConditionalOnClass;
import org.springframework.boot.autoconfigure.condition.ConditionalOnMissingBean;
import org.springframework.boot.context.properties.EnableConfigurationProperties;
import org.springframework.context.annotation.Bean;
import org.springframework.context.annotation.Configuration;

import twitter4j.Twitter;
import twitter4j.TwitterFactory;
import twitter4j.conf.ConfigurationBuilder;

@Configuration
@ConditionalOnClass({ TwitterFactory.class })
@EnableConfigurationProperties(Twitter4jProperties.class)
public class Twitter4jAutoConfiguration {

    private static Log log = LogFactory.getLog(Twitter4jAutoConfiguration.class);

    @Autowired
    private Twitter4jProperties properties;

    @Bean
    @ConditionalOnMissingBean
    public TwitterFactory twitterFactory(){

        if (this.properties.getOauth().getConsumerKey() == null
            || this.properties.getOauth().getConsumerSecret() == null
            || this.properties.getOauth().getAccessToken() == null
            || this.properties.getOauth().getAccessTokenSecret() == null)
        {
            log.error("Twitter4j properties not configured properly. Please check
            twitter4j.* properties settings in configuration file.");
```

```
        throw new RuntimeException("Twitter4j properties not configured properly.
        Please check twitter4j.* properties settings in configuration file.");
    }

    ConfigurationBuilder cb = new ConfigurationBuilder();
    cb.setDebugEnabled(properties.getDebug())
      .setOAuthConsumerKey(properties.getOauth().getConsumerKey())
      .setOAuthConsumerSecret(properties.getOauth().getConsumerSecret())
      .setOAuthAccessToken(properties.getOauth().getAccessToken())
      .setOAuthAccessTokenSecret(properties.getOauth().getAccessTokenSecret());
    TwitterFactory tf = new TwitterFactory(cb.build());
    return tf;
    }

    @Bean
    @ConditionalOnMissingBean
    public Twitter twitter(TwitterFactory twitterFactory){
        return twitterFactory.getInstance();
    }

}
```

This example uses `@ConditionalOnClass({ TwitterFactory.class})` to specify that this autoconfiguration should take place only when the `TwitterFactory.class` class is present.

It also uses `@ConditionalOnMissingBean` on bean definition methods to consider this bean definition only if the `TwitterFactory` bean is not already defined explicitly.

Also note that the example annotated with `@EnableConfigurationProperties(Twitter4jProperties.class)` to enable support for `ConfigurationProperties` and injected the `Twitter4jProperties` bean.

Now you need to configure the custom `Twitter4jAutoConfiguration` in the `src/main/resources/METAINF/spring.factories` file as follows:

```
org.springframework.boot.autoconfigure.EnableAutoConfiguration=\ com.apress.spring.boot.
autoconfigure.Twitter4jAutoConfiguration
```

Next you are going to create the starter module called `twitter4j-spring-boot-starter`.

Create the twitter4j-spring-boot-starter Module

Now you'll create a module called `twitter4j-spring-boot-starter` and configure its dependencies, as shown in Listing 16-6.

Listing 16-6. twitter4j-spring-boot-starter/pom.xml

```xml
<?xml version="1.0" encoding="UTF-8"?>
<project xmlns="http://maven.apache.org/POM/4.0.0"
    xmlns:xsi="http://www.w3.org/2001/XMLSchema-instance"
    xsi:schemaLocation="http://maven.apache.org/POM/4.0.0
                        http://maven.apache.org/maven-v4_0_0.xsd">
    <modelVersion>4.0.0</modelVersion>
```

```xml
<groupId>com.apress</groupId>
<artifactId>twitter4j-spring-boot-starter</artifactId>
<packaging>jar</packaging>
<version>1.0-SNAPSHOT</version>

<properties>
    <project.build.sourceEncoding>UTF-8</project.build.sourceEncoding>
    <maven.compiler.source>1.8</maven.compiler.source>
    <maven.compiler.target>1.8</maven.compiler.target>
    <spring-boot.version>2.0.0.BUILD-SNAPSHOT</spring-boot.version>
    <twitter4j.version>4.0.4</twitter4j.version>
</properties>

<dependencyManagement>
    <dependencies>
        <dependency>
            <groupId>org.springframework.boot</groupId>
            <artifactId>spring-boot-dependencies</artifactId>
            <version>${spring-boot.version}</version>
            <type>pom</type>
            <scope>import</scope>
        </dependency>
    </dependencies>
</dependencyManagement>

<dependencies>
    <dependency>
        <groupId>org.springframework.boot</groupId>
        <artifactId>spring-boot-starter</artifactId>
    </dependency>
    <dependency>
        <groupId>com.apress</groupId>
        <artifactId>twitter4j-spring-boot-autoconfigure</artifactId>
        <version>${project.version}</version>
    </dependency>
    <dependency>
        <groupId>org.twitter4j</groupId>
        <artifactId>twitter4j-core</artifactId>
        <version>${twitter4j.version}</version>
    </dependency>
</dependencies>

</project>
```

Note that in this Maven module, you are actually pulling in the `twitter4j-core` dependency.

You don't need to add any code to this module, but you can optionally specify the dependencies you are going to provide through this starter in the `src/main/resources/METAINF/spring.provides` file, as follows:

```
provides: twitter4j-core
```

That's all for this starter. Next, you see how to create a sample using `twitter4j-spring-boot-starter`.

Application Using twitter4j-spring-boot-starter

We are going to create a simple Maven-based Spring Boot application and use `twitter4j-spring-boot-starter` to fetch the latest tweets. First, you create a simple Spring Boot application and add the `twitter4j-spring-boot-starter` dependency, as shown in Listing 16-7.

Listing 16-7. twitter4j-spring-boot-sample/pom.xml

```xml
<?xml version="1.0" encoding="UTF-8"?>
<project xmlns="http://maven.apache.org/POM/4.0.0"
        xmlns:xsi="http://www.w3.org/2001/XMLSchema-instance"
        xsi:schemaLocation="http://maven.apache.org/POM/4.0.0
                    http://maven.apache.org/maven-v4_0_0.xsd">
    <modelVersion>4.0.0</modelVersion>

    <groupId>com.apress</groupId>
    <artifactId>twitter4j-spring-boot-sample</artifactId>
    <packaging>jar</packaging>
    <version>1.0-SNAPSHOT</version>

    <parent>
        <groupId>org.springframework.boot</groupId>
        <artifactId>spring-boot-starter-parent</artifactId>
        <version>2.0.0.BUILD-SNAPSHOT</version>
    </parent>

    <properties>
        <project.build.sourceEncoding>UTF-8</project.build.sourceEncoding>
        <java.version>1.8</java.version>
    </properties>

    <build>
        <plugins>
            <plugin>
                <groupId>org.springframework.boot</groupId>
                <artifactId>spring-boot-maven-plugin</artifactId>
            </plugin>
        </plugins>
    </build>

    <dependencies>

        <dependency>
            <groupId>com.apress</groupId>
            <artifactId>twitter4j-spring-boot-starter</artifactId>
            <version>1.0-SNAPSHOT</version>
        </dependency>
        <dependency>
        <groupId>org.springframework.boot</groupId>
        <artifactId>spring-boot-starter-test</artifactId>
            <scope>test</scope>
        </dependency>
    </dependencies>

</project>
```

Create the entry point class SpringbootTwitter4jDemoApplication, as shown in Listing 16-8.

Listing 16-8. SpringbootTwitter4jDemoApplication.java

```java
package com.apress.demo;

import org.springframework.boot.SpringApplication;
import org.springframework.boot.autoconfigure.SpringBootApplication;

@SpringBootApplication
public class SpringbootTwitter4jDemoApplication
{
    public static void main(String[] args)
    {
        SpringApplication.run(SpringbootTwitter4jDemoApplication.class, args);
    }
}
```

Next, create TweetService, as shown in Listing 16-9.

Listing 16-9. TweetService.java

```java
package com.apress.demo;

import java.util.ArrayList;
import java.util.List;
import org.springframework.beans.factory.annotation.Autowired;
import org.springframework.stereotype.Service;

import twitter4j.ResponseList;
import twitter4j.Status;
import twitter4j.Twitter;
import twitter4j.TwitterException;

@Service
public class TweetService
{
    @Autowired
    private Twitter twitter;

    public List<String> getLatestTweets()
    {
        List<String> tweets = new ArrayList<>();
        try {
            ResponseList<Status> homeTimeline = twitter.getHomeTimeline();
            for (Status status : homeTimeline)
            {
                tweets.add(status.getText());
            }
        }
```

```java
        catch (TwitterException e) {
            throw new RuntimeException(e);
        }
        return tweets;
    }
}
```

Now create a test to verify the Twitter4j autoconfiguration (see Listing 16-10). Before that, make sure you have set your Twitter4j OAuth configuration parameter to your actual values. You can get them from https://apps.twitter.com/.

Listing 16-10. SpringbootTwitter4jDemoApplicationTest.java

```java
package com.apress.demo;

import java.util.List;
import org.junit.Test;
import org.junit.runner.RunWith;
import org.springframework.beans.factory.annotation.Autowired;
import org.springframework.boot.test.context.SpringBootTest;
import org.springframework.test.context.junit4.SpringRunner;
import twitter4j.TwitterException;

@RunWith(SpringRunner.class)
@SpringBootTest
public class SpringbootTwitter4jDemoApplicationTest
{
    @Autowired
    private TweetService tweetService;

    @Test
    public void testGetTweets() throws TwitterException
    {
        List<String> tweets = tweetService.getLatestTweets();

        for (String tweet : tweets)
        {
            System.err.println(tweet);
        }
    }
}
```

Now when you run this JUnit test, you should be able to see the latest tweets on your console output.

Summary

In this chapter, you learned how to create your own autoconfiguration classes and your own Spring Boot Starter. In the next chapter, you will learn how to develop Spring Boot applications using JVM languages like Groovy, Scala, and Kotlin.

CHAPTER 17

Spring Boot with Groovy, Scala, and Kotlin

Java is the most widely used programming language that runs on Java Virtual Machine (JVM). There are many other JVM-based languages, such as Groovy, Scala, JRuby, Jython, Kotlin, etc. Among them, Groovy and Scala are widely adopted and very popular among the Java community and Kotlin adoption is growing very rapidly.

Spring Boot is a Java-based framework that can also be used with other JVM-based languages. This chapter looks at how to use Spring Boot with the Groovy, Scala, and Kotlin programming languages.

Using Spring Boot with Groovy

Groovy is a dynamically typed language that runs on JVM. As Groovy's syntax is very close to Java's, it is very easy for Java developers to get started with Groovy. Spring Boot applications can be developed using the Groovy programming language.

Introducing Groovy

Groovy is a JVM-based programming language with Java-like syntax. But Groovy supports dynamic typing, closures, meta-programming, operator overloading, and more. In addition to these, Groovy provides many cool features, such as multi-line strings, string interpolation, elegant looping structures, and easy property access. Also, semicolons are optional. These all help to improve developer productivity.

Groovy Strings

You can create strings in Groovy using either single quotes or double quotes. When using single quotes, the string is treated as an instance of java.lang.String, whereas when using double quotes, it is treated as an instance of groovy.lang.Gstring, which supports string interpolation.

```
def name = "John"
def amount = 125
println('My name is ${name}')
println("My name is ${name}")
println("He paid \$$ {amount}")
```

© K. Siva Prasad Reddy 2017

K. S. Prasad Reddy, *Beginning Spring Boot 2*, DOI 10.1007/978-1-4842-2931-6_17

When you run this code, it will print the following output:

```
My name is ${name}
My name is John
He paid $125
```

As single quotes are used in the first `println()` statement, `${name}` is printed as it is, whereas it is interpolated in the second `println()` statement because double quotes are used there. This code also uses the escape character \$ to print the $ symbol.

Groovy supports multi-line strings using triple quotes (`"""` or `'''`) as follows:

```
//using single quotes
def content = '''My Name is John.
                    I live in London.
                    I am a software developer'''

def name = 'John'
def address = 'London'
def occupation = 'software developer'
//using double quotes
def bio = """My name is ${name}.
                I live in ${address}.
                I am a ${occupation}."""
```

Groovy's multi-line supports come in very handy while creating strings that span multiple lines, like table creation scripts, HTML templates with placeholders, etc.

JavaBean Properties

In Java, you usually create Java beans by creating private properties and setters and getters for those properties. Although you can generate the setters and getters using IDE support, it is verbose and unnecessary noisy.

In Groovy, you can create beans just by declaring the properties and then access them using the `object.propertyName` syntax without having to create setters and getters.

```
class Person
{
    def id
    def name
    def email
}
def p = new Person()
p.id = 1
p.name = 'Jon'
p.email = 'john@mail.com'
println("Id: ${p.id}, Name: ${p.name}, Email: ${p.email}")
```

Here, you can see that the values are assigned to the bean properties directly, like `p.id=1`, without having to create a setter for `id`. Similarly, you can read the property `id` using `p.id`, without requiring a getter for `id`. Behind the scenes, Groovy will generate setters and getters for the properties.

Looping

Groovy supports a variety of looping structures in addition to the regular while and for loops.
Iterate using the range operator (..):

```
for(i in 0..5) { print "${i}" }
```

The output is as follows:

```
0 1 2 3 4 5
```

Iterate using upto() with the lower and upper limits inclusive:

```
0.upto(3) { print "$it " }
```

The output is as follows:

```
0 1 2 3
```

Iterate using times(), starting from 0:

```
5.times { print "$it " }
```

The output is as follows:

```
0 1 2 3 4
```

Iterate using step() with the lower and upper limits and a step value:

```
0.step(10, 2) { print "$it "}
```

The output is as follows:

```
0 2 4 6 8
```

There are many other features provided by Groovy that help you build the application faster:

- Working with collections—http://docs.groovy-lang.org/latest/html/
  documentation/#_working_with_collections

- Closures—http://groovy-lang.org/closures.html

- Regular expressions—http://docs.groovy-lang.org/latest/html/
  documentation/#_regular_expression_operators

- Traits—http://docs.groovy-lang.org/latest/html/documentation/#_traits

- Groovy truth—http://docs.groovy-lang.org/latest/html/
  documentation/#Groovy-Truth

- Typing—http://docs.groovy-lang.org/latest/html/documentation/#_typing

- Parsing and producing JSON—http://groovy-lang.org/json.html

- Processing XML—http://docs.groovy-lang.org/latest/html/documentation/#_processing_xml

- Meta programming—http://docs.groovy-lang.org/latest/html/documentation/#_metaprogramming

To learn more about Groovy, refer to the official documentation at: http://groovy-lang.org/documentation.html.

Creating a Spring Boot Application Using Groovy

You can create a Spring Boot application using Groovy either from the IDE or using the online Spring Boot application generator http://start.spring.io and selecting Groovy as the language.

If you are using the Maven build tool, gmavenplus-plugin is configured to compile Groovy code. You can put the Groovy main source code in the src/main/groovy folder and then test the Groovy code in the src/test/groovy folder. See Listing 17-1.

Listing 17-1. pom.xml

```xml
<?xml version="1.0" encoding="UTF-8"?>
<project xmlns="http://maven.apache.org/POM/4.0.0"
    xmlns:xsi="http://www.w3.org/2001/XMLSchema-instance"
    xsi:schemaLocation="http://maven.apache.org/POM/4.0.0 http://maven.apache.org/xsd/
    maven-4.0.0.xsd">
    <modelVersion>4.0.0</modelVersion>

    <groupId>com.apress</groupId>
    <artifactId>springboot-groovy-demo</artifactId>
    <version>0.0.1-SNAPSHOT</version>
    <packaging>jar</packaging>

    <name>springboot-groovy-demo</name>

    <parent>
        <groupId>org.springframework.boot</groupId>
        <artifactId>spring-boot-starter-parent</artifactId>
        <version>2.0.0.BUILD-SNAPSHOT</version>
        <relativePath/>
    </parent>

    <properties>
        <project.build.sourceEncoding>UTF-8</project.build.sourceEncoding>
        <project.reporting.outputEncoding>UTF-8</project.reporting.outputEncoding>
        <java.version>1.8</java.version>
    </properties>

    <dependencies>
        <dependency>
            <groupId>org.springframework.boot</groupId>
            <artifactId>spring-boot-starter-web</artifactId>
        </dependency>
```

```xml
    <dependency>
        <groupId>org.codehaus.groovy</groupId>
        <artifactId>groovy</artifactId>
    </dependency>
    <dependency>
        <groupId>org.springframework.boot</groupId>
        <artifactId>spring-boot-starter-test</artifactId>
        <scope>test</scope>
    </dependency>
</dependencies>

<build>
    <plugins>
        <plugin>
            <groupId>org.springframework.boot</groupId>
            <artifactId>spring-boot-maven-plugin</artifactId>
        </plugin>
        <plugin>
            <groupId>org.codehaus.gmavenplus</groupId>
            <artifactId>gmavenplus-plugin</artifactId>
            <version>1.5</version>
            <executions>
                <execution>
                    <goals>
                        <goal>addSources</goal>
                        <goal>addTestSources</goal>
                        <goal>generateStubs</goal>
                        <goal>compile</goal>
                        <goal>testGenerateStubs</goal>
                        <goal>testCompile</goal>
                        <goal>removeStubs</goal>
                        <goal>removeTestStubs</goal>
                    </goals>
                </execution>
            </executions>
        </plugin>
    </plugins>
</build>

<repositories>
    ...
    ...
</repositories>

<pluginRepositories>
    ...
    ...
</pluginRepositories>

</project>
```

If you selected Gradle as the build tool, the groovy plugin will be configured, as shown in Listing 17-2.

Listing 17-2. build.gradle

```
...
...

apply plugin: 'groovy'
apply plugin: 'org.springframework.boot'
apply plugin: 'io.spring.dependency-management'

...
...

dependencies {
    compile('org.springframework.boot:spring-boot-starter-web')
    compile('org.codehaus.groovy:groovy')
    testCompile('org.springframework.boot:spring-boot-starter-test')
}
```

You'll now see how to develop a simple Spring Boot web application using Groovy, Spring Data JPA, and Thymeleaf. Add the Web, Thymeleaf, JPA, and H2 starters dependencies to your application.

Create a JPA entity called User.groovy, as shown in Listing 17-3.

Listing 17-3. User.groovy

```
import javax.persistence.*

@Entity
@Table(name="users")
class User {
    @Id @GeneratedValue(strategy = GenerationType.AUTO)
    Long id
    String name
    String email
}
```

As you are using Groovy, you don't need to create setters and getters for your entity properties.

Create a Spring Data JPA repository for the User entity, as shown in Listing 17-4.

Listing 17-4. UserRepository.groovy

```
interface UserRepository extends JpaRepository<User, Long>
{
    User findByEmail(String email);
}
```

Create a SpringMVC controller to show the list of users, as shown in Listing 17-5.

Listing 17-5. HomeController.groovy

```groovy
import org.springframework.beans.factory.annotation.Autowired
import org.springframework.stereotype.Controller
import org.springframework.ui.Model
import org.springframework.web.bind.annotation.GetMapping

@Controller
class HomeController
{

    @Autowired
    UserRepository repo;

    @GetMapping("/")
    String home(Model model) {
        model.addAttribute("users", repo.findAll())
        "home"
    }
}
```

In Groovy, the last statement in the method is treated as a returned value, so you can just mention "home" instead of return "home".

Create the Thymeleaf view home.html to render users, as shown in Listing 17-6.

Listing 17-6. src/main/resources/templates/home.html

```html
<!DOCTYPE HTML>
<html xmlns:th="http://www.thymeleaf.org">
<head>
    <title>Users List</title>
    <meta http-equiv="Content-Type" content="text/html; charset=UTF-8" />
</head>
<body>
<table>
    <thead>
    <tr>
        <th>Id</th>
        <th>Name</th>
    </tr>
    </thead>
    <tbody>
    <tr th:each="user : ${users}">
        <td th:text="${user.id}">Id</td>
        <td th:text="${user.name}">Name</td>
    </tr>
    </tbody>
</table>
</body>
</html>
```

When you generate the application, the main entry point class is created, as shown in Listing 17-7.

Listing 17-7. SpringbootGroovyDemoApplication.groovy

```
import org.springframework.boot.SpringApplication
import org.springframework.boot.autoconfigure.SpringBootApplication

@SpringBootApplication
class SpringbootGroovyDemoApplication {

    static void main(String[] args) {
        SpringApplication.run SpringbootGroovyDemoApplication, args
    }
}
```

Initialize the database with sample data using a SQL script, as shown in Listing 17-8.

Listing 17-8. src/main/resources/data.sql

```
insert into users(id, name, email) values
(1,'admin','admin@gmail.com'),
(2,'john','john@gmail.com'),
(3,'test','test@gmail.com');
```

Now you can run the application by executing the SpringbootGroovyDemoApplication.main() method or using the mvn spring-boot:run or gradle bootRun commands. If you point your browser to http://localhost:8080/, you should be able to see user details.

Using Spring Boot with Scala

Scala is one of the most popular JVM-based programming languages. It mixes functional programming and object oriented programming idioms into a single language.

Spring Initializer (http://start.spring.io) doesn't provide support for Scala yet, but you can create Spring Boot applications using the Scala programming language by configuring appropriate plugins based on the build tool you are using.

Introducing Scala

Scala is a JVM-based statically typed programming language that supports both the functional programming and object oriented programming paradigms. You can write programs in Scala in a concise and expressive manner instead of using the verbose and imperative style of coding.

The next few sections look at a few of the Scala features that are slightly different from Java.

Type Inference

In Scala, a variable declaration syntax looks like var variable_name : data_type = value. But Scala can infer the data type of the variable based on the assigned value. That means you can omit the :data_type part in the declaration.

```
var n : Int = 5 //with explicit type declaration
var n = 5 //with type inference
```

Classes and Objects

The classes in Scala are similar to Java and can contain variables, methods, etc. But in Scala, a class can contain one primary constructor and zero or more auxiliary constructors. The auxiliary constructors should invoke primary constructors directly or through another auxiliary constructor.

```
class Person (val firstName: String, val lastName: String){
  def this(firstName: String) { this(firstName, "")}
}

object Main extends App {
  val p1 = new Person("Siva","Prasad")
  val p2 = new Person("Siva")
}
```

In Scala, there is no concept of `static`. If you want to mimic the behavior of `static` in Scala, you create a *companion object* with the same name as the class and put all the members, including properties and methods, in there. The object in Scala is a singleton and you can access members without creating an instance of it.

```
class StringUtils {}

object StringUtils {

  def toUpper(str : String): String = {
    return str.toUpperCase()
  }
}
val str = "john"
println(StringUtils.toUpper(str))
```

Traits

Traits in Scala are similar to Java 8 interfaces, which encapsulate fields, methods, and abstract methods. Classes can extend any number of traits.

```
trait ReportSender {

  def sendReport(report: String): Unit = {
    //send email with report content
  }

  def generateReport() : String
}

class HTMLReportSender extends ReportSender {
  override def generateReport(): String = "<html><body>ReportData</body></html>"
}
```

To learn more about Scala, refer to Scala's official documentation at: `http://docs.scala-lang.org/index.html`.

Creating a Spring Boot Application Using Scala

You can develop Spring Boot applications using the Scala programming language. If you want to use Maven as a build tool, you can use `scala-maven-plugin` to compile your Scala code. You can place the main Scala code in `src/main/scala` and the test Scala code in the `src/test/scala` folder. See Listing 17-9.

Listing 17-9. pom.xml

```xml
<?xml version="1.0" encoding="UTF-8"?>
<project xmlns="http://maven.apache.org/POM/4.0.0"
    xmlns:xsi="http://www.w3.org/2001/XMLSchema-instance"
    xsi:schemaLocation="http://maven.apache.org/POM/4.0.0
    http://maven.apache.org/xsd/maven-4.0.0.xsd">
    <modelVersion>4.0.0</modelVersion>

    <groupId>com.apress</groupId>
    <artifactId>springboot-scala-demo</artifactId>
    <version>0.0.1-SNAPSHOT</version>
    <packaging>jar</packaging>

    <name>springboot-scala-demo</name>

    <parent>
        <groupId>org.springframework.boot</groupId>
        <artifactId>spring-boot-starter-parent</artifactId>
        <version>2.0.0.BUILD-SNAPSHOT</version>
        <relativePath/>
    </parent>

    <properties>
        <kotlin.compiler.incremental>true</kotlin.compiler.incremental>
        <project.build.sourceEncoding>UTF-8</project.build.sourceEncoding>
        <project.reporting.outputEncoding>UTF-8</project.reporting.outputEncoding>
        <java.version>1.8</java.version>
        <scala.version>2.11.1</scala.version>
    </properties>

    <dependencies>
        <dependency>
            <groupId>org.scala-lang</groupId>
            <artifactId>scala-library</artifactId>
            <version>${scala.version}</version>
        </dependency>
        <dependency>
            <groupId>org.springframework.boot</groupId>
            <artifactId>spring-boot-starter-test</artifactId>
            <scope>test</scope>
        </dependency>
    </dependencies>
```

```xml
<build>
    <sourceDirectory>src/main/scala</sourceDirectory>
    <testSourceDirectory>src/test/scala</testSourceDirectory>
    <plugins>
        <plugin>
            <groupId>org.springframework.boot</groupId>
            <artifactId>spring-boot-maven-plugin</artifactId>
        </plugin>
        <plugin>
            <groupId>net.alchim31.maven</groupId>
            <artifactId>scala-maven-plugin</artifactId>
            <version>3.2.1</version>
            <executions>
              <execution>
                <goals>
                  <goal>compile</goal>
                  <goal>testCompile</goal>
                </goals>
              </execution>
            </executions>
            <configuration>
              <jvmArgs>
                <jvmArg>-Xms64m</jvmArg>
                <jvmArg>-Xmx1024m</jvmArg>
              </jvmArgs>
            </configuration>
        </plugin>
    </plugins>
</build>

<repositories>
    ...
    ...
</repositories>

<pluginRepositories>
    ...
    ...
</pluginRepositories>
</project>
```

Note that this code adds src/main/scala and src/test/scala folders as source folders using the <sourceDirectory> and <testSourceDirectory> configurations. It also adds the scala-library dependency to use Scala.

If you want to use the Gradle build tool, you can use the scala plugin, which automatically uses the src/main/scala and src/test/scala folders as Scala source code directories. See Listing 17-10.

Listing 17-10. build.gradle

```
apply plugin: 'java'
apply plugin: 'scala'
apply plugin: 'application'
apply plugin: 'org.springframework.boot'
apply plugin: 'io.spring.dependency-management'

mainClassName = 'com.apress.demo.Application'
...
...

dependencies {
    ...
    ...
    compile('org.scala-lang:scala-library:2.11.1')
    ...
    ...
}
```

Now you'll see how to develop a simple web application using Spring Boot and Scala. Add the Web, Spring Data JPA, Thymeleaf, and H2 starter dependencies.

Create a JPA entity called User.scala, as shown in Listing 17-11.

Listing 17-11. User.scala

```
import javax.persistence._

import scala.beans.BeanProperty

@Entity
@Table(name="users")
class User {

  @Id
  @GeneratedValue(strategy = GenerationType.AUTO)
  @BeanProperty
  var id: Long = _

  @BeanProperty
  var name: String = _

  @BeanProperty
  var email: String = _

}
```

You are using the @BeanProperty to generate setters and getters for fields based on the JavaBean naming conventions.

Now you'll see how to create the Spring Data JPA repository for the User entity. As Scala doesn't have interfaces, you are going to create UserRepository as a trait, as shown in Listing 17-12.

Listing 17-12. UserRepository.scala

```scala
import org.springframework.data.jpa.repository.JpaRepository
import org.springframework.data.repository.query.Param

trait UserRepository extends JpaRepository[User, java.lang.Long] {
  def findByEmail(@Param("email") name: String): List[User]
}
```

You will create a Spring MVC controller to show the list of users, as shown in Listing 17-13.

Listing 17-13. HomeController.scala

```scala
import org.springframework.beans.factory.annotation.Autowired
import org.springframework.stereotype.Controller
import org.springframework.ui.Model
import org.springframework.web.bind.annotation.{GetMapping}

@Controller
class HomeController
{
  @Autowired
  var repo: UserRepository = _

  @GetMapping(Array("/"))
  def home(model: Model) : String = {
    model.addAttribute("users", repo.findAll())
    "home"
  }
}
```

You can use the same home.html Thymeleaf template you created for the Groovy sample application. Next, you are going to create the application main entry point class. As Scala doesn't support static methods, you have to create a companion object and write the main() method, as shown in Listing 17-14.

Listing 17-14. Application.scala

```scala
import org.springframework.boot.SpringApplication
import org.springframework.boot.autoconfigure.SpringBootApplication

@SpringBootApplication
class Application {

}

object Application {
  def main(args: Array[String]) : Unit = {
    SpringApplication.run(classOf[Application], args:_*)
  }
}
```

Now you can run Application.main(), which starts your Spring Boot application and accesses it at http://localhost:8080/. This shows a list of users.

Using Spring Boot with Kotlin

Spring Boot officially supports the Kotlin programming language and you can create Spring Boot applications using Kotlin from Spring Initializer at http://start.spring.io or from your IDE. Kotlin support is introduced in the new Spring Framework 5 release. You can read more about it at https://spring.io/blog/2017/01/04/introducing-kotlin-support-in-spring-framework-5-0.

Introducing Kotlin

Kotlin (https://kotlinlang.org/) is a JVM-based statically typed programming language created by JetBrains. One of the key goals of Kotlin is to be interoperable with Java so that you can use Java and Kotlin together in the same project.

Here's how you write a simple Hello World program in Kotlin.

```
package demo

fun main(args: Array<String>){
    println("Hello World");
}
```

In Kotlin, there are no static methods like in Java, so you can write those methods that you want to be static as top-level functions.

Classes

Classes in Kotlin are similar to Scala classes in that they have a class name with one primary constructor and one or more secondary constructors.

```
class Person(val firstname: String,val lastname: String) {
    constructor(name: String) : this(name, "")

    fun printDetails() = println("FirstName: ${firstname}, LastName: ${lastname}")
}
```

Interfaces

Interfaces in Kotlin are similar to Java 8 interfaces in that they can have abstract method declarations as well as implemented methods.

```
interface ReportSender
{
    fun generateReport() : String

    fun sendReport() {
        val report = generateReport()
        println("Report: "+ report)
        //send email with report content
    }
}
```

```kotlin
class HTMLReportSender : ReportSender
{
    override fun generateReport(): String = "<html><body>ReportData</body></html>"
}

fun main(args: Array<String>)
{
    val rs = HTMLReportSender()
    rs.sendReport()
}
```

Data Classes

In Java, you usually create data holder classes as POJOs (plain old Java objects) with just private properties and setters and getters. Then you implement the equals(), hashCode(), and toStirng() methods. Kotlin makes creating such classes very easy by using *data classes*.

```kotlin
data class Person(val name: String, val email: String)
```

Just by declaring a class as a data class, the Kotlin compiler will automatically generate the equals(), hashCode(), and equals() methods.

You can learn more about Kotlin at https://kotlinlang.org/docs/reference/.

Creating a Spring Boot Application Using Kotlin

You can create Spring Boot applications using Kotlin from the IDE or from http://start.spring.io by selecting Kotlin as the language of choice.

If you are using the Maven build tool, kotlin-maven-plugin will be configured to use src/main/kotlin and src/test/kotlin as the main and test source code folders, respectively. See Listing 17-15.

Listing 17-15. pom.xml

```xml
<?xml version="1.0" encoding="UTF-8"?>
<project xmlns="http://maven.apache.org/POM/4.0.0"
    xmlns:xsi="http://www.w3.org/2001/XMLSchema-instance"
    xsi:schemaLocation="http://maven.apache.org/POM/4.0.0
    http://maven.apache.org/xsd/maven-4.0.0.xsd">
    <modelVersion>4.0.0</modelVersion>

    <groupId>com.apress</groupId>
    <artifactId>springboot-kotlin-demo</artifactId>
    <version>0.0.1-SNAPSHOT</version>
    <packaging>jar</packaging>

    <name>springboot-kotlin-demo</name>

    <parent>
        <groupId>org.springframework.boot</groupId>
        <artifactId>spring-boot-starter-parent</artifactId>
        <version>2.0.0.BUILD-SNAPSHOT</version>
        <relativePath/>
    </parent>
```

```xml
<properties>
    <kotlin.compiler.incremental>true</kotlin.compiler.incremental>
    <project.build.sourceEncoding>UTF-8</project.build.sourceEncoding>
    <project.reporting.outputEncoding>UTF-8</project.reporting.outputEncoding>
    <java.version>1.8</java.version>
    <kotlin.version>1.1.2-5</kotlin.version>
</properties>

<dependencies>
    ...
    ...
    <dependency>
        <groupId>org.jetbrains.kotlin</groupId>
        <artifactId>kotlin-stdlib-jre8</artifactId>
        <version>${kotlin.version}</version>
    </dependency>
    <dependency>
        <groupId>org.jetbrains.kotlin</groupId>
        <artifactId>kotlin-reflect</artifactId>
        <version>${kotlin.version}</version>
    </dependency>
    ...
    ...
</dependencies>

<build>
    <sourceDirectory>${project.basedir}/src/main/kotlin</sourceDirectory>
    <testSourceDirectory>${project.basedir}/src/test/kotlin</testSourceDirectory>
    <plugins>
        <plugin>
            <groupId>org.springframework.boot</groupId>
            <artifactId>spring-boot-maven-plugin</artifactId>
        </plugin>
        <plugin>
            <artifactId>kotlin-maven-plugin</artifactId>
            <groupId>org.jetbrains.kotlin</groupId>
            <version>${kotlin.version}</version>
            <configuration>
                <compilerPlugins>
                    <plugin>spring</plugin>
                </compilerPlugins>
                <jvmTarget>1.8</jvmTarget>
            </configuration>
            <executions>
                <execution>
                    <id>compile</id>
                    <phase>compile</phase>
                    <goals>
                        <goal>compile</goal>
                    </goals>
                </execution>
```

```xml
                    <execution>
                        <id>test-compile</id>
                        <phase>test-compile</phase>
                        <goals>
                            <goal>test-compile</goal>
                        </goals>
                    </execution>
                </executions>
                <dependencies>
                    <dependency>
                        <groupId>org.jetbrains.kotlin</groupId>
                        <artifactId>kotlin-maven-allopen</artifactId>
                        <version>${kotlin.version}</version>
                    </dependency>
                </dependencies>
            </plugin>
        </plugins>
    </build>

    <repositories>
        ...
    </repositories>

    <pluginRepositories>
        ...
    </pluginRepositories>

</project>
```

Note that the Kotlin library dependencies `kotlin-stdlib-jre8` and `kotlin-reflect` are also added. With this configuration, you can place your Kotlin source code in `src/main/kotlin`, which will be automatically compiled using the Kotlin compiler.

If you are using the Gradle build tool, the `build.gradle` file will be generated, as shown in Listing 17-16.

Listing 17-16. build.gradle

```groovy
buildscript {
    ext {
        kotlinVersion = '1.1.2-4'
        springBootVersion = '2.0.0.BUILD-SNAPSHOT'
    }
    repositories {
        mavenCentral()
        maven { url "https://repo.spring.io/snapshot" }
        maven { url "https://repo.spring.io/milestone" }
    }
    dependencies {
        classpath("org.springframework.boot:spring-boot-gradle-plugin:${springBootVersion}")
        classpath("org.jetbrains.kotlin:kotlin-gradle-plugin:${kotlinVersion}")
        classpath("org.jetbrains.kotlin:kotlin-allopen:${kotlinVersion}")
    }
}
```

```
apply plugin: 'kotlin'
apply plugin: 'kotlin-spring'
apply plugin: 'eclipse'
apply plugin: 'org.springframework.boot'
apply plugin: 'io.spring.dependency-management'

version = '0.0.1-SNAPSHOT'
sourceCompatibility = 1.8
compileKotlin {
    kotlinOptions.jvmTarget = "1.8"
}
compileTestKotlin {
    kotlinOptions.jvmTarget = "1.8"
}

...
...

dependencies {
    ...
    compile("org.jetbrains.kotlin:kotlin-stdlib-jre8:${kotlinVersion}")
    compile("org.jetbrains.kotlin:kotlin-reflect:${kotlinVersion}")
    ...
}
```

The Spring framework needs configuration classes (classes annotated with `@Configuration`, `@Service`, `@Component`, `@Repository`, etc.) to be non-final so that it can create CGLIB proxies. But Kotlin classes are final by default. If you want to make a class non-final in Kotlin, you need to add the open modifier to the class.

```
open class Application {
}
```

As this is a common requirement to be interoperable with many Java-based frameworks, Kotlin provides the `all-open` compiler plugin, which allows you to specify a list of annotations and make the classes with those annotations open by default. Then you don't have to manually add the open modifier.

The `spring` plugin opens classes annotated with Spring annotations—such as `@Component`, `@Async`, `@Transactional`, and `@Cacheable`—automatically. As other Spring annotations—such as `@Configuration`, `@Controller`, `@RestController`, `@Service`, and `@Repository`—are meta-annotated with the `@Component` annotation, these classes will also be opened automatically. When you generate a Spring Boot application with Kotlin from the Spring Initializer, the `kotlin-spring` plugin is configured by default.

Now you'll see how to develop a simple web application with Spring Boot and Kotlin. Add the Web, Spring Data JPA, and Thymeleaf starter dependencies.

Create a JPA entity called User, as shown in Listing 17-17.

Listing 17-17. User.kt

```
import javax.persistence.*

@Entity
@Table(name="users")
class User(
        @Id @GeneratedValue(strategy = GenerationType.AUTO)
        var id: Long = -1,
        var name: String = "",
        var email: String = ""
        ) {

    override fun toString(): String {
        return "User(id=$id, name='$name', email='$email')"
    }
}
```

JPA entities should have a default constructor. One option is to have a User entity with a primary constructor using the var type properties with their default values. Another option is to create a no-arg default constructor as a secondary constructor and pass default values to the primary constructor.

■ **Note** You can also use kotlin-jpa plugin to generate a no-arg constructor for JPA entities. Refer to https://kotlinlang.org/docs/reference/compiler-plugins.html#kotlin-jpa-compiler-plugin for more information.

Listing 17-18 shows you how to create a Spring Data JPA repository for the User entity.

Listing 17-18. UserRepository.kt

```
import org.springframework.data.jpa.repository.JpaRepository

interface UserRepository : JpaRepository<User, Long> {

    fun findByEmail(email: String): Iterable<User>
}
```

Create a SpringMVC controller to display the list of users, as shown in Listing 17-19.

Listing 17-19. HomeController.kt

```
import org.springframework.stereotype.Controller
import org.springframework.ui.Model
import org.springframework.web.bind.annotation.GetMapping

@Controller
class HomeController(val repository:UserRepository) {
```

```kotlin
@GetMapping("/")
fun home(model: Model): String {
    model.addAttribute("users", repository.findAll())
    return "home"
}
}
```

You can reuse the `home.html` Thymeleaf template and `data.sql` script to populate sample users that you created in the previous section.

Finally, create the main entry point class, as shown in Listing 17-20.

Listing 17-20. SpringbootKotlinDemoApplication.kt

```kotlin
import org.springframework.boot.SpringApplication
import org.springframework.boot.autoconfigure.SpringBootApplication


@SpringBootApplication
class SpringbootKotlinDemoApplication

fun main(args: Array<String>) {
    SpringApplication.run(SpringbootKotlinDemoApplication::class.java, *args)
}
```

This code creates the `main()` method as a top-level function. Now if you run the `main()` method, it will start the application. You can then access `http://localhost:8080/`, which shows the list of users.

Summary

This chapter discussed how to a create Spring Boot application using the JVM-based languages Groovy, Scala, and Kotlin. In the next chapter, you will learn about JHipster, which is a Yeoman-based Spring Boot application generator.

CHAPTER 18

Introducing JHipster

JHipster is a Yeoman-based generator that creates Spring Boot based web applications. JHipster configures a wide variety of tools and frameworks that are commonly used in Spring Boot applications, which improves developer productivity.

This chapter covers how to install JHipster and create a monolithic application. It explores the generated application features and looks at how to create entities using the sub-generator as well as JDL Studio.

Introducing JHipster

Technology is evolving very rapidly and new tools, frameworks, and libraries are being created everyday. In recent years, there has been a lot of innovation in the JavaScript ecosystem and lot of high-quality modern web development tools were born. There are build tools like Grunt, Gulp, Webpack, etc. There are Single Page Application (SPA) frameworks like AngularJS, ReactJS, VueJS, etc. And there are many JavaScript testing libraries like Mocha, Jasmine, Jest, etc. Integrating all these tools manually is tedious and repetitive.

Yeoman (`http://yeoman.io/`) is a scaffolding tool that generates web projects following best practices. Yeoman provides various generators to scaffold web projects using various technologies. For example, if you want to create an AngularJS 1.x based project, you can use `generator-angular`, which will generate an AngularJS project with the Grunt build tool, with karma based testing support.

JHipster (`https://jhipster.github.io/`) is a Yeoman-based generator that generates Spring Boot based web projects with a wide variety of options for building tools, front-end frameworks, relational databases, NoSQL databases, Spring security strategies, caching options, and more.

With JHipster you can generate Spring Boot applications with most of the configuration configured properly and then start implementing the business use cases. JHipster also provides sub-generators to generate JPA entities and scaffolding UI for typical CRUD (Create, Read, Update, Delete) operations, which makes development faster.

Installing JHipster

JHipster is a Yeoman-based generator that depends on the NPM (Node Package Manager). The next section covers the prerequisites for using JHipster.

Prerequisites

Follow these steps to install JHipster:

1. Install JDK 8.

2. Install Git from `https://git-scm.com/`.

3. Install Node.js from `https://nodejs.org/`.

4. You can use NPM or Yarn to install JHipster. These examples use Yarn. You install Yarn from `https://yarnpkg.com/`.

5. Install Yeoman using `yarn global add yo`.

6. If you want to use AngularJS 1.x for the front-end, you need to install bower and `gulp-cli`. If you want to use Angular 2.x onward, you don't need to install them. The commands are as follows:

   - `yarn global add bower`

   - `yarn global add gulp-cli`

7. Install JHipster generator using `yarn global add generator-jhipster`.

Now you should be able to run `jhipster --help` and see the various commands that JHipster supports.

Creating a JHipster Application

Creating a JHipster application is very easy; you simply run the `jhipster` command and answer the questions based on your technology's preferences and application's needs. JHipster can generate a monolithic application or a microservices based application.

In this chapter, you are going to create a simple monolithic blog application and then use the relational database H2 for development and MySQL for production.

```
> mkdir jhipster-blog
> cd jhipster-blog
> jhipster
```

The `jhipster` command will ask you a series of questions. Select the options shown here:

```
? (1/16) Which *type* of application would you like to create? Monolithic application
(recommended for simple projects)
? (2/16) What is the base name of your application? jhipsterblog
? (3/16) Would you like to install other generators from the JHipster Marketplace? No
? (4/16) What is your default Java package name? com.apress.jhblog
? (5/16) Do you want to use the JHipster Registry to configure, monitor and scale your
application? No
? (6/16) Which *type* of authentication would you like to use? JWT authentication
(stateless, with a token)
? (7/16) Which *type* of database would you like to use? SQL (H2, MySQL, MariaDB,
PostgreSQL, Oracle, MSSQL)
? (8/16) Which *production* database would you like to use? MySQL
? (9/16) Which *development* database would you like to use? H2 with in-memory persistence
```

```
? (10/16) Do you want to use Hibernate 2nd level cache? Yes, with ehcache
(local cache, for a single node)
? (11/16) Would you like to use Maven or Gradle for building the backend? Maven
? (12/16) Which other technologies would you like to use?
(Press <space> to select, <a> to toggle all, <i> to inverse selection)
? (13/16) Which *Framework* would you like to use for the client? [BETA] Angular 4
? (14/16) Would you like to use the LibSass stylesheet preprocessor for your CSS? No
? (15/16) Would you like to enable internationalization support? No
? (16/16) Besides JUnit and Karma, which testing frameworks would you like to use?
(Press <space> to select, <a> to toggle all, <i> to inverse selection)
```

Based on the options selected here, JHipster will generate a Spring Boot application with the following features:

- Angular 4-based front-end with Webpack configuration

- H2 in-memory database used in development and MySQL used for production

- Liquibase migration support for database migrations

- Spring Data JPA configured for database interaction

- Caching support is configured using EHCache

- Application is secured with Spring Security JWT token based authentication

- Provides an Administration dashboard showing application metrics using the Spring Boot Actuator

- Ability to change log levels at runtime through UI

- Swagger-based REST API documentation

- Provides a few user accounts out-of-the-box with Login, Change Password, and New User Registration functionality

Now you can run the application by running ./mvnw on Linux/MacOS or mvnw.cmd on Windows. This command will start the application dev profile and is accessible at http://localhost:8080/. Next, you'll explore the generated application.

As shown on the home page, you can log in with admin/admin, which has both the ROLE_USER and ROLE_ADMIN roles, or with user/user, which has only the ROLE_USER role.

Log in as the admin user using admin/admin. After a successful login, you will be redirected to the home page. The top navigation bar includes the Entities, Administration, and Account menus. As you haven't created any entities yet, there won't be any entities listed in the Entities menu.

Choose Administration ➤ Metrics to view the application metrics, such as memory consumption, thread states, garbage collection details, HTTP request statistics, etc., which are provided by the Spring Boot Actuator (Figure 18-1). You can also view cache statistics, datasource statistics, and service method execution metrics provided by GaugeService.

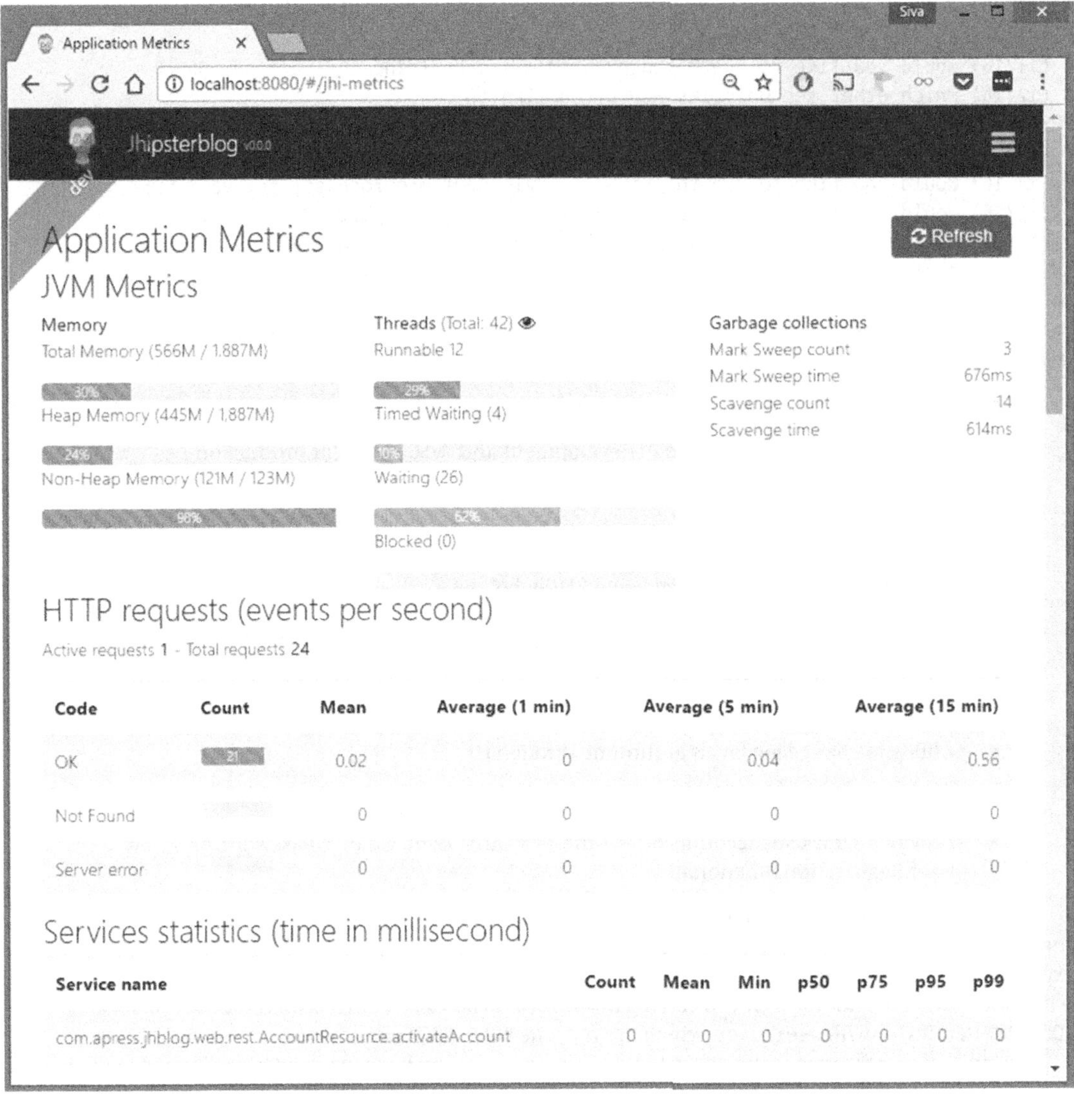

Figure 18-1. *JHipster metrics dashboard*

You can also explore the Health info, which shows the disk space and database health information.

You can explore Configuration, which shows the current running application's aggregated configuration from the default YAML configuration files, profile-specific YAML configuration files, system properties, and more.

You can view the application logger and its current log levels by choosing Administration ➤ Logs. You can search for loggers and change the log level by clicking on the desired level.

You can click on Administration ➤ Database to open the H2 in-memory database console, where you can explore the current state of the database.

The JHipster application is configured to capture events like authentication for audit purposes. You can view the audit log by choosing Administration ➤ Audits.

You can also manage the application's users by clicking on Administration ➤ User Management, where you can perform CRUD operations on users. See Figure 18-2.

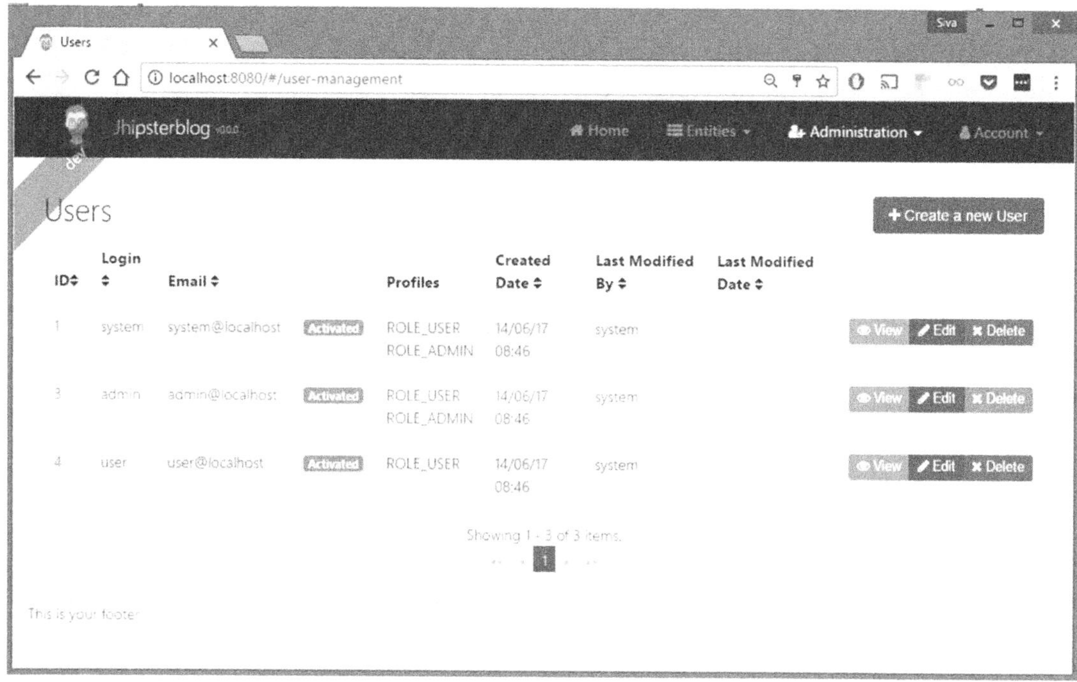

Figure 18-2. *JHipster user management*

You can view the Swagger documentation for the REST API by choosing Administration ➤ API. You can also view the Request and Response formats for each endpoint and trigger REST API calls by providing inputs if needed.

Creating Entities

Once the application is created, you may want to create entities and scaffold UI for that entity to perform CRUD operations on it. JHipster provides ways to create entities and perform the following tasks:

- Create a JPA entity
- Create a database table based on the properties information provided
- Create a Liquibase changeset for database migration
- Create a Spring data JPA repository for the entity
- Create a Spring MVC REST controller with basic CRUD operations
- Create an Angular router, component, and service
- Create HTML views
- Generate integration and performance tests

You can generate entities using the `jhipster entity` sub-generator, the JHipster Domain Language (JDL) Studio, or the JHipster UML (`https://jhipster.github.io/jhipster-uml/`). The next section looks at how to use the JHipster entity sub-generator and JDL Studio to generate entities.

Using the JHipster Entity Sub-Generator

You can generate entities using the `jhipster entity` sub-generator by providing a table name and column details, as follows:

```
jhipster entity Post --table-name posts
```

This command will ask whether you want to add a field to your entity. In this example, you'll add three fields—`title`, `content`, and `createdOn`—and specify type and validation rules as follows:

- Name: `title`, Type: `String`, Validation: Required

- Name: `content`, Type: `String`, Validation: Required

- Name: `createdOn`, Type: `LocalDate`

Next it will ask if you want to add a relationship to another entity. Answer no. You will learn how to manage relationships in the next section.

The following questions will be asked; answer them as follows:

```
? Do you want to use a Data Transfer Object (DTO)? No, use the entity directly
? Do you want to use separate service class for your business logic? No, the REST controller
should use the repository directly
? Do you want pagination on your entity? No
```

You can choose to create Data Transfer Objects (DTOs), which will be used to create a response for the REST API, but for now you can choose to return entities. You can also choose to create a service layer to perform any business logic, but you are choosing to directly use the Spring Data JPA repositories because there is no business logic involved. Lastly, you can choose whether you need pagination support or not.

After running the `jhipster entity` sub-generator command successfully, you can run the application and see the `Post` menu item in the Entities menu. You can perform the CRUD operations on the `Post` entity.

Instead of running the `entity` sub-generator and answering all these questions, you can use JDL Studio to create entities.

Using JDL Studio

JDL Studio is an online utility that creates entities and configures relationships among entities using the JHipster Domain Language (JDL). You can read about JDL at `https://jhipster.github.io/jdl/`.

If you go to `https://jhipster.github.io/jdl-studio/`, a sample domain model is configured with various entity definitions and relationship among those entities. Remove all of that and add the `Post` entity definition as follows:

```
entity Post {
        title String required
    content String required
    createdOn LocalDate
}
```

Click on the "Download Text File of This JDL" link in the top-right corner. The `jhipster-jdl.jh` file will download. Now you can run `jhipster import-jdl` command to create the entities from the JDL file.

```
> jhipster import-jdl jhipster-jdl-file.jh
```

After running this command, the Post entity, Spring Data JPA repository, Spring MVC controller, Angular front-end components, and more, will be generated. If you already have a Post entity, it will update the entity.

Managing Relationships

You can use the JHipster entity command not only for creating entities but also to specify relationships among entities. For example, you can create a Comment entity, then establish a *one-to-many* relationship from Post to Comment and a *many-to-one* entity from Comment to Post.

While creating the Post entity using the `jhipster entity` sub-generator, you can specify the relationship to the Comment entity as follows:

```
> jhipster entity Post --table-name posts
```

As you already have a Post entity, it will display options to regenerate, add, and remove fields and relationships. Choose `Yes, add more fields and relationships`.

```
? Do you want to add a field to your entity? No
? Do you want to add a relationship to another entity? Yes
? What is the name of the other entity? Comment
? What is the name of the relationship? comments
? What is the type of the relationship? one-to-many
? What is the name of this relationship in the other entity? post
```

Now you can generate a Comment entity with the `name`, `email`, `content`, and `createdOn` fields. When prompted to add a relationship to another entity, you can add a many-to-one relationship from Comment to the Post entity as follows:

```
? What is the name of the other entity? Post
? What is the name of the relationship? post
? What is the type of the relationship? many-to-one
? When you display this relationship with Angular, which field from 'Post' do you want to
use? id
? Do you want to add any validation rules to this relationship? No
```

You can use JDL Studio to create entities and specify relationships among them as well. Configure the Post and Comment entities and the OneToMany relationship as follows:

```
entity Post {
    title String required
  content String required
  createdOn LocalDate
}
```

```
entity Comment {
        name String required
    email String required
    content String required
    createdOn LocalDate
}

relationship OneToMany {
  Post{comments} to Comment{post}
}
```

Now you can download this JDL file and import it as you did earlier. This will create JPA entities and establish JPA relationship as follows:

```
@Entity
@Table(name = "post")
@Cache(usage = CacheConcurrencyStrategy.NONSTRICT_READ_WRITE)
public class Post implements Serializable {

    ...
    ...

    @OneToMany(mappedBy = "post")
    @JsonIgnore
    @Cache(usage = CacheConcurrencyStrategy.NONSTRICT_READ_WRITE)
    private Set<Comment> comments = new HashSet<>();

    ...
    ...
}

@Entity
@Table(name = "comment")
@Cache(usage = CacheConcurrencyStrategy.NONSTRICT_READ_WRITE)
public class Comment implements Serializable {

    ...
    ...

    @ManyToOne
    private Post post;

}
```

JHipster scaffolding will generate a dropdown with posts to select while creating a comment.

You can read more about managing relationships at https://jhipster.github.io/managing-relationships/.

By default, when you run ./mvnw, the application will start in development mode using the dev profile. If you want to run the application in production mode, you can run it using the prod profile, as in ./mvnw -Pprod.

You can also generate a runnable WAR file using the `./mvnw -Pprod package` command and run the application as follows:

```
java -jar jhipsterblog-0.0.1-SNAPSHOT.war
```

When you run the application in the production profile, various optimizations will be performed. For example, static assets like HTML, JS, and CSS files will be optimized and GZip compression will be configured.

Note You can also use JHipster to generate Spring Boot-based microservices. To learn how to create microservices using JHipster, refer to `https://jhipster.github.io/microservices-architecture`.

Summary

In this chapter, you learned how to use JHipster to generate Spring Boot-based web applications with the Angular front-end. In the next chapter, you will look at how to run applications in production and how to deploy a Spring Boot application on the Heroku Cloud platform.

CHAPTER 19

Deploying Spring Boot Applications

Spring Boot supports embedded servlet containers, which makes deploying applications much easier, because you don't need an external application server setup. You can simply package your Spring Boot application as a JAR module and run it using the java -jar command. However, you need to consider a few things while running applications in a production environment.

You can use profiles to externalize configuration properties per environment and run your application, activating desired profiles. But you don't want to specify sensitive data in configuration properties and commit it in the source code. Spring Boot provides various mechanisms to override the configuration properties when starting the application.

In recent years, *containerization* technologies like Docker have become a very popular way to run applications in both development and production environments. In complex applications, you may need to run multiple services like databases, search engines, log monitoring tools, etc. Installing all these services on the development environment is tedious. You can use Docker to spin up multiple containers with all the required services, without having to install all of them locally.

This chapter you looks into how to run Spring Boot applications in production mode and how to override configuration properties. You will also look at deploying Spring Boot applications on the Heroku Cloud platform. Finally, you will learn about running Spring Boot applications on Docker containers.

Running Spring Boot Applications in Production Mode

Spring Boot applications with JAR-type packaging are self-contained applications that can run easily and don't require any external application server setup. Once the application is packaged as a JAR, you can simply run the application as follows:

```
java -jar app.jar
```

As discussed in Chapter 4, you can have multiple profile configuration files, such as application-qa. properties and application-prod.properties, and can activate the desired profiles using the spring. profiles.active system property. Suppose you configured the datasource properties in the dev and prod profile configuration files, as shown in Listing 19-1.

© K. Siva Prasad Reddy 2017
K. S. Prasad Reddy, *Beginning Spring Boot 2*, DOI 10.1007/978-1-4842-2931-6_19

Listing 19-1. src/main/resources/application-dev.properties

```
spring.datasource.driver-class-name=com.mysql.jdbc.Driver
spring.datasource.url=jdbc:mysql://localhost:3306/myapp
spring.datasource.username=root
spring.datasource.password=admin
```

Listing 19-1 shows how to configure your local MySQL server properties for the dev profile.

Listing 19-2. src/main/resources/application-prod.properties

```
spring.datasource.driver-class-name=com.mysql.jdbc.Driver
spring.datasource.url=jdbc:mysql://prodmysqlsrv:3306/myapp
spring.datasource.username=appuser
spring.datasource.password=S3*(Hi)@32vi
```

Listing 19-2 configuration is pointing to remote MySQL server properties for the prod profile.
Now you can run the application in production by activating the prod profile, as follows:

```
java -jar -Dspring.profiles.active=prod app.jar
```

Suppose you have Spring components that should be activated only when you're running in a cloud environment. In that case, you can activate multiple profiles by specifying a comma-separated list of profile names.

```
java -jar -Dspring.profiles.active=prod,cloud app.jar
```

By activating prod and cloud profiles, all the default profile components (ie, components which are not associated to any specific environment) and components associated with prod and cloud profiles will be activated. But you don't want to configure sensitive information like actual production server credentials in these properties files and commit them to version control systems.

Spring Boot allows you to override the configuration parameters in various ways. You can override the properties using system properties as follows:

```
java -jar -Dserver.port=8585 app.jar
```

By specifying system properties, even if you configure the `server.port` property in the `application-*.properties` files, it will be overridden with `server.port=8585` and the application will start on port 8585. Specifying a long list of properties like this can be cumbersome, so Spring Boot provides another mechanism to override the properties.

You can load the properties from multiple locations. `SpringApplication` will load properties from the `application-*.properties` files in the following locations:

- A `/config` subdirectory of the current directory

- The current directory

- A classpath `/config` package

- The classpath root

The properties defined in the top location take higher precedence over the properties defined in lower locations.

Suppose you have the `app.jar` in the `/home/appserver/app1.0/` directory from which you run the application using the `java -jar` command.

Now you can create an `application-prod.properties` file in the `/home/appserver/app1.0/config` directory, which overrides the properties defined in the `application-prod.properties` file in classpath. So you can configure all the default properties in the `src/main/resources/application-*.properties` files and override them using the `config/application-*.properties` file while running the application.

Note that you should not commit the `config/applzication-*.properties` files into version control systems, as they contain sensitive configuration details.

Spring Boot also provides support for running applications as native executable services on Unix-based systems or as a Windows service. For more information on installing Spring Boot applications as services, read `http://docs.spring.io/spring-boot/docs/current/reference/htmlsingle/#deployment-install`.

Deploying Spring Boot Application on Heroku

Heroku (`https://www.heroku.com/`) is a platform as a service (PaaS) that enables developers to build and run applications in the cloud. Heroku supports a wide variety of programming languages, including Ruby, Java, NodeJS, Python, PHP, Scala, and Go.

In this section, you learn how to deploy a Spring Boot application on Heroku. First familiarize yourself with Heroku by reading the "Getting Started on Heroku with Java" guide at: `https://devcenter.heroku.com/articles/getting-started-with-java#introduction`.

Create an account on Heroku and install the Heroku Toolbelt based on your operating system.

You can create an application using the `heroku create` command, which will automatically create a GIT remote (called `heroku`) and associate it with your local GIT repository.

Another option is to host your application code on a GitHub repository and link that repository to your Heroku application. This chapter follows the second approach.

1. Create a repository on GitHub.

    Create an account on GitHub, if you don't have one, and create a repository named `springboot-heroku-demo`. I created a repository at `https://github.com/sivaprasadreddy/springboot-heroku-demo`.

2. Create a Spring Boot application.

    You are going to create a simple Spring Boot application with the Web and Data-JPA starters. You are going to use the Postgres database, which is a free add-on for your application. See Listing 19-3.

Listing 19-3. pom.xml

```
<?xml version="1.0" encoding="UTF-8"?>
<project xmlns="http://maven.apache.org/POM/4.0.0"
        xmlns:xsi="http://www.w3.org/2001/XMLSchema-instance"
        xsi:schemaLocation="http://maven.apache.org/POM/4.0.0
        http://maven.apache.org/xsd/maven-4.0.0.xsd">
    <modelVersion>4.0.0</modelVersion>

    <groupId>com.apress</groupId>
    <artifactId>springboot-heroku-demo</artifactId>
    <version>1.0</version>
```

```xml
<parent>
    <groupId>org.springframework.boot</groupId>
    <artifactId>spring-boot-starter-parent</artifactId>
    <version>2.0.0.BUILD-SNAPSHOT</version>
</parent>

<properties>
    <java.version>1.8</java.version>
</properties>

<build>
    <finalName>${project.artifactId}</finalName>
    <plugins>
        <plugin>
            <groupId>org.springframework.boot</groupId>
            <artifactId>spring-boot-maven-plugin</artifactId>
        </plugin>
    </plugins>
</build>

<dependencies>

    <dependency>
        <groupId>org.springframework.boot</groupId>
        <artifactId>spring-boot-starter-test</artifactId>
        <scope>test</scope>
    </dependency>

    <dependency>
        <groupId>org.springframework.boot</groupId>
        <artifactId>spring-boot-starter-web</artifactId>
    </dependency>
    <dependency>
        <groupId>org.springframework.boot</groupId>
        <artifactId>spring-boot-starter-thymeleaf</artifactId>
    </dependency>
    <dependency>
        <groupId>org.springframework.boot</groupId>
        <artifactId>spring-boot-starter-data-jpa</artifactId>
    </dependency>
    <dependency>
        <groupId>com.h2database</groupId>
        <artifactId>h2</artifactId>
    </dependency>
    <dependency>
        <groupId>org.postgresql</groupId>
        <artifactId>postgresql</artifactId>
    </dependency>
</dependencies>

</project>
```

3. Create a JPA entity and a Spring Data repository.

    Now you need to create a simple JPA entity called User and a Spring Data JPA
    repository called UserRepository, as shown in Listings 19-4 and 19-5.

Listing 19-4. User.java

```
@Entity
@Table(name="USERS")
public class User
{
    @Id
    @GeneratedValue(strategy = GenerationType.IDENTITY)
    private long id;
    private String name;

    //setters & getters
}
```

Listing 19-5. UserRepository.java

```
@Repository
public interface UserRepository extends JpaRepository<User, Long>
{

}
```

4. Configure the datasource properties.

    As you have the H2 database driver in the classpath, if you don't configure any
    datasource properties, Spring Boot will create an in-memory datasource. While
    running the application locally, you can configure datasource properties by
    pointing to your local Postgres database in src/main/resources/application-
    dev.properties, as shown in Listing 19-6.

Listing 19-6. src/main/resources/application-dev.properties

```
spring.datasource.url=jdbc:postgresql://localhost:5432/demodb
spring.datasource.driver-class-name=org.postgresql.Driver
spring.datasource.username=postgres
spring.datasource.password=secret123
spring.datasource.maxActive=10
spring.datasource.maxIdle=5
spring.datasource.minIdle=2
spring.datasource.initialSize=5
spring.datasource.removeAbandoned=true
spring.jpa.hibernate.ddl-auto=update
```

But when deploying on Heroku, you have to use the Postgres database provided
by the Heroku platform. So you can configure the datasource properties in
src/main/resources/application-heroku.properties, as shown in Listing 19-7,
and enable the heroku profile.

Listing 19-7. src/main/resources/application-heroku.properties

```
spring.datasource.url=${JDBC_DATABASE_URL}
spring.datasource.driver-class-name=org.postgresql.Driver
spring.datasource.maxActive=10
spring.datasource.maxIdle=5
spring.datasource.minIdle=2
spring.datasource.initialSize=5
spring.datasource.removeAbandoned=true
spring.jpa.hibernate.ddl-auto=update
```

JDBC_DATABASE_URL is an environment variable that's generated dynamically by pointing to the Postgres database server. You can check the value of the JDBC_DATABASE_URL environment variable by running the following command:

```
heroku run echo \$JDBC_DATABASE_URL
```

5. Initialize the database with sample data. This example uses a SQL script to populate sample user data, as shown in Listing 19-8.

Listing 19-8. src/main/resources/data.sql

```
delete from users;

insert into users(id,name) values (1, 'Admin');
insert into users(id,name) values (2, 'Test');
```

6. Create a controller to display the users.

Listing 19-9 shows how to create a SpringMVC request handler method to display a list of users.

Listing 19-9. HomeController.java

```
@Controller
public class HomeController
{

    private UserRepository repository;

    @Autowired
    public HomeController(UserRepository repository) {
        this.repository = repository;
    }

    @GetMapping("/")
    public String home(Model model) {
        List<User> users = repository.findAll();
        model.addAttribute("users", users);
        return "home";
    }

}
```

7. Create a Thymeleaf view to render the users list, as shown in Listing 19-10.

Listing 19-10. src/main/resources/templates/home.html

```
<!DOCTYPE HTML>
<html xmlns:th="http://www.thymeleaf.org">
<head>
    <title>SpringBoot Heroku Demo</title>
</head>
<body>
    <table>
        <thead>
            <tr>
                <th>List of Users</th>
            </tr>
        </thead>
        <tbody>
            <tr th:each="user : ${users}">
                <td th:text="${user.name}">user name</td>
            </tr>
        </tbody>
    </table>
</body>
</html>
```

8. Create a `Procfile`.

In order to run an application on Heroku, you need to create a `Procfile` in the root directory of the project. The `Procfile` is a text file that declares what command should be executed to start your application. Add the command shown in Listing 19-11 in the `Procfile` to run your Spring Boot application.

Listing 19-11. Procfile in Project Root Directory

```
web java -Dserver.port=$PORT -Dspring.profiles.active=heroku $JAVA_OPTS -jar target/
springboot-heroku-demo.jar
```

Note that the code configures the `server.port` property as a system property using `-Dserver.port=$PORT`, where the $PORT value is provided by Heroku dynamically. The code enables the heroku profile by specifying the `-Dspring.profiles.active=heroku` system property.

Now that you have the application code ready, you need to create an application on Heroku and link to the GitHub repository.

Go to `https://www.heroku.com/` and log in with your credentials. After a successful login, you will be redirected to the dashboard. On the Dashboard page, you can click on the New button on the top-right corner and select Create New App. There, you can provide the app name and select Runtime Selection. If you don't provide an app name, Heroku will generate a random name. Enter the application name and click on Create New App; it will take you to the application's Deploy configuration screen.

Click on the Resources tab and search for Postgres Add-on. Add the Heroku Postgres database. Click on the Deploy tab and, in the Deployment Method section, click on GitHub. Select your GitHub username, search for repository, and click Connect on the repository you want to link to.

Now you can click on Deploy Branch to deploy your application on Heroku. You can also enable automatic deployment of your application whenever you push changes to the GitHub repository by clicking on the Enable Automatic Deploys button.

Once the application is deployed, you can click on the Open App button in top-right corner, which will open your application home page in a new tab. If something goes wrong or you want to check the logs, choose More --> View Logs. You can also view logs from the terminal by running the following command.

```
heroku logs --tail --app <application_name>
```

To learn more about the Heroku platform, visit https://devcenter.heroku.com/.

Running a Spring Boot Application on Docker

Docker (https://www.docker.com/) is an open source platform for packaging and running applications. Docker is becoming more and more popular because it quickly packages and runs the application in lightweight containers with the required dependencies installed and configured.

First, you should familiarize yourself with some Docker terminology.

- A *Docker image* is a kind of blueprint from which you can create a container. For example, there is a Docker Ubuntu image from which you can create a container and perform actions just like you do on any Ubuntu OS.

- A *Docker container* is an instance of a Docker image that can be started, stopped, paused, and restarted. Each Docker container is assigned a unique identifier.

- A *Docker host* is the host operating system from which you are spinning up the Docker containers.

- A *Docker hub* is a cloud-based registry service that hosts plenty of free Docker images that you can use. You can also build your own image and publish them.

You can create Docker containers using various Docker commands, but using *Dockerfile* is the preferred approach. Dockerfile contains the instructions on how to build the Docker image so that you can easily repeat the image building process on any machine.

Installing Docker

Docker is a rapidly evolving technology and hence the Docker installation process may change over time. I strongly recommend you refer to the official Docker installation documentation at https://docs.docker.com/engine/installation/ to install Docker based on your operating system. Once Docker is installed, you can determine whether the installation is successful by running the following command.

```
sudo docker info
```

If the installation is successful, you should be able to see various details about Docker. Listing 19-12 shows a sample Dockerfile.

Listing 19-12. Sample Dockerfile

```
# Base image is Ubuntu
FROM ubuntu:14.04

# Author: Siva
MAINTAINER Siva <sivaprasadreddy.k@gmail.com>
```

```
# Install apache2 package
RUN apt-get update && apt-get install -y apache2 && apt-get clean

# run command on startup
CMD ["echo", "Dockerfile demo"]
```

This file creates a base image called `ubuntu:14.04` by using the `FROM` command. You can optionally provide author details using the `MAINTAINER` command.

Next, the code runs the commands to install the apache2 web server using the `RUN` command, which will be executed during the image-building time.

Finally, this code runs the `echo` command with the `Dockerfile demo` argument, using the `CMD` command. You can use the `CMD` command to specify which command should be executed when you launch the container. You can override the `CMD` command while launching the container by specifying the command as an argument to the `docker run` command.

You should have only one `CMD` command in a `Dockerfile`. Even if you specify multiple `CMD` commands, only the last one will be considered.

You can use the `docker build` command to build an image from `Dockerfile` and tag it with name using the `-t` flag. Run the following command from the same directory having `Dockerfile`:

```
sudo docker build -t my-apache2 .
```

Note the dot at the end of the command. This indicates the location of `Dockerfile`, which is the current directory.

You can use the `docker images` command to list all the images that are available locally.

Now you can launch a container from the `my-apache2` image by using the `docker run` command as follows:

```
sudo docker run my-apache2
```

This command should print `Dockerfile demo` on the console.

You can use the `sudo docker ps` command to display the running container details.

Now that you have a basic understand of how to work with Docker, in the next section, you will see how to package and run a Spring Boot application in a Docker container.

Running a Spring Boot Application in a Docker Container

You are going to use the application you built for deploying Spring Boot on Heroku in the previous section. Create `Dockerfile` in the root of the project, as follows:

```
FROM java:8
ADD target/springboot-heroku-demo.jar app.jar
RUN bash -c 'touch /app.jar'
ENTRYPOINT ["java","-Djava.security.egd=file:/dev/./urandom","-jar","/app.jar"]
```

This code uses `java:8` as the base image. It copies `target/springboot-heroku-demo.jar` into the target image with the name `app.jar`. Finally, it invokes the `java -jar app.jar` command using `ENTRYPOINT`.

Before building the Docker image, you first need to build the application:

```
springboot-heroku-demo> mvn clean package
```

Now you can run the `docker build` command as follows:

```
docker build -t sivaprasadreddy/springboot-heroku-demo .
```

Here, you are tagging the image with the name `sivaprasadreddy/springboot-heroku-demo`. As you haven't activated any profiles, the default profile will be active and the application will use the H2 in-memory database.

Now launch the container from the `sivaprasadreddy/springboot-heroku-demo` image, as follows.

```
docker run -d \
            --name springboot-heroku-demo \
            -p 80:8080 \
            sivaprasadreddy/springboot-heroku-demo
```

You are running the container by giving it the name `springboot-heroku-demo` and exposing the container's port 8080 on the Docker host machine at port 80.

Now you'll see how to launch a Postgres database in one Docker container and then launch the application in another container using the Postgres database from the first container.

You can launch a Postgres database container by using the `postgres` image as follows:

```
docker run --name demo-postgres \
        -e POSTGRES_DB=demodb   \
        -e POSTGRES_USER=postgres \
        -e POSTGRES_PASSWORD=secret123 \
        -d postgres
```

This code launches a `postgres` container in detached mode by using the `-d` flag and gives it the name `demo-postgres`. It also specifies the database name, username, and password as environment variables by using `-e` flags.

Now you'll create the Docker profile configuration file `application-docker.properties` as follows:

```
spring.datasource.driver-class-name=org.postgresql.Driver
spring.datasource.url=jdbc:postgresql://${POSTGRES_PORT_5432_TCP_ADDR}:${POSTGRES_PORT_5432_TCP_PORT}/demodb
spring.datasource.username=${POSTGRES_ENV_POSTGRES_USER}
spring.datasource.password=${POSTGRES_ENV_POSTGRES_PASSWORD}
spring.jpa.hibernate.ddl-auto=update
```

You can modify the `Dockerfile` to run the application by activating the docker profile:

```
FROM java:8
ADD target/springboot-heroku-demo.jar app.jar
RUN bash -c 'touch /app.jar'
ENTRYPOINT ["java","-Djava.security.egd=file:/dev/./urandom","-Dspring.profiles.active=docker","-jar","/app.jar"]
```

Note that the code specifies -Dspring.profiles.active=docker to activate the docker profile so that the application will use the Postgres database running in another Docker container instead of using the H2 in-memory database.

Now build the project using the mvn clean package command and build your application Docker image.

```
docker build -t sivaprasadreddy/springboot-heroku-demo .
```

Before launching your container, you need to delete the existing container. You can remove the existing container as follows:

```
sudo docker rm springboot-heroku-demo
```

You need to link the application's Docker container with the demo-postgres Docker container in order to be able to use the Postgres database from the application.

Launch the application container using the following command:

```
docker run -d \
            --name springboot-heroku-demo \
            --link demo-postgres:postgres \
            -p 80:8080 \
            sivaprasadreddy/springboot-heroku-demo
```

Note that you linked the demo-postgres container using the --link flag and gave it an alias called postgres. Now the application is running in one container and is talking to the Postgres database running in another container.

Running Multiple Containers Using docker-compose

If your application depends on multiple services and you need to start all of them in Docker containers, it is tedious to start them individually. You can use the docker-compose tool to orchestrate multiple containers required to run your application. You need to create a docker-compose.yml file and configure the services that you want to run.

Create docker-compose.yml in the root directory of your application, as shown in Listing 19-13.

Listing 19-13. docker-compose.yml

```
demo-postgres:
  image: postgres:latest
  environment:
    - POSTGRES_DB=demodb
    - POSTGRES_USER=postgres
    - POSTGRES_PASSWORD=secret123

springboot-heroku-demo:
  image: sivaprasadreddy/springboot-heroku-demo
  links:
    - demo-postgres:postgres
  ports:
    - 80:8080
```

Now you can simply run the docker-compose up command from the directory where you have the docker-compose.yml file to start the application and the Postgres containers.

■ **Note** You can use docker-maven-plugin to build Docker images. Visit https://github.com/spotify/ docker-maven-plugin to learn more about docker-maven-plugin. If you are using the Gradle build tool, you can use the gradle-docker plugin (https://github.com/Transmode/gradle-docker) to build Docker images.

To learn more about Docker, visit https://docs.docker.com/.

Summary

This chapter discussed how to run applications in production and how to deploy a Spring Boot application on the Heroku Cloud platform. You also learned about running Spring Boot applications on the Docker container.

Index

© K. Siva Prasad Reddy 2017

K. S. Prasad Reddy, *Beginning Spring Boot 2*, DOI 10.1007/978-1-4842-2931-6

■ T

■ U, V

■ W, X

■ Y, Z

Get the eBook for only $5!

Why limit yourself?

With most of our titles available in both PDF and ePUB format, you can access your content wherever and however you wish—on your PC, phone, tablet, or reader.

Since you've purchased this print book, we are happy to offer you the eBook for just $5.

To learn more, go to http://www.apress.com/companion or contact support@apress.com.

Apress®

Made in the USA
Monee, IL
07 July 2026

56552663R00181